G.A. HENTY

December 8, 1832   ---
                November 16, 1902

WINNING HIS SPURS

SPURS

A TALE OF THE CRUSADES

by
G.A. Henty

WITH NUMEROUS ILLUSTRATIONS

Preston Speed *ublications*

Pennsylvania

A note about our name: Preston/Speed Publications
In an age where it has become fashionable to denigrate fathers, we
have decided to honor ours.   Our name is in loving memory of Preston
Louis Schmitt and Speed - Lester Herbert Maynard ("Speed" was a
nickname that was earned for prowess in baseball).

This book is printed on acid-free paper, and its binding
materials have been chosen for strength and durability.

© Preston/Speed 1997

Published 1882 by
Samson Low, London

Samson Low Title Page Date 1893

Hardcover Edition ISBN 1-887159-13-4
Softcover Edition ISBN 1-887159-34-7
Printed in the U.S.A.

PRESTON/SPEED PUBLICATIONS
RR #4, BOX 705
MILL HALL, PENNSYLVANIA 17751
(570) 726-7844
1997

INTRODUCTION:

G. A. Henty's life was filled with exciting adventure. Completing Westminster School, he attended Cambridge University. Along with a rigorous course of study, Henty participated in boxing, wrestling and rowing. The strenuous study and healthy, competitive participation in sports prepared Henty to be with the British army in Crimea, as a war correspondent witnessing Garibaldi fight in Italy, visiting Abyssinia, being present in Paris during the Franco-Prussian war, in Spain with the Carlists, at the opening of the Suez Canal, touring India with the Prince of Wales (later Edward VII) and a trip to the California gold fields. These are only a few of his exciting adventures.

G. A. Henty lived during the reign of Queen Victoria (1837-1901) and began his story telling career with his own children. After dinner, he would spend an hour or two in telling them a story that would continue the next day. Some stories took weeks! A friend was present one day and watched the spell-bound reaction of his children suggesting that he write down his stories so others could enjoy them. He did. Henty wrote approximately 144 books plus stories for magazines and was dubbed as "The Prince of Story-Tellers" and "The Boy's Own Historian." One of Mr. Henty's secretaries reported that he would quickly pace back and forth in his study dictating stories as fast as the secretary could record them.

Henty's stories revolve around a fictional boy hero during fascinating periods of history. His heroes are diligent, courageous, intelligent and dedicated to their country and cause in the face, at times, of great peril. His histories, particularly battle accounts, have been recognized by historian scholars for their accuracy. There is nothing dry in Mr. Henty's stories and thus he removes the drudgery and laborious task often associated with the study of history.

Henty's heroes fight wars, sail the seas, discover land, conquer evil empires, prospect for gold, and a host of other exciting adventures. They meet famous personages like Josephus, Titus, Hannibal, Robert the Bruce, Sir William Wallace, General Marlborough, General Gordon, General Kitchner, Robert E. Lee, Frederick the Great, the Duke of Wellington, Huguenot leader Coligny, Cortez, King Alfred, Napoleon, and Sir Francis Drake just to mention a *few*. The heroes go through the fall of Jerusalem, the Roman invasion of Britain, the Crusades, the Viking invasion of Europe, the Reformation in various countries, the Reign of Terror, etc. In short, Henty's heroes live through tumultuous historic eras meeting the leaders of that time. Understanding the culture of the time period becomes second nature as well as comparing/contrasting the society of various European and heathen cultures.

Preston/Speed Publications is delighted to offer again the works of G. A. Henty. Action-packed exciting adventure awaits adults and a whole new generation. The books have been reproduced with modern typesetting. However, the original grammar, spellings and punctuation remains the same as the original versions.

FOREWORD

The Crusade era (1096-1291) was not a glorious one for the Catholic Church. Enlivened by Pope Urban II's words, "Deus vult" ("God wills it") thousands of individuals set out in one of several crusades to reclaim Jerusalem from Moslem captivity.

The word "crusade" is rooted in the Latin word for cross — crux. The crusaders were marked by a cross on the breast of their clothing as a reminder that they were on a mission to advance God's kingdom by driving out the Moslems from land deemed holy by the Catholic Church. In *Winning His Spurs*, Henty provides his readers with the fascinating story of the Third Crusade. That Crusade lasted from 1188-92. It originated as a result of the capable Turkish leader, Saladin, capturing Jerusalem in 1187. The following year under the joint efforts of Philip August, King of France, Frederick Barbarossa, emperor of the Holy Roman Empire, and King Richard of England, a crusade was initiated to recapture Jerusalem. The Crusade lasted longer than this unity. Some miles from Antioch, Emperor Frederick drowned while swimming in a river. After the capture of Acre, King Philip and his followers returned home following a disagreement with King Richard. This left the burden of future battles on the broad shoulders of King Richard. I will allow you, the readers of this volume, to read Henty's stirring description of King Richard's valiant battles. I will only point out that "the Lion-Hearted" was appended to King Richard's name as a result of the bravery and leadership he exemplified in this Crusade.

As one might expect, the Crusades changed the Western World in numerous ways. Many began to see theological problems within the Catholic Church. Crusaders had been told that involvement in a Crusade would suffice for the absolution of sin. Forgiveness with God could come through this "good work". Forgotten was the key teaching of Scripture that "But we are all like an unclean thing, and all our righteousness are like filthy rags" (Isaiah 64:6). Christ is central to salvation. "But God demonstrates His own love toward us, in that while we were still sinners Christ died for us" (Romans 5:8). Thus, it is only through repentance and faith in Christ's finished work that salvation comes. Seeds of awareness were sown in the Crusade era that would later blossom into the fruit of the Reformation.

Likewise, the crusaders were mistaken in their belief that the kingdom of God could be advanced by warfare. The Moslem Turks did not become Christians when Jerusalem was conquered by Christians. Spiritual warfare is not ended by physical means. What is needed in all ages is Christians going forth teaching the heart-changing Gospel to those who need it.

The Third Crusade had a long-standing impact on several fronts. As I have already mentioned, Christianity held no appeal to the Moslems because of the ongoing attacks and subsequent massacres of Moslems and pillaging of towns by the crusaders. No doubt Richard the Lion-Hearted brought some change to this feeling of heightened animosity between the crusaders and the Turks. The English leader showed respect to Saladin. That respect was reciprocated as Henty points out. Viewing one another as human beings allows communication to begin on important life and death issues.

Secondly, the capture of Acre was a highlight of this Crusade. The importance of this capture has been lost to many of the generations that have lived since that time. Following the king's victorious battle, became the capital of the Kingdom of Jerusalem. In time, the city grew in its economic importance. Acre also became the headquarters for the Knights Hospitaller. These men, under the auspices of the Catholic Church, provided much help over the years to the pilgrims who journeyed to Jerusalem. They greatly aided members of the First Crusade. These Knights provided shelter and took care of the sick. As a result, when the crusaders arrived home, they gave much land to the Knights Hospitaller. With this added wealth, more hospices were established in the Mediterranean area. In a day when many were removing themselves from society by entering monasteries, these Knights sought to serve the Lord by ministering to the needs of many in the world.

Another group, the Knights Templar, were so named because they lived in the Temple of Solomon. They protected pilgrims in their journey to the Jordan River. Their military ability was called into service in a much more broad way as they sought to defend Jerusalem in the Second Crusade. Prior to the Third Crusade, these Knights met stunning defeats at the hands of Saladin's forces.

With Acre becoming the power base of the Hospitallers after King Richard's victory, they continued to remain organized and involved both militarily and as servants in aiding the needs of the crusaders and travelers in their area. Perhaps the Knights' finest day came in 1565. On the island of Malta, situated between Libya and Sicily, some nine thousand Knights faced the onslaught of forty thousand Turkish troops under the leadership of Suleiman the Magnificent. The Turkish goal was not Malta, but southern Europe itself. With their invasion they would bring their Moslem religion.

Many readers will no doubt remember that the Moslem Moors had been driven out of Spain less than a century earlier. The Reformation under Luther had taken root and was spreading its tender shoots throughout Europe. Thus, it was vital that the Turks be defeated. What could nine thousand do against forty thousand? One thing. Win. Win, they did. According to Ernle Bradford's account in his *The Great Siege*, more than eight thousand Knights were killed. The Turks lost far more, thirty thousand. Yet the island did not come under Turkish rule, nor did Turkish conquest reach southern Europe.

The Knights' staunch defense is a story in itself with its own heroes and cruelty. In these brief paragraphs, I do not want to imply that these Knights were never cruel or blameless in their actions. Realizing this, we cannot overlook their important job of aiding travelers and ministry to the sick, as well as their military aid over several centuries.

The Third Crusade's legacy was far more than the failure to capture Jerusalem. Thousands of lives were affected in ways unknown to them as they began their arduous journey. Many never returned home. Others returned forever changed by their experiences and shaped by what they had seen.

This volume is a welcomed addition to available literature today. Henty has a well-earned reputation as an accurate historian. In *Winning His Spurs*, Henty shows that ramifications of our actions can touch the lives of many and put us in many a situation far more perilous than what we can imagine. As the reader will soon discover, King Richard and his closest followers were in life-threatening danger before and after their numerous confrontations with Saladin. The reader most likely will never face such danger. However, our actions will have impact and influence on the lives of others, many times unknown to us. As a comfort, we must never forget the overarching plan of a loving God that rules and overrules in all situations for His glory and the good of those who trust in Him.

Byron Snapp, Associate Pastor
Calvary Reformed Presbyterian Church
Hampton, Virginia

SPECIAL NOTE:

Winning His Spurs (1882) has been the most difficult book yet to produce from the G. A. Henty historical fiction series. The editors at Preston/Speed Publications were sorely tempted on numerous occasions to have this work photoshot directly from the original text. However, due to the numerous errors in the first edition as well as following editions, Preston/Speed Publications was dissuaded from this course. We would like to thank Fred West of Columbus, Ohio, without whose hard work the production of *Winning His Spurs* would have been almost impossible. Another special thank you must be extended to Ann King of Great Britain for her expertise on Mr. Henty.

Winning His Spurs was first published in 1882 by Sampson Low, which would later become Sampson Low, Murston, Scarle and Rivington, London, England. Interestingly enough, *Winning His Spurs* was also published under the title of *Fighting the Saracens: Or the Boy Knight* (1892) by Charles E. Brown of Boston, U.S.A. This edition made several changes from the original work by Mr. Henty. Moreover, *Winning His Spurs* was also published under the title of *The Boy Knight: A Tale of the Crusades* (1882) by Robert Bros. of Boston, U.S.A. Unfortunately, *The Boy Knight* had, basically, no illustrations, numerous changes and so many errors that it was deemed worthless for use by Preston/Speed Publications.

Finally, it is generally accepted that Mr. Henty only began to write his 'My Dear Lads' prefaces during his long association with his primary publisher. Preston/Speed Publications trusts, however, that you will enjoy the Foreword by Rev. Byron Snapp.

CONTENTS

WINNING HIS SPURS.

CHAPTER I.

THE OUTLAWS

IT WAS a bright morning in the month of August, when a lad of some fifteen years of age, sitting on a low wall, watched party after party of armed men riding up to the castle of the Earl of Evesham. A casual observer glancing at his curling hair and bright open face, as also at the fashion of his dress, would at once have assigned to him a purely Saxon origin; but a keener eye would have detected signs that Norman blood ran also in his veins, for his figure was lither and lighter, his features more straightly and shapely cut, than was common among Saxons. His dress consisted of a tight fitting jerkin, descending nearly to his knees. The material was light-blue cloth, while over his shoulder hung a short cloak of a darker hue. His cap was of Saxon fashion, and he wore on one side a little plume of a heron. In a somewhat costly belt hung a light short sword, while across his knees lay a crossbow, in itself almost a sure sign of its bearer being of other than Saxon blood. The boy looked anxiously as party after party rode past towards the castle.

"I would give something," he said, "to know what wind blows these knaves here. From every petty castle in the Earl's feu the retainers seem hurrying here. Is he bent, I wonder, on settling once and for all his quarrels with the

Baron of Wortham? or can he be intending to make a clear sweep of the woods? Ah! here comes my gossip Hubert; he may tell me the meaning of this gathering."

Leaping to his feet, the speaker started at a brisk walk to

meet a jovial-looking personage coming down from the direction of the castle. The new comer was dressed in the attire of a falconer, and two dogs followed at his heels.

"Ah, Master Cuthbert," he said, "what brings you so near to the castle? It is not often that you favour us with your presence."

"I am happier in the woods, as you well know, and was on my way thither but now, when I paused at the sight of all these troopers flocking in to Evesham. What enterprise has Sir Walter on hand now, think you?"

"The earl keeps his own counsel," said the falconer, "but methinks a shrewd guess might be made at the purport of the gathering. It was but three days since that his foresters were beaten back by the landless men, whom they caught in the very act of cutting up a fat buck. As thou knowest, my lord though easy and well-disposed to all, and not fond of harassing and driving the people as are many of his neighbours, is yet to the full as fanatical anent his forest privileges as the worst of them. They tell me that when the news came in of the poor figure that his foresters cut with broken bows and draggled plumes—for the varlets had soused them in a pond of not over savoury water—he swore a great oath that he would clear the forest of the bands. It may be, indeed, that this gathering is for the purpose of falling in force upon that evil-disposed and most treacherous baron, Sir John of Wortham, who has already begun to harry some of the outlying lands, and has driven off, I hear, many heads of cattle. It is a quarrel which will have to be fought out sooner or later, and the sooner the better, say I. Although I am no man of war, and love looking after my falcons or giving food to my dogs far more than exchanging hard blows, yet would I gladly don the buff and steel coat to aid in levelling the keep of that robber and tyrant, Sir John of Wortham."

"Thanks, good Hubert," said the lad. "I must not stand gossiping here. The news you have told me, as you know, touches me closely, for I would not that harm should come to the forest men."

"Let it not out, I beseech thee, Cuthbert, that the news came from me, for temperate as Sir Walter is at most times, he would, methinks, give me short shift did he know that the wagging of my tongue might have given warning through which the outlaws of the Chase should slip through his fingers."

"Fear not, Hubert; I can be mum when the occasion needs. Can you tell me farther, when the bands now gathering are likely to set forth?"

"In brief breathing space," the falconer replied. "Those who first arrived I left swilling beer, and devouring pies and other provisions cooked for them last night, and from what I hear, they will set forth as soon as the last comer has arrived. Whichever be their quarry, they will try to fall upon it before the news of their arrival is bruited abroad."

With a wave of his hand to the falconer the boy started. Leaving the road, and striking across the slightly undulated country dotted here and there by groups of trees, the lad ran at a brisk trot, without stopping to halt or breathe, until after half an hour's run he arrived at the entrance of a building, whose aspect proclaimed it to be the abode of a Saxon franklin of some importance. It would not be called a castle, but was rather a fortified house, with a few windows looking without, and surrounded by a moat crossed by a drawbridge, and capable of sustaining anything short of a real attack. Erstwood had but lately passed into Norman hands, and was indeed at present owned by a Saxon. Sir William de Lance, the father of the lad who is now entering its portals, was a friend and follower of the Earl of Evesham; and soon after his lord had married Gweneth the heiress of all these fair lands—given to him by the will of the king, to whom by the death of her father she became a ward—Sir William had married Editha, the daughter and heiress of the franklin of Erstwood, a cousin and dear friend of the new Countess of Evesham.

In neither couple could the marriage at first have been called one of inclination on the part of the ladies, but love came after marriage. Although the knights and barons of the Norman invasion would, no doubt, be considered rude and rough in these days of broadcloth and civilization, yet their manners were gentle and polished by the side of those of the rough though kindly Saxon franklins; and although the

Saxon maids were doubtless as patriotic as their fathers and mothers, yet the female mind is greatly led by gentle manners and courteous address. Thus then, when bidden or forced to give their hands to the Norman knights, they speedily accepted their lot, and for the most part grew contented and happy enough. In their changed circumstances it was pleasanter to ride by the side of their Norman husbands, surrounded by a gay cavalcade, to hawk and to hunt, than to discharge the quiet duties of mistress of a Saxon farm-house. In many cases, of course, their lot was rendered wretched by the violence and brutality of their lords; but in the majority they were well satisfied with their lot, and these mixed marriages did more to bring the peoples together and weld them in one, than all the laws and decrees of the Norman sovereigns.

This had certainly been the case with Editha, whose marriage with Sir William had been one of the greatest happiness. She had lost him, three years before the story begins, fighting in Normandy, in one of the innumerable wars in which our first Norman kings were constantly involved. On entering the gates of Erstwood, Cuthbert had rushed hastily to the room where his mother was sitting with three or four of her maidens, engaged in work.

"I want to speak to you at once, mother," he said.

"What is it now, my son?" said his mother, who was still young and very comely. Waving her hand to the girls, they left her.

"Mother," he said, when they were alone, "I fear me that Sir Walter is about to make a great raid upon the outlaws. Armed men have been coming in all the morning from the castles round, and if it be not against the Baron de Wortham that these preparations are intended, and methinks it is not, it must needs be against the landless men."

"What would you do, Cuthbert?" his mother asked anxiously. "It will not do for you to be found meddling in these matters. At present you stand well in the favour of the Earl, who loves you for the sake of his wife, to whom you are kin, and of your father, who did him good liegeman's service."

"But, mother, I have many friends in the wood. There is Cnut, their chief, your own first cousin, and many others of our friends, all good men and true, though forced by the cruel Norman laws to refuge in the woods."

"What would you do" again his mother asked.

"I would take Ronald my pony and ride to warn them of the danger that threatens."

"You had best go on foot, my son. Doubtless men have been set to see that none from the Saxon homesteads carry the warning to the woods. The distance is not beyond your reach, for you have often wandered there, and on foot you can evade the eye of the watchers; but one thing, my son, you must promise, and that is, that in no case, should the Earl and his bands meet with the outlaws, will you take part in any fray or struggle."

"That will I willingly, mother," he said. "I have no cause for offence against the castle or the forest, and my blood and my kin are with both. I would fain save shedding of blood in a quarrel like this. I hope that the time may come when Saxon and Norman may fight side by side, and I may be there to see."

A few minutes later, having changed his blue doublet for one of more sober and less noticeable colour, Cuthbert started for the great forest, which then stretched to within a mile of Erstwood.

In those days a large part of the country was covered with forest, and the policy of the Normans in preserving these woods for the chase, tended to prevent the increase of cultivation.

The farms and cultivated lands were all held by Saxons, who although nominally handed over to the nobles to whom William and his successors had given the fiefs, saw but little of their Norman masters. These stood, indeed, much in the position in which landlords stand to their tenants, payment being made, for the most part, in produce. At the edge of the wood the trees grew comparatively far apart, but as Cuthbert proceeded farther into its recesses, the trees in the virgin forest stood thick and close together. Here and there

open glades ran across each other, and in these his sharp eye. accustomed to the forest, could often see the stags starting away at the sound of his foot-steps.

It was a full hour's journey before Cuthbert reached the point for which he was bound. Here, in an open space, probably cleared by a storm ages before, and overshadowed by giant trees, was a group of men of all ages and appearances, some were occupied in stripping the skin off a buck which hung from the bough of one of the trees. Others were roasting portions of the carcase of another deer. A few sat apart, some talking others busy in making arrows, while a few lay asleep on the greensward. As Cuthbert entered the clearing, several of the party rose to their feet.

"Ah, Cuthbert," shouted a man of almost gigantic stature, who appeared to be one of the leaders of the party, "what brings you here, lad, so early? You are not wont to visit us till even, when you can lay your crossbow at a stag by moon-light."

"No, no, Cousin Cnut," Cuthbert said, "thou canst not say that I have ever broken the forest laws, though I have looked on often and often, whilst you have done so."

"The abettor is as bad as the thief," laughed Cnut, "and if the foresters caught us in the act, I wot they would make but little difference whether it was the shaft of my longbow or the quarrel from thy crossbow which brought down the quarry. But again, lad, why comest thou here? for I see by the sweat on your face and by the heaving of your sides that you have run fast and far."

"I have, Cnut; I have not once stopped for breathing since I left Erstwood. I have come to warn you of danger. The earl is preparing for a raid."

Cnut laughed somewhat disdainfully.

"He has raided here before, and I trow has carried off no game. The landless men of the forest can hold their own against a handful of Norman knights and retainers in their own home."

"Ay," said Cuthbert, but this will be no common raid. This morning bands from all the holds within miles round are riding in, and at least 500 men-at-arms are likely to do chase to-day."

"Is it so?" said Cnut, while exclamations of surprise, but not of apprehension, broke from those standing round. "If that be so, lad, you have done us good service indeed. With fair warning we can slip through the fingers of ten times 500 men, but if they came upon us unawares, and hemmed us in, it would fare but badly with us, though we should, I doubt not, give a good account of them before their battle-axes and maces ended the strife. Have you any idea by which road they will enter the forest, or what are their intentions?"

"I know not," Cuthbert said; "all that I gathered was that the earl intended to sweep the forest, and to put an end to the breaches of the laws, not to say of the rough treatment that his foresters have met with at your hands. You had best, methinks, be off before Sir Walter and his heavily-armed men are here. The forest, large as it is, will scarce hold you both, and methinks you had best shift your quarters to Langholm Chase until the storm has passed."

"To Langholm be it, then," said Cnut, "though I love not the place. Sir John of Wortham is a worse neighbour by far than the earl. Against the latter we bear no malice, he is a good knight and a fair lord; and could he free himself of the Norman notions that the birds of the air, and the beasts of the field, and the fishes of the water, all belong to Normans, and that we Saxons have no share in them, I should have no quarrel with him. He grinds not his neighbours, he is content with a fair tithe of the produce, and as between man and man is a fair judge without favour. The baron is a fiend incarnate; did he not fear that he would lose by so doing, he would gladly cut the throats, or burn, or drown, or hang every Saxon within twenty miles of his hold. He is a disgrace to his order, and some day when our band gathers a little stronger, we will burn his nest about his ears."

"It will be a hard nut to crack," Cuthbert, said, laughing. "With such arms as you have in the forest the enterprise would be something akin to scaling the skies."

"Ladders and axes will go far, lad, and the Norman men-at-arms have learned to dread our shafts. But enough of the baron; if we must be his neighbours for a time, so be it."

"You have heard, my mates," he said, turning to his comrades gathered around him, "what Cuthbert tells us. Are you of my opinion, that it is better to move away till the storm is past, than to fight against heavy odds, without much chance of either booty or victory?"

A general chorus proclaimed that the outlaws approved of the proposal for a move to Langholm Chase. The preparations were simple. Bows were taken down from the boughs on which they were hanging, quivers slung across the backs, short cloaks thrown over the shoulders. The deer was hurriedly dismembered, and the joints fastened to a pole slung on the shoulders of two of the men. The drinking-cups, some of which were of silver, looking strangely out of place among the rough horn implements and platters, were bundled together, carried a short distance and dropped among some thick bushes for safety; and then the band started for Wortham.

With a cordial farewell and many thanks to Cuthbert, who declined their invitations to accompany them, the retreat to Langholm commenced.

Cuthbert, not knowing in which direction the bands were likely to approach, remained for a while motionless, intently listening.

In a quarter of an hour he heard the distant note of a bugle.

It was answered in three different directions, and Cuthbert, who knew every path and glade of the forest, was able pretty accurately to surmise those by which the various bands were commencing to enter the wood.

Knowing that they were still a long way off, he advanced as rapidly as he could in the direction in which they were coming. When by the sound of distant voices and the breaking of branches he knew that one at least of the parties was near at hand, he rapidly climbed a thick tree and ensconced himself in the branches, and there watched, secure and hidden from the sharpest eye, the passage of a body of men-at-arms fully a hundred strong, led by Sir Walter himself, accompanied by some half dozen of his knights.

When they had passed, Cuthbert again slipped down the tree and made at all speed for home. He reached it, so far as he knew without having been observed by a singe passer-by.

After a brief talk with his mother, he started for the castle, as his appearance there would divert any suspicion

that might arise; and it would also appear natural that seeing the movements of so large a body of men, he should go up to gossip with his acquaintances there.

When distant a mile from Evesham, he came upon a small party.

On a white palfrey rode Margaret, the little daughter of the earl. She was accompanied by her nurse and two retainers on foot.

Cuthbert—who was a great favourite with the earl's daughter, for whom he frequently brought pets, such as nests of young owlets, falcons, and other creatures—was about to join the party when from a clump of trees near burst a body of ten mounted men. Without a word they rode straight at the astonished group. The retainers were cut to the ground before they had thought of drawing a sword in defence.

The nurse was slain by a blow with a battle-axe, and Margaret, snatched from her palfrey, was thrown across the saddlebow of one of the mounted men, who then with his comrades dashed off at full speed.

CHAPTER II.

A RESCUE.

THE whole of the startling scene of the abduction of the Earl of Evesham's daughter occupied but a few seconds. Cuthbert was so astounded at the sudden calamity that he remained rooted to the ground at the spot where, fortunately for himself, unnoticed by the assailants, he had stood when they first burst from their concealment.

For a short time he hesitated as to the course he should take.

The men-at-arms who remained in the castle were scarce strong enough to rescue the child, whose captors would no doubt be reinforced by a far stronger party lurking near.

The main body of Sir Walter's followers were deep in the recesses of the forest, and this lay altogether out of the line for Wortham, and there would be no chance whatever of bringing them up in time to cut off the marauders on their way back.

There remained only the outlaws, who by this time would be in Langholm Forest, perhaps within a mile or two of the castle itself.

The road by which the horsemen could travel would be far longer than the direct line across country, and he resolved at once to strain every nerve to reach his friends in time to get them to interpose between the captors of the Lady Margaret and their stronghold.

For an instant he hesitated whether to run back to Erstwood to get a horse; but he decided that it would be as quick to go on foot, and far easier so to find the outlaws.

These thoughts occupied but a few moments, and he at once started at the top of his speed for his long run across the country.

Had Cuthbert been running in a race of hare and hound, he would assuredly have borne away the prize from most boys of his age. At headlong pace he made across the country, every foot of which, as far as the edge of Langholm Chase, he knew by heart.

The distance to the woods was some twelve miles, and in an hour and a half from the moment of his starting Cuthbert was deep within its shades. Where he would be likely to find the outlaws he knew not; and, putting a whistle to his lips, he shrilly blew the signal, which would, he knew, be recognized by any of the band within hearing.

He thought that he heard an answer, but was not certain, and again dashed forward, almost as speedily as if he had but just started.

Five minutes later a man stood in the glade up which he was running. He recognized him at once as one of Cnut's party.

"Where are the band?" he gasped.

"Half a mile or so to the right," replied the man.

Guided by the man, Cuthbert ran at full speed, till, panting and scarce able to speak, he arrived at the spot where Cnut's band were gathered.

In a few words he told them what had happened, and although they had just been chased by the father of the captured child, there was not a moment of hesitation in promising their aid to rescue her from a man whom they regarded as a far more bitter enemy, both of themselves and their race.

"I fear we shall be too late to cut them off," Cnut said, "they have so long a start; but at least we will waste no time in gossiping."

Winding a horn to call together some of the members of the band who had scattered, and leaving one at the meeting-place to give instructions to the rest, Cnut, followed by those assembled there, went off at a swinging trot through the glades towards Wortham Castle.

After a rapid calculation of distances, and allowing for the fact that the baron's men – knowing that Sir Walter's retainers and friends were all deep in the forest, and even if they heard of the outrage could not be on their traces for hours – would take matters quietly, Cnut concluded that they had arrived in time.

Turning off, they made their way along the edge of the wood, to the point where the road from Evesham ran through the forest.

Scarcely had the party reached this point when they heard a faint clatter of steel.

"Here they come!" exclaimed Cuthbert.

Cnut gave rapid directions, and the band took up their posts behind the trees, on either side of the path.

"Remember," Cnut said, "above all things be careful not to hit the child, but pierce the horse on which she is riding. The instant he falls, rush forward. We must trust to surprise to give us the victory."

Three minutes later the head of a band of horsemen was seen through the trees. They were some thirty in number, and, closely grouped as they were together, the watchers behind the trees could not see the form of the child carried in their midst.

When they came abreast of the concealed outlaws, Cnut gave a sharp whistle, and fifty arrows flew from tree and bush into the closely gathered party of horsemen. More than half their number fell at once; some, drawing their swords, endeavoured to rush at their concealed foes, while others dashed forward in the hope of riding through the snare into which they had fallen. Cuthbert had levelled his crossbow, but had not fired; he was watching with intense anxiety for a glimpse of the bright-coloured dress of the child. Soon he saw a horseman separate himself from the rest and dash forward at full speed. Several arrows flew by him, and one or two struck the horse on which he rode.

The animal, however, kept on its way.

Cuthbert levelled his crossbow on the low arm of a tree,

and as the rider came abreast of him touched the trigger, and the steel-pointed quarrel flew true and strong against the temple of the passing horseman. He fell from his horse like a stone and the well-trained animal at once stood still by the side of his rider.

Cuthbert leapt forward, and to his delight the child at once opened her arms and cried in a joyous tone, —

"Cuthbert!"

The fight was still raging fiercely, and Cuthbert, raising her from the ground, ran with her into the wood, where they remained hidden until the combat ceased, and the last survivors of the Baron's band had ridden past towards the castle.

Then Cuthbert went forward with his charge and joined the band of outlaws, who, absorbed in the fight, had not witnessed the incident of her rescue, and now received them with loud shouts of joy and triumph.

"This is a good day's work indeed for all," Cuthbert said; "it will make of the earl a firm friend instead of a bitter enemy; and I doubt not that better days are dawning for Evesham Forest."

A litter was speedily made with boughs, on this Margaret was placed, and on the shoulders of two stout foresters started for home, Cnut and Cuthbert walking beside, and a few of the band keeping at a short distance behind, as a sort of rearguard should the Baron attempt to regain his prey.

There was now no cause for speed, and Cuthbert in truth could scarce drag one foot before another, for he had already traversed over twenty miles, the greater portion of the distance at his highest rate of speed.

Cnut offered to have a litter made for him also, but this Cuthbert indignantly refused; however, in the forest they came upon the hut of a small cultivator, who had a rough forest pony, which was borrowed for Cuthbert's use.

It was late in the afternoon before they came in sight of Evesham Castle. From the distance could be seen bodies of armed men galloping towards it, and it was clear that only now the party were returning from the wood, and had learned the news of the disappearance of the Earl's daughter, and of the finding of the bodies of her attendants.

Presently they met one of the mounted retainers riding at headlong speed.

"Have you heard or seen anything," he shouted, as he approached, "of the Lady Margaret? She is missing, and foul play has taken place."

"Here I am, Rudolph," cried the child, sitting up on the rude litter.

The horseman gave a cry of astonishment and pleasure, and without a word wheeled his horse and galloped past back at headlong speed towards the castle.

As Cuthbert and the party approached the gate, the earl himself, surrounded by his knights and followers, rode out hastily from the gate and halted in front of the little party. The litter was lowered, and as he dismounted from his horse his daughter sprang out and leapt into his arms.

For a few minutes the confusion and babble of tongues were too great for anything to be heard, but Cuthbert, as soon as order was somewhat restored, stated what had happened, and the earl was moved to fury at the news of the outrage which had been perpetrated by the Baron of Wortham upon his daughter and at the very gates of his castle, and also at the thought that she should have been saved by the bravery and devotion of the very men against whom he had so lately been vowing vengeance in the depths of the forest.

"This is not a time," he said to Cnut, "for talking or making promises, but be assured that henceforth the deer of Evesham Chase are as free to you and your men as to me. Forest laws or no forest laws, I will no more lift a hand against men to whom I owe so much. Come when you will to the castle, my friends, and let us talk over what can be done to rase your outlawry and restore you to an honest career again."

Cuthbert returned home tired, but delighted with his day's work, and Dame Editha was surprised indeed with the tale of adventure he had to tell. The next morning he went over to the castle, and heard that a grand council had been held the evening before, and that it had been determined to attack Wortham Castle and to raze it to the ground.

Immediately on hearing of his arrival, the earl, after again expressing his gratitude for the rescue of his daughter, asked him if he would go into the forest and invite the outlaws to join their forces with those of the castle to attack the baron.

Cuthbert willingly undertook the mission, as he felt that this alliance would further strengthen the position of the forest men.

When he arrived there was some considerable consultation and discussion between the outlaws as to the expediency of mixing themselves in the quarrels between the Norman barons. However, Cnut persuaded them that as the Baron of Wortham was an enemy and oppressor of all Saxons, it was in fact their own quarrel that they were fighting rather than that of the earl, and they therefore agreed to give their aid, and promised to be at the rendezvous outside the castle to be attacked, soon after dawn next morning. Cuthbert returned with the news, which gave great satisfaction to the earl.

The castle was now a scene of bustle and business; armourers were at work repairing head-pieces and breastplates, sharpening swords and battle-axes, while the fletchers prepared sheaves of arrows. In the courtyard a number of men were engaged oiling the catapults, ballistas, and other machines for hurling stones. All were discussing the chances of the assault for it was no easy matter which they had set themselves to do. Wortham Hold was an extremely strong one, and it needed all and more than all the machines at their disposal to undertake so formidable an operation as a siege.

The garrison, too, were strong and desperate; and the baron, knowing what must follow his outrage of the day before, would have been sure to send off messengers round the country begging his friends to come to his assistance. Cuthbert had begged permission of his mother to ask the earl to allow him to join as a volunteer, but she would not hear of it. Neither would she suffer him to mingle with the foresters. The utmost that he could obtain was that he might go as a spectator, with strict injunctions to keep himself out of the fray, and as far as possible beyond bow-shot of the castle wall.

It was a force of some 400 strong that issued from the wood early next morning to attack the stronghold at Wortham. The force consisted of some ten or twelve knights and barons, some 150 or 160 Norman men-at-arms, a miscellaneous gathering of other retainers, 200 strong, and some eighty of the forest men. These last were not to fight under the earl's banner, but were to act on their own account. There were among them outlaws, escaped serfs, and some men guilty of bloodshed. The earl then could not have suffered these men to fight under his flag until purged in some way of their offences.

This arrangement suited the foresters well.

Their strong point was shooting; and by taking up their own position, and following their own tactics, under the leadership of Cnut, they would be able to do far more execution, and that with less risk to themselves, than if compelled to fight according to the fashion of the Normans.

As they approached the castle a trumpet was blown, and the herald, advancing, demanded its surrender, stigmatized the Baron of Wortham as a false knight and a disgrace to his class, and warned all those within the castle to abstain from giving him aid or countenance, but to submit themselves to the earl, Sir Walter of Evesham, the representative of King Richard.

The reply to the summons was a burst of taunting laughter from the walls; and scarcely had the herald withdrawn, than a flight of arrows showed that the besieged were perfectly ready for the fray.

Indeed, the baron had not been idle. Already the dispute between himself and the earl had come to such a point that it was certain that sooner or later open hostilities would break out.

He had therefore been for some time quietly accumulating a large store of provisions and munitions of war, and strengthening the castle in every way.

The moat had been cleaned out, and filled to the brim

with water. Great quantities of heavy stones had been
accumulated on the most exposed points of the walls, in
readiness to hurl upon any who might try to climb. Huge
sheaves of arrows and piles of crossbow bolts, were in
readiness, and in all, save the number of men, Wortham
had for weeks been prepared for the siege.

On the day when the attempt to carry off the earl's
daughter had failed, the baron, seeing that his bold stroke to
obtain a hostage which would have enabled him to make his
own terms with the earl, had been thwarted, knew that the
struggle was inevitable.

Fleet messengers had been sent in all directions. To
Gloucester and Hereford, Stafford, and even Oxford, men
had ridden, with letters to the baron's friends, beseeching
them to march to his assistance.

"I can," he said, "defend my hold for weeks. But it is
only by aid from without that I can finally hope to break the
power of this braggart earl."

Many of those to whom he addressed his call had
speedily complied with his demand, while those at a
distance might be expected to reply later to the appeal.

There were many among the barons who considered the
mildness of the Earl of Evesham towards the Saxons in his
district to be a mistake, and who, although not actually
approving of the tyranny and brutality of the Baron of
Wortham, yet looked upon his cause to some extent as their
own.

The Castle of Wortham stood upon ground but very
slightly elevated above the surrounding country. A deep and
wide moat ran round it, and this could, by diverting a rivulet,
be filled at will.

From the edge of the moat the walls rose high, and with
strong flanking towers and battlements.

There were strong works also beyond the moat opposite
to the drawbridge; while in the centre of the castle rose the
keep, from whose summit the archers, and the machines for

casting stones and darts, could command the whole circuit of defence.

As Cuthbert, accompanied by one of the hinds of the farm, took his post high up in a lofty tree, where at his ease he could command a view of the proceedings, he marvelled

much in what manner an attack upon so fair a fortress would be commenced.

"It will be straightforward work to attack the outwork," he said, "but that once won, I see not how we are to proceed against the castle itself. The machines that the earl has will scarcely hurl stones strong enough even to knock the mortar from the walls. Ladders are useless where they cannot be planted; and if the garrison are as brave as the castle is strong, methinks that the earl has embarked upon a business that will keep him here till next spring."

There was little time lost in commencing the conflict.

The foresters, skirmishing up near to the castle, and taking advantage of every inequality in the ground, of every bush and tuft of high grass, worked up close to the moat, and then opened a heavy fire with their bows against the men-at-arms on the battlements, and prevented their using the machines against the main force now advancing to the attack upon the outwork.

This was stoutly defended. But the impetuosity of the earl, backed as it was by the gallantry of the knights serving under him, carried all obstacles.

The narrow moat which encircled this work was speedily filled with great bundles of brushwood, which had been prepared the previous night. Across these the assailants rushed.

Some thundered at the gate with their battle-axes, while others placed ladders by which, although several times hurled backwards by the defenders, they finally succeeded in getting a footing on the wall.

Once there, the combat was virtually over.

The defenders were either cut down or taken prisoners, and in two hours after the assault began, the outwork of Wortham Castle was taken.

This, however, was but the commencement of the undertaking, and it had cost more than twenty lives to the assailants.

They were now, indeed, little nearer to capturing the castle than they had been before.

The moat was wide and deep. The drawbridge had been lifted at the instant that the first of the assailants gained a footing upon the wall. And now that the outwork was captured, a storm of arrows, stones, and other missiles was poured into it from the castle walls, and rendered it impossible for any of its new masters to show themselves above it.

Seeing that any sudden attack was impossible, the earl now directed a strong body to cut down trees, and prepare a movable bridge to throw across the moat.

This would be a work of fully two days; and in the meantime Cuthbert returned to the farm.

CHAPTER III.

THE CAPTURE OF WORTHAM HOLD.

UPON his return home, after relating to his mother the events of the morning's conflict, Cuthbert took his way to the cottage inhabited by an old man who had in his youth been a mason.

"Have I not heard, Gurth," he said, "that you helped to build the Castle of Wortham?"

"No, no, young sir," he said; "old as I am, I was a child when the castle was built. My father worked at it, and it cost him, and many others, his life."

"And how was that, prithee?" asked Cuthbert.

"He was, with several others, killed by the baron, the grandfather of the present man, when the work was finished."

"But why was that, Gurth?"

"We were but Saxon swine," said Gurth bitterly, "and a few of us more or less mattered not. We were then serfs of the baron. But my mother fled with me on the news of my father's death. For years we remained far away, with some friends in a forest near Oxford. Then she pined for her native air, and came back and entered the service of the franklin."

"But why should your mother have taken you away?" Cuthbert asked.

"She always believed, Master Cuthbert, that my father was killed by the baron, to prevent him giving any news of the secrets of the castle. He and some others had been kept in the walls for many months, and were engaged in the making of secret passages."

"That is just what I came to ask you, Gurth. I have heard something of this story before, and now that we are attacking Wortham Castle, and the earl has sworn to level it to the ground, it is of importance if possible to find out whether any of the secret passages lead beyond the castle, and if so, where. Almost all the castles have, I have been told, an exit by which the garrison can at will make sorties or escape; and I thought that maybe you might have heard enough to give us some clue as to the existence of such a passage at Wortham."

The old man thought for some time in silence, and then said,—

"I may be mistaken, but methinks a diligent search in the copse near the stream might find the mouth of the outlet."

"What makes you think that this is so, Gurth?"

"I had been with my mother to carry some clothes to my father on the last occasion on which I saw him. As we neared the castle I saw my father and three other of the workmen, together with the baron, coming down from the castle towards the spot. As my mother did not wish to approach while the baron was at hand, we stood within the trees at the edge of the wood, and watched what was being done. The baron came with them down to the bushes, and then they again came out, crossed the river, and one of them cut some willows, peeled them, and erected the white staves in a line towards the castle. They walked for a bit on each side, and seemed to be making calculations. Then they went back into the castle, and I never saw my father again."

"Why did you not go in at once according to your intention?"

"Because my mother said that she thought some important work was on hand, and that maybe the baron would not like that women should know aught of it, for he was of suspicious and evil mind. More than this I know not. The castle had already been finished, and most of the masons discharged. There were, however, a party of serfs kept at work, and also some masons, and rumour had it that they were engaged in making the secret passages. Whether it was so or not I cannot say, but I know that none of that party ever left the castle alive. It was given out that a bad fever had raged there, but none believed it; and the report went about, and was I doubt not true, that all had been killed, to preserve the secret of the passage."

Cuthbert lost no time in making use of the information that he had gained.

Early next morning, at daybreak, he started on his pony to Wortham.

As he did not wish the earl or his followers to know the facts that he had learned until they were proved, he made his way round the camp of the besiegers, and by means of his whistle called one of the foresters to him.

"Where is Cnut?" he asked.

"He is with a party occupied in making ladders."

"Go to him," Cuthbert said, "and tell him to withdraw quietly and make his way here. I have an important matter on which I wish to speak to him."

Cnut arrived in a few minutes, somewhat wondering at the message. He brightened greatly when Cuthbert told him what he had learned.

"This is indeed important," he said. "We will lose no time in searching the copse you speak of. You and I, together with two of my most trusty men, with axes to clear away the brush, will do. At present a thing of this sort had best be kept between as few as may be."

They started at once and soon came down upon the stream.

It ran at this point in a little valley, some twenty or thirty feet deep. On the bank not far from the castle grew a small wood, and it was in this that Cuthbert hoped to find the passage spoken of by Gurth.

The trees and brushwood were so thick that it was apparent at once that if the passage had ever existed it had been unused for some years.

The woodmen were obliged to chop down dozens of young saplings to make their way up from the water towards the steeper part of the bank.

The wood was some fifty yards in length, and as it was uncertain at which point the passage had come out, a very minute search had to be made.

"What do you think it would be like, Cnut?" Cuthbert asked.

"Like enough to a rabbit-hole, or more likely still there would be no hole whatever. We must look for moss and greenery, for it is likely that such would have been planted, so as to conceal the door from any passerby, while yet allowing a party from inside to cut their way through it without difficulty."

After a search of two hours, Cnut decided that the only place in the copse in which it was likely that the entrance to a passage could be hidden, was a spot where the ground was covered thickly with ivy and trailing plants.

"It looks level enough with the rest," Cuthbert said.

"Ay, lad, but we know not what lies behind this thick screen of ivy. Thrust in that staff."

One of the woodmen began to probe with the end of a staff among the ivy. For some time he was met by the solid ground, but presently the butt of the staff went through suddenly, pitching him on his head, amidst a suppressed laugh from his comrades.

"Here it is, if anywhere," said Cnut, and with their billhooks they at once began to clear away the thickly grown creepers.

Five minutes' work was sufficient to show a narrow cut, some two feet wide, in the hill side, at the end of which stood a low door.

"Here it is," said Cnut, with triumph, "and the castle is ours. Thanks, Cuthbert, for your thought and intelligence. It has not been used lately, that is clear," he went on. "These creepers have not been moved for years. Shall we go and tell the earl of our discovery? What think you, Cuthbert?"

"I think we had better not," Cuthbert said. "We might not succeed in getting in, as the passage may have fallen farther along; but I will speak to him and tell him that we have something on hand which may alter his dispositions for fighting to-morrow."

Cuthbert made his way to the earl, who had taken possession of a small cottage a short distance from the castle.

"What can I do for you?" Sir Walter said.

"I want to ask you, sir, not to attack the castle to-morrow until you see a white flag waved from the keep."

"But how on earth is a white flag to be raised from the keep?"

"It may be," Cuthbert said, "that I have some friends inside who will be able to make a diversion in our favour. However sir, it can do no harm if you will wait till then, and may save many lives. At what hour do you mean to attack?"

"The bridges and all other preparations to assist us across the moat will be ready to-night. We will advance then under cover of darkness, and as soon after dawn as may be attack in earnest."

"Very well, sir," Cuthbert said. "I trust that within five minutes after your bugle has sounded, the white flag will make its appearance on the keep, but it cannot do so until after you have commenced an attack, or at least a pretence of an attack."

Two or three hours before daylight Cuthbert accompanied Cnut and twenty-five picked men of the foresters to the copse. They were provided with crowbars, and all carried heavy axes. The door was soon prised open. It opened silently and without a creak.

"It may be," Cnut said, "that the door has not been opened as you say for years, but it is certain," and he placed his torch to the hinges, "that it has been well oiled within the last two or three days. No doubt the baron intended to make his escape this way, should the worst arrive. Now that we have the door open we had better wait quiet until the dawn commences. The earl will blow his bugle as a signal for the advance; it will be another ten minutes before they are fairly engaged, and that will be enough for us to break open any doors that there may be between this and the castle, and to force our way inside."

It seemed a long time waiting before the dawn fairly broke—still longer before the earl's bugle was heard to sound the attack. Then the band, headed by Cnut and two or three of the strongest of the party, entered the passage.

Cuthbert had had some misgivings as to his mother's injunctions to take no part in the fray, and it cannot be said that in accompanying the foresters he obeyed the letter of her instructions. At the same time as he felt sure that the effect of a surprise would be complete and crushing, and that the party would gain the top of the keep without any serious resistance, he considered the risk was so small as to justify him in accompanying the foresters.

The passage was some five feet high, and little more than two feet wide. It was dry and dusty, and save the marks on the ground of a human foot going and returning, doubtless that of the man who had oiled the lock the day before, the passage appeared to have been unused from the time that it left the hands of its builders.

Passing along for some distance they came to another strong oaken door. This, like the last, yielded to the efforts of the crowbars of the foresters, and they again advanced. Presently they came to a flight of steps.

"We must now be near the castle," Cnut said. "In fact, methinks I can hear confused noises ahead."

Mounting the steps, they came to a third door; this was thickly studded with iron, and appeared of very great strength. Fortunately the lock was upon their side, and they were enabled to shoot the bolt; but upon the other side the door was firmly secured by large bolts, and it was fully five minutes before the foresters could succeed in opening it. It was not without a good deal of noise that they at last did so; and several times they paused, fearing that the alarm must have been given in the castle. As, however, the door remained closed, they supposed that the occupants were fully engaged in defending themselves from the attacks of the earl's party.

When the door gave way, they found hanging across in front of them a very thick arras, and pressing this aside they entered a small room in the thickness of the wall of the keep. It contained the merest slit for light, and was clearly unused. Another door, this time unfastened, led into a larger apartment, which was also at present unoccupied. They could hear now the shouts of the combatants without, the loud orders given by the leaders on the walls, the crack, as the stones hurled by the mangonels struck the walls, and the ring of steel as the arrows struck against steel cap and cuirass.

"It is fortunate that all were so well engaged, or they would certainly have heard the noise of our forcing the door, which would have brought all of them upon us. As it is, we are in the heart of the keep. We have now but to make a rush up these winding steps, and methinks we shall find ourselves on the battlements. They will be so surprised, that no real resistance can be offered to us. Now let us advance."

So saying Cnut led the way upstairs, followed by the foresters, Cuthbert, as before, allowing five or six of them to intervene between him and the leader. He carried his short sword and a quarterstaff, a weapon by no means to be despised in the hands of an active and experienced player.

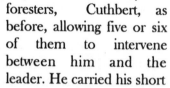

Presently, after mounting some fifty or sixty steps, they issued on the platform of the keep.

Here were gathered some thirty or forty men, who were so busied in shooting with cross-bows, and in working machines casting javelins, stones, and other missiles upon the besiegers, that they were unaware of the addition to their numbers until the whole of the foresters had gathered on the summit and at the order of Cnut, suddenly fell upon them with a loud shout.

Taken wholly by surprise by the foe, who seemed to have risen from the bowels of the earth by magic, the soldiers of the Baron of Wortham offered but a feeble resistance. Some were cast over the battlement of the keep, some driven down staircases, others cut down, and then Cuthbert, fastening a small white flag he had prepared to his quarterstaff, waved it above the battlements.

Even now the combatants on the outer wall were in ignorance of what had happened in the keep; so great was the din that the struggle which had there taken place had passed unnoticed; and it was not until the fugitives, rushing out into the courtyard, shouted that the keep had been captured, that the besieged became aware of the imminence of the danger.

Hitherto the battle had been going well for the defenders of the castle. The Baron of Wortham was indeed surprised at the feebleness of the assault. The arrows which had fallen in clouds upon the first day's attack upon the castle among his soldiers were now comparatively few and ineffective. The besiegers scarcely appeared to push forward their bridges with any vigour, and it seemed to him that a coldness had fallen upon them, and that some disagreement must have arisen between the foresters and the earl, completely crippling the energy of the attack.

When he heard the words shouted from the courtyard below he could not believe his ears. That the keep behind should have been carried by the enemy appeared to him impossible. With a roar he called upon the bravest of his men to follow, and rushing across the courtyard, rapidly ascended the staircase. The movement was observed from the keep, and Cnut and a few of his men, stationed themselves with their battle-axes at the top of various stairs leading below.

The signal shown by Cuthbert had not passed unobserved. The earl, who had given instructions to his followers to make a mere feint of attacking, now blew the signal for the real onslaught. The bridges were rapidly run across the moat, ladders were planted, and the garrison being paralyzed and confused by the attack in their rear, as well as hindered by the arrows which now flew down upon them from the keep above, offered but a feeble resistance, and the assailants, led by Sir Walter himself, poured over the walls.

Now there was a scene of confusion and desperate strife. The baron had just gained the top of the stairs, and was engaged in a fierce conflict with Cnut and his men, when the news reached him that the wall was carried from without. With an execration he again turned and rushed down the stairs, hoping by a vigorous effort to cast back the foe.

It was, however, all too late: his followers, disheartened and alarmed, fought without method or order in scattered groups of threes and fours. They made their last stand in corners and passages. They knew there was but little hope of mercy from the Saxon foresters, and against these they fought to the last. To the Norman retainers, however, of the earl they offered a less determined resistance, throwing down their arms and surrendering at discretion.

The baron, when fiercely fighting, was slain by an arrow from the keep above, and with his fall the last resistance ceased. A short time was spent in searching the castle, binding the prisoners, and carrying off the valuables that the baron had collected in his raids. Then a light was set to the timbers, the granaries were fired, and in a few minutes the smoke wreathing out of the various loopholes and openings told the country round that the stronghold had fallen, and that they were free from the oppressor at last.

CHAPTER IV.

THE CRUSADES.

WARM thanks and much praise were bestowed upon Cuthbert for his share in the capture of the castle, and the earl, calling the foresters round him, then and there bestowed freedom upon any of them who might have been serfs of his, and called upon all his knights and neighbours to do the same, in return for the good service which they had rendered.

This was willingly done, and a number of Cnut's party who had before borne the stigma of escaped serfs were now free men.

We are too apt to forget, in our sympathy with the Saxons, that fond as they were of freedom for themselves, they were yet severe masters, and kept the mass of the people in a state of serfage. Although their laws provided ample justice as between Saxon man and man, there was no justice for the unhappy serfs, who were either the original inhabitants or captives taken in war, and who were distinguished by a collar of brass or iron round their neck.

Cnut's party had indeed long got rid of these badges, the first act of a serf when he took to the woods being always to file off his collar; but they were liable when caught to be punished, even by death, and were delighted at having achieved their freedom.

"And what can I do for you, Cuthbert?" Sir Walter said, as they rode homewards. "It is to you that I am indebted: in the first place for the rescue of my daughter, in the second for the capture of that castle, which I doubt me much whether we should ever have taken in fair fight had it not been for your aid."

"Thanks, Sir Walter," the lad replied. "At present I need nothing, but should the time come when you may go to the wars, I would fain ride with you as your page, in the hope of some day winning my spurs also in the field."

"So shall it be," the earl said, "and right willingly. But who have we here?"

As he spoke a horseman rode up and presented a paper to the earl.

"This is a notice," the earl said, after perusing it, "that King Richard has determined to take up the cross, and that he calls upon his nobles and barons to join him in the effort to free the holy sepulchre from the infidels. I doubt whether the minds of the people are quite prepared, but I hear that there has been much preaching by friars and monks in some parts, and that many are eager to join in the war."

"Think you that you will go to the war, Sir Walter?"

Cuthbert asked.

"I know not as yet; it must much depend upon the king's mood. For myself, I care not so greatly as some do about this question of the Holy Land. There has been blood enough shed already to drown it, and we are no nearer than when the first swarms of pilgrims made their way thither."

On Cuthbert's returning home and telling his mother all that had passed, she shook her head, but said that she could not oppose his wishes to go with the earl when the time should come, and that it was only right he should follow in the footsteps of the good knight his father.

"I have heard much of these Crusades," he said; "canst tell me about them?"

"In truth I know not much, my son; but Father Francis, I doubt not, can tell you all the particulars anent the affair."

The next time that Father Francis, who was the special adviser of Dame Editha, rode over from the convent on his ambling nag, Cuthbert eagerly asked him if he would tell him what he knew of the Crusades.

"Hitherto, my son," he said, "the Crusades have, it must be owned, brought many woes upon Europe. From the early times great swarms of pilgrims were accustomed to go from all parts of Europe to the holy shrines.

"When the followers of the evil prophet took possession of the land, they laid grievous burdens upon the pilgrims, heavily they fined them, persecuted them in every way, and treated them as if indeed they were but the scum of the earth under their feet.

"So terrible were the tales that reached Europe that men came to think that it would be a good deed truly, to wrest the sepulchre of the Lord from the hands of these heathens. Pope Urban was the first to give authority and strength to the movement, and at a vast meeting at Claremont of 30,000 clergy and 4000 barons, it was decided that war must be made against the infidel. From all parts of France men flocked to hear Pope Urban preach there; and when he had finished his oration, the vast multitude, carried away by enthusiasm, swore to win the holy sepulchre or to die.

"Mighty was the throng that gathered for the First Crusade. Monks threw aside their gowns and took to the sword and cuirass; even women and children joined in the throng. What, my son, could be expected from a great army so formed? Without leaders, without discipline, without tactics, without means of getting food, they soon became a scourge of the country through which they passed.

"Passing through Hungary, where they greatly ravaged the fields, they came to Bulgaria. Here the people, struck with astonishment and dismay at this great horde of hungry people who arrived among them like locusts, fell upon them with the sword, and great numbers fell. The first band that passed into that country perished miserably, and of all that huge assembly, it may be said that, numbering, at the start, not less than 250,000 persons, only about 100,000 crossed into Asia Minor. The fate of these was no better than that of those who had perished in Hungary and Bulgaria. After grievous suffering and loss they at last reached Nicæa. There they fell into an ambuscade; and out of the whole of the undisciplined masses who had followed Peter the Hermit, it is doubtful whether 10,000 ever returned home.

"This first attempt to rescue the holy sepulchre was followed by others equally wild, misguided, and unfortunate. Some of them indeed began their evil deeds as soon as they had left their home. The last of these bodies fell upon the Jews, who are indeed enemies of the Christian faith, but who have now, at least, nothing to do with the question of the holy sepulchre. As soon as they entered into Germany the Crusaders put them to death with horrible torture. Plunder and rapine indeed appeared to be the object of the crusaders. On this as well as on most other preceding bands, their misdeeds drew down the vengeance of the people. At an early period of their march, and as soon as they reached Hungary, the people fell upon them, and put the greater portion to the sword.

"Thus, in these irregular expeditions no less than 500,000 people are supposed to have perished. Godfrey de Bouillon was the first who undertook to lead a Crusade according to the military knowledge of the day. With him were his brothers Eustace and Baldwin, the Counts of

Anault and St. Paul, and many other nobles and gentlemen, with their retainers, well armed and under good order; and so firm was the discipline of Duke Godfrey that they were allowed to pass freely, by the people of the countries who had opposed the previous bands.

"Through Hungary, Bulgaria, and Thrace he made his way; and though he met with many difficulties from Alexius, the crafty and treacherous Emperor of the Greeks, he at last succeeded in crossing into Asia. There he was joined by many from England, as well as from France and other countries. Duke Robert, the son of our first William, led a strong band of Normans to the war, as did the other great princes of France and Spain.

"The army which crossed the narrow passage of the Hellespont is estimated at no less than 700,000 fighting men. Of these 100,000 were knights clad in complete armour, the remainder were men-at-arms and bowmen.

"Nicæa, the place which had been the scene of the massacre of Peter the Hermit's hosts, was taken after a desperate conflict, lasting for many weeks, and the crusaders afterwards defeated the Turks in a great battle near the town of Doryleum. After these successes disputes arose among the leaders, and Count Baldwin, brother of Duke Godfrey, left the main body with about 1500 men, and founded a kingdom for himself in Mesopotamia.

"The main body, slowly and painfully, and suffering from disease, famine, and the heat, made its way south. Antioch, a city of great strength and importance, was besieged, but it proved so strong that it resisted for many months, and was at last only taken by treachery.

"After the capture of this place the sufferings of the crusaders so far from being diminished were redoubled. They themselves during the siege had bought up all the food that could be brought from the surrounding country, while the magazines of the town were found, when an entry was effected, to be entirely deserted. The enemy, aided by a great Persian host, came down, and those who had been the besiegers were now besieged. However, when in the last strait the Christian army sallied out, and inspired with supernatural strength, defeated the Turks and Persians, with a slaughter of 100,000 men. Another slow movement to the south brought them into the Holy Land, and pressing forward, they came at last within sight of Jerusalem itself.

"So fearful had been the losses of the crusaders that of 700,000 who crossed the Hellespont, not more than 40,000 reached the end of the pilgrimage. This fragment of an army, which had appeared before a very strongly fortified town, possessed no means of capturing the place—none of the machines of war necessary for the purpose, no provisions or munitions of any kind. Water was scarce also; and it appeared as if the remnant of the great army of Godfrey de Bouillon had arrived before Jerusalem only to perish there.

"Happily just at this time a further band of crusaders from Genoa, who had reached Jaffa, made their appearance. They were provided with stores, and had skilled workmen capable of making the machines for the siege. On July 14th, 1099, the attack was made, and after resistance gallant and desperate as the assault, the crusaders burst into the city, massacred the whole of the defenders and inhabitants, calculated at 70,000 in number, and so became masters of the holy sepulchre.

"The Sultan of Egypt was meanwhile advancing to the assistance of the Mohammedans of Syria; but Godfrey, with 20,000 of his best men, advanced to meet the vast host, and scattered them as if they had been sheep. Godfrey was now chosen King of Jerusalem, and the rest of his army—save 300 knights and 200 soldiers, who agreed to remain with him—returned to their home. The news of the victory led other armies of crusaders to follow the example of that of Godfrey; but as these were almost as completely without organization or leadership as those of Peter the Hermit, they suffered miserably on their way, and few indeed ever reached the Holy Land. Godfrey died in 1100, and his brother Baldwin succeeded him.

"The history of the last 100 years has been full of fresh efforts to crush the Moslem power, but hitherto it cannot be said that fortune has attended the efforts of the Christians. Had it not been indeed for the devotion of the Knights of St. John and of the Templars, two great companies formed of men who devoted their lives to the holding of the sepulchre against the infidel, our hold of the Holy Land would have been lost.

"Gradually the Saracens have wrested post after post from our hands. Edessa was taken in 1144, and the news of this event created an intense excitement. The holy St. Bernard stirred up all France, and Louis VII. himself took the vow and headed a noble army. The ways of God are not our ways, and although the army of Germany joined that of France, but little results came of this great effort. The Emperor Conrad, with the Germans, was attacked by the Turk Saladin of Iconium, and was defeated with a loss of 60,000 men. The King of France, with his army, was also attacked with fury, and a large portion of his force were slaughtered. Nothing more came of this great effort, and while the first Crusade seemed to show that the men-at-arms of Europe were irresistible, the second on the contrary gave proof that the Turks were equal to the Christian knights. Gradually the Christian hold of the Holy Land was shaken. In 1187, although fighting with extraordinary bravery, the small army of Christian Knights of the Temple and of St. John were annihilated, the King of Jerusalem was made prisoner, and the Christian power was crushed. Then Saladin, who commanded the Turks, advanced against Jerusalem, and forced it to capitulate.

"Such, my boy, is the last sad news which has reached us; and no wonder that it has stirred the hearts of the monarchs of Europe, and that every effort will be again made to recapture the holy sepulchre, and to avenge our brethren who have been murdered by the infidels."

"But, Father Francis, from your story it would seem that Europe has already sacrificed an enormous number of lives to take the holy sepulchre, and that after all the fighting, when she has taken it, it is only to lose it again."

"That is so, my son; but we will trust that in future things will be better managed. The Templars and Hospitallers now number so vast a number of the best lances in Europe, and are grown to be such great powers, that we may believe that when we have again wrested the holy sepulchre from the hands of the infidels they will be able to maintain it against all assaults. Doubtless the great misfortunes which have fallen upon the Christian armies have been a punishment from heaven, because they have not gone to work in the right spirit. It is not enough to take up lance and shield, and to place a red cross upon the shoulder. Those who desire to fight the battle of the Lord must cleanse their hearts, and go forth in the spirit of pilgrims rather than knights. I mean, not that they should trust wholly to spiritual weapons—for in truth the infidel is a foe not to be despised—but I mean, that they should lay aside all thoughts of worldly glory, and rivalry one against another."

"And think you, Father, that such is the spirit with which King Richard and the other kings and nobles now preparing to go to the Holy Land are animated?"

Father Francis hesitated.

"It is not for me, my son, to judge motives, or to speak

well or ill the instruments who have been chosen for this great work. It is of all works the most praiseworthy, most holy. It is horrible to think that the holy shrines of Jerusalem should be in the hands of men who believe not in our Redeemer; and I hold it to be the duty of every man who can bear arms, no matter what his rank or his station, to don his armour and to go forth to battle in the cause. Whether success will crown the effort, or whether God wills it otherwise, it is not for man to discuss; it is enough that the work is there, and it is our duty to do it."

"And think you, Father, that it will do good to England?"

"That do I, my son, whether we gain the Holy Land or no. Methinks that it will do good service to the nation that Saxon and Norman should fight together under the holy cross. Hitherto the races have stood far too much apart. They have seen each other's bad qualities rather than good; but methinks that when the Saxon and the Norman stand side by side on the soil of the Holy Land, and shout together for England, it must needs bind them together, and lead them to feel that they are no longer Normans and Saxons, but Englishmen. I intend to preach on the village green at Evesham next Sunday morning on this subject, and as I know you are in communication with the forest men, I would, Cuthbert, that you would persuade them to come in to hear me. You were wondering what could be found for these vagrants. They have many of them long since lost the habits of honest labour. Many of them are still serfs, although most have been freed by the good earl and the knights his followers. Some of those who would fain leave the life in the woods, still cling to it because they think that it would be mean to desert their comrades, who being serfs are still bound to lurk there; but methinks that this is a great opportunity for them. They are valiant men, and the fact that they are fond of drawing an arrow at a buck does not make them one whit the worse Christians. I will do my best to move their hearts, and if they will but agree together to take the cross, they would make a goodly band of footmen to accompany the earl."

"Is the earl going?" Cuthbert asked eagerly.

"I know not for certain," said Father Francis; "but I think from what I hear from his chaplain, Father Eustace, that his mind turns in that direction."

"Then, Father, if he goes, I will go too," Cuthbert exclaimed. "He promised to take me as his page the first time he went to war."

Father Francis shook his head.

"I fear me, Cuthbert, this is far from the spirit in which we a while ago agreed that men should go to the holy war."

Cuthbert hung his head a little.

"Ay, Father Francis, men; but I am a boy," he said, "and after all, boys are fond of adventure for adventure's sake. However, Father," he said, with a smile, "no doubt your eloquence on the green will turn me mightily to the project, for you must allow that the story you have told me this morning is not such as to create any very strong yearning in one's mind to follow the millions of men who have perished in the Holy Land."

"Go to," said Father Francis, smiling, "thou art a pert varlet. I will do my best on Sunday to turn you to a better frame of mind."

CHAPTER V.

PREPARATIONS.

NEXT Sunday a large number of people from some miles round were gathered on the green at Evesham, to hear Father Francis preach on the holy sepulchre. The forest men in their green jerkins mingled with the crowd, and a look of attention and seriousness was on the faces of all, for the news of the loss of the holy sepulchre had really exercised a great effect upon the minds of the people in England as elsewhere.

Those were the days of pilgrimage to holy places, when

the belief in the sanctity of places and things was overwhelming, and when men believed that a journey to the holy shrines was sufficient to procure for them a pardon for all their misdeeds. The very word "infidel" in those days was full of horror, and the thought that the holy places of the Christians were in the hands of Moslems, affected all Christians throughout Europe with a feeling of shame as well as of grief.

Among the crowd were many of the Norman retainers from the castle and from many of the holds around, and several knights with the ladies of their family stood a little apart from the edge of the gathering; for it was known that Father Francis would not be alone, but that he would be accompanied by a holy friar who had returned from the East, and who could tell of the cruelties which the Christians had suffered at the hands of the Saracens.

Father Francis, at ordinary times a tranquil preacher, was moved beyond himself by the theme on which he was holding forth. He did not attempt to hide from those who stood around that the task to be undertaken was one of grievous peril and trial; that disease and heat, hunger and thirst, must be dared, as well as the sword of the infidel. But he spoke of the grand nature of the work, of the humiliation to Christians of the desecration of the shrines, and of the glory which awaited those who joined the crusade, whether they lived or whether they died in the Holy Land.

His words had a strong effect upon the simple people who listened to him, but the feelings so aroused were as nought to the enthusiasm which greeted the address of the friar.

Meagre and pale, with a worn, anxious face as one who had suffered much, the friar, holding aloft two pieces of wood from the Mount of Olives tied together in the form of a cross, harangued the crowd. His words poured forth in a fiery stream, kindling the hearts, and stirring at once the devotion and the anger of his listeners.

He told of the holy places, he spoke of the scenes of
Holy Writ, which had there been enacted; and then he
depicted the men who had died for them. He told of the
knights and men-at-arms, each of whom proved himself
again and again a match for a score of infidels. He spoke of
the holy women, who, fearlessly and bravely, as the knights
themselves, had borne their share in the horrors of the siege
and in the terrible times which had preceded it.

He told them that this misfortune had befallen
Christianity because of the lukewarmness which had come
upon them.

"What profited it," he asked, "if the few knights who
remained to defend the holy sepulchre were heroes? A few
heroes cannot withstand an army. If Christendom after
making a mighty effort to capture the holy sepulchre had not
fallen away, the conquest which had been made with so vast
an expenditure of blood would not have been lost. This is a
work in which no mere passing fervour will avail; bravery at
first, endurance afterwards, are needed. Many men must
determine not only to assist to wrest the holy sepulchre from
the hands of the infidels, but to give their lives, so long as
they might last, to retaining it. It is scarce to be expected that
men with wives and families will take a view like this, indeed
it is not to be desired. But there are single men, men of no
ties, who can devote their whole lives, as did the Knights of
the Orders of the Cross, to this great object. When their life
has come to an end, doubtless others will take up the
banner that their hands can no longer hold. But for life it is,
indeed, that many of humble as well as of princely class
must bind themselves to take and defend to death the holy
sepulchre."

So, gradually raising the tone of his speech, the friar
proceeded; until at length by his intense earnestness, his wild
gesticulations, his impassioned words, he drew the whole of
his listeners along with him; and when he ceased, a mighty

shout of "To the Holy Land!" burst from his hearers.

Falling upon their knees, the crowd begged of him to give them the sign of the cross, and to bestow his blessing upon their swords, and upon their efforts.

Father Francis had prepared, in contemplation of such a movement, a large number of small white crosses of cloth. These he and the friar now fastened to the shoulders of the men as they crowded up to receive it, holding their hands aloft, kissing the cross that the Friar extended to them, and swearing to give their lives, if need be, to rescue the holy shrines from the infidel.

When all had received the holy symbol, Father Francis again ascended the bank from which they had addressed the crowd:

"Now go to your homes, my sons," he said. "Think of the oath that you have taken, and of the course that lies open to you when the time comes. When King Richard is prepared to start, then will you be called upon to fulfil your vows. It may be that all who have sworn may not be called upon to go. It needs that the land here should be tilled, it needs that there should be protectors for the women and children, it needs that this England of ours should flourish, and we cannot give all her sons, however willing they might be to take the cross. But the willingness which you will, I am sure, show to go if needs be, and to redeem your vows, will be sufficient. Some must go and some must stay; these are matters to be decided hereafter; for the time let us separate; you will hear when the hour for action arrives."

A fortnight later the Earl of Evesham, who had been on a long journey to London, returned with full authority to raise and organize a force as his contingent to the holy wars.

All was now bustle and activity in the castle.

Father Francis informed him of the willingness of such of the forest men as he deemed fit to enlist under his banner; and the earl was much gratified at finding that the ranks of heavily armed retainers whom he would take with him, were to be swollen by the addition of so useful a contingent as that of 100 skilful archers.

Cuthbert was not long in asking for an interview with the earl.

He had indeed great difficulty in persuading Dame Editha that he was old enough to share in the fatigues of so great an expedition, but he had Father Francis on his side; and between the influence of her confessor, and the importunities of her son, the opposition of the good lady fell to the ground.

Cuthbert was already, for his age, well trained to arms. Many of the old soldiers at the castle who had known and loved his father, had been ever ready to give lessons in the use of arms to Cuthbert, who was enthusiastic in his desire to prove as good a knight as his father had been. His friends, the outlaws, had taught him the use of the bow and of the quarter-staff; and Cuthbert, strong and well-built for his age, and having little to do save to wield the sword and the bow, had attained a very considerable amount of skill with each.

He had too, which was unusual, a certain amount of book learning, although this, true to say, had not been acquired so cheerfully or willingly as the skill at arms. Father Francis had, however, taught him to read and to write—accomplishments which were at that time rare, except in the cloister. In those days if a knight had a firm seat in his saddle, a strong arm, a keen eye, and high courage, it was thought to be of little matter whether he could or could not do more than make his mark on the parchment. The whole life of the young was given to acquiring skill in arms; and unless intended for the convent, any idea of education would in the great majority of cases have been considered as preposterous.

To do Cuthbert justice, he had protested with all his might against the proposition of Father Francis to his mother to teach him some clerkly knowledge. He had yielded most unwillingly at last to her entreaties, backed as they were by the sound arguments and good sense of Father Francis.

The Earl of Evesham received Cuthbert's application very graciously.

"Certainly, Cuthbert," he said, "you shall accompany me; first, on account of my promise to you; secondly, because from the readiness you displayed both in the matter of my daughter and of the attack on Wortham, you will be a notable aid and addition to my party; thirdly, from my friendship for your father and Dame Editha."

This point being settled, Cuthbert at once assumed his new duties. There was plenty for him to do—to see that the orders of the earl were properly carried out; to bear messages to the knights who followed the earl's fortunes, at their various holds; to stand by and watch the armourers at work, and the preparation of the stores of arms and missiles which would be necessary for the expedition.

Sometimes he would go round to summon the tenants of the various farms and lands, who held from the earl, to come to the castle; and here Sir Walter would, as far as might be without oppression, beg of them to contribute largely to the expedition.

In these appeals he was in no slight way assisted by Father Francis, who pointed out loudly to the people that those who stayed behind were bound to make as much sacrifice of their worldly goods, as those who went to the war might make of their lives. Life and land are alike at the service of God. Could the land be sold, it would be a good deed to sell it; but as this could not be, they should at least sell all that they could, and pledge their property if they could find lenders, in order to contribute to the needs of their lord, and the fitting out of this great enterprise.

The preparations were at last complete, and a gallant band gathered at the castle ready for starting. It consisted of some 200 men-at-arms led by six knights, and of 100 bowmen dressed in Lincoln green, with quilted jerkins to keep out the arrows of the enemy. All the country from

around gathered to see the start. Dame Editha was there, and by her side stood the earl's little daughter. The earl himself was in armour, and beside him rode Cuthbert in the gay attire of a page.

Just at that moment, however, his face did not agree with his costume for although he strove his best to look bright and smiling, it was a hard task to prevent the tears from filling his eyes at his departure from his mother. The good lady cried unrestrainedly, and Margaret joined in her tears. The people who had gathered round cheered lustily; the trumpets blew a gay fanfaronade; and the squire threw to the wind the earl's colours.

It was no mere pleasure trip on which they were starting, for all knew that, of the preceding crusades, not one in ten of those who had gone so gladly forth had ever returned.

It must not be supposed that the whole of those present were animated by any strong religious feeling. No doubt there existed a desire, which was carefully fanned by the preaching of the priests and monks, to rescue the holy sepulchre from the hands of the Saracens; but a far stronger feeling was to be found in the warlike nature of the people in those days. Knights, men-at-arms, and indeed men of all ranks, were full of a combative spirit. Life in the castle and hut was alike dull and monotonous, and the excitement of war and adventure was greatly looked for, both as a means of obtaining glory and booty, and for the change they afforded to the dreary monotony of life.

There is little to tell of the journey of the Earl of Evesham's band through England to Southampton, at which place they took ship and crossed to France—or rather to Normandy, for in those days Normandy was regarded, as indeed it formed, a part of England.

Cuthbert, as was natural to his age, was full of delight at all the varying scenes through which they passed. The towns were to him an especial source of wonder, for he had never visited any other than that of Worcester, to which he had once or twice been taken on occasions of high festival. Havre was in those days an important place, and being the landing-place of a great portion of the English bands, it was full of bustle and excitement. Every day ships brought in nobles and their followings.

The King of England was already in Normandy hastening the preparations, and each band, as it landed, marched down to the meeting-place on the plains of Vezelay. Already they began to experience a taste of the hardships which they were to endure.

In those days there was no regular supply train for an army, but each division or band supported itself by purchase or pillage, as the case might be, from the surrounding country.

As the English troops were marching through a friendly

country, pillage was of course strictly forbidden; but while many of the leaders paid for all they had, it must be owned that among the smaller leaders were many who took anything that they required with or without payment.

The country was eaten up.

The population in those days was sparse, and the movement of so large a number of men along a certain route completely exhausted all the resources of the inhabitants; and although willing to pay for all that his men required, the Earl of Evesham had frequently to lie down on the turf supperless himself.

"If this is the case now," he said to Cuthbert, "what will it be after we have joined the French army? Methinks whatever we may do if we reach the Holy Land, that we have a fair chance of being starved before we sail."

After a long succession of marches they arrived in sight of the great camp at Vezelay. It was indeed rather a canvas town than a camp. Here were gathered nearly 100,000 men, a vast host at any time, but in those days far greater in proportion to the strength of the countries than at present. The tents of the leaders, nobles, and other knights and gentlemen, rose in regular lines, forming streets and squares.

The great mass of troops, however, were contented to sleep in the open air; indeed the difficulties of carriage were so great that it was only the leaders who could carry with them their canvas abodes. Before each tent stood the lance and colours of its owner, and side by side in the centre of the camp stood the royal pavilions of Phillip of France and Richard of England, round which could be seen the gonfalons of all the nobles of Western Europe.

Nothing could be gayer than the aspect of this camp as the party rode into it. They were rather late, and the great body of the host were already assembled.

Cuthbert gazed with delight at the varied colours, the gay dresses, the martial knights, and the air of discipline and order which reigned everywhere.

This was indeed war in its most picturesque form, a form which, as far as beauty is concerned, has been altogether altered, and indeed destroyed, by modern arms.

In those days individual prowess and bravery went for everything. A handful of armoured knights were a match for thousands of footmen, and battles were decided as much by the prowess and bravery of the leader and his immediate following as by that of the great mass of the army.

The earl had the day before sent on a messenger to state that he was coming, and as the party entered the camp they were met by a squire of the camp-marshal, who conducted them to the position allotted to them.

The earl's tent was soon erected, with four or five grouped around it for his knights, one being set aside for his squires and pages.

When this was done, Cuthbert strolled away to look at the varied sights of the camp. A military officer in these days would be scandalized at the scenes which were going on, but the strict, hard military discipline of modern times was then absolutely unknown.

A camp was a moving town, and to it flocked the country people with their goods; smiths and armourers erected their forges; minstrels and troubadours flocked in to sing of former battles, and to raise the spirits of the soldiers by merry lays of love and war; simple countrymen and women came in to bring their presents of fowls or cakes to their friends in camp; knights rode to and fro on their gaily caparisoned horses through the crowd; the newly raised levies, in many cases composed of woodmen and peasants who had not in the course of their lives wandered a league from their birthplaces, gaped in unaffected wonder at the sights around them; while last, but by no means least, the maidens and good wives of the neighbourhood, fond then as now of brave men and gay dresses, thronged the streets of the camp, and joined in, and were the cause of, merry laughter and jest.

Here and there, a little apart from the main stream of traffic, the minstrels would take up their position, and playing a gay air, the soldier lads and lasses would fall to and foot it merrily to the strains. Sometimes there would be a break in the gaiety, and loud shouts, and perhaps fierce oaths, would rise. Then the maidens would fly like startled fawns, and men hasten to the spot; though the quarrel might be purely a private one, yet should it happen between the retainers of two nobles, friends of each would be sure to strike in, and serious frays would arise before the marshal of the camp with his posse could arrive to interfere. Sometimes indeed these quarrels became so serious and desperate that alliances were broken up and great intentions frustrated by the quarrels of the soldiery.

Here and there, on elevated platforms, or even on the top of a pile of tubs, were friars occupied in haranguing the soldiers, and in inspiring them with enthusiasm for the cause upon which they were embarked. The conduct of their listeners showed easily enough the motives which had brought them to war. Some stood with clasped hands and eager eyes listening to the exhortations of the priests, and ready, as might be seen from their earnest gaze, to suffer martyrdom in the cause. More, however, stood indifferently round, or after listening to a few words walked on with a laugh or a scoff; indeed preaching had already done all that lay in its power. All those who could be moved by exhortations of this kind were there, and upon the rest the discourses and sermons were thrown away.

Several times in the course of his stroll round the camp Cuthbert observed the beginnings of quarrels, which were in each case only checked by the intervention of some knight or other person in authority coming past, and he observed that these in every instance occurred between men of the English and those of the French army.

Between the Saxon contingent of King Richard's army and the French soldiers there could indeed be no quarrel, for the Saxons understood no word of their language; but with the Normans the case was different, for the Norman-French, which was spoken by all the nobles and their retainers in Britain, was as nearly as possible the same as that in use in France.

It seemed, however, to Cuthbert, watching narrowly what was going on, that there existed by no means a good feeling between the men of the different armies; and he thought that this divergence so early in the campaign boded but little good for the final success of the expedition.

When he returned to the tent the earl questioned him as to what he had seen, and Cuthbert frankly acknowledged that it appeared to him that the feeling between the men of the two armies was not good.

"I have been," the earl said, "to the royal camp, and from what I hear, Cuthbert, methinks that there is reason for what you say. King Richard is the most loyal and gallant of kings, but he is haughty, and hasty in speech. The Normans, too, have been somewhat accustomed to conquer our neighbours, and it may well be that the chivalry of France love us not. However, it must be hoped that this feeling will die away, and that we shall emulate each other only in our deeds on the battlefield."

CHAPTER VI.

THE LISTS.

THE third day after the arrival of the Earl of Evesham there was a great banquet given by the King of France to King Richard and his principal nobles.

Among those present was the Earl of Evesham, and Cuthbert as his page followed him to the great tent where the banquet was prepared.

Here, at the top of the tent, on a raised dais, sat the King of France surrounded by his courtiers.

The Earl of Evesham, having been conducted by the herald to the dais, paid his compliments to the king, and was saluted by him with many flattering words.

The sound of a trumpet was heard, and Richard of England, accompanied by his principal nobles, entered.

It was the first time that Cuthbert had seen the king.

Richard was a man of splendid stature and of enormous strength. His appearance was in some respects rather Saxon than Norman, for his hair was light and his complexion clear and bright. He wore the moustache and pointed beard at that time in fashion; and although his expression was generally that of frankness and good humour, there might be observed in his quick motions and piercing glances signs of the hasty temper and unbridled passion which went far to wreck the success of the enterprise upon which he was embarked.

Richard possessed most of the qualities which make a man a great king and render him the idol of his subjects, especially in a time of semi-civilization, when personal prowess is placed at the summit of all human virtues. In all his dominions there was not one man who in personal conflict was a match for his king.

Except during his fits of passion, King Richard was generous, forgiving, and royal in his moods. He was incapable of bearing malice. Although haughty of his dignity, he was entirely free from any personal pride, and while he would maintain to the death every right and privilege against another monarch, he could laugh and joke with the humblest of his subjects on terms of hearty good fellowship. He was impatient of contradiction, eager to carry out whatever he had determined upon; and nothing enraged him so much as hesitation or procrastination. The delays which were experienced in the course of the Crusade angered him more than all the opposition offered by the Saracens, or than the hardships through which the Christian host had to pass.

At a flourish of trumpets all took their seats at dinner, their places being marked for them by a herald, whose duty it was to regulate nicely the various ranks and dignities.

The Earl of Evesham was placed next to a noble of Brabant. Cuthbert took his place behind his lord and served him with wines and meats, the Brabant being attended by a tall youth, who was indeed on the verge of manhood.

As the dinner went on the buzz of conversation became fast and furious. In those days men drank deep, and quarrels often arose over the cups. From the time that the dinner began, Cuthbert noticed that the manner of Sir de Jacquelin Barras, Count of Brabant, was rude and offensive.

It might be that he was accustomed to live alone with his retainers, and that his manners were rude and coarse to all. It might be that he had a special hostility to the English. At any rate, his remarks were calculated to fire the anger of the earl.

He began the conversation by wondering how a Norman baron could live in a country like England, inhabited by a race but little above pigs.

The earl at once fired up at this, for the Normans were now beginning to feel themselves English, and to resent attacks upon a people for whom their grandfathers had entertained contempt.

He angrily repelled the attack upon them by the Brabant knight, and asserted at once that the Saxons were every bit as civilized, and in some respects superior, to the Normans or French.

The ill-feeling thus begun at starting clearly waxed stronger as dinner went on. The Brabant knight drank deeply, and although his talk was not clearly directed against the English, yet he continued to throw out inuendos and side attacks, and to talk with a vague boastfulness, which greatly irritated Sir Walter.

Presently, as Cuthbert was about to serve his master with a cup of wine, the tall page pushed suddenly against him, spilling a portion of the wine over his dress.

"What a clumsy child!" he said scoffingly.

"You are a rough and ill-mannered loon," Cuthbert said

angrily. "Were you in any other presence I would chastise you as you deserve."

The tall page burst into a mocking laugh.

"Chastise me!" he said. "Why, I could put you in my pocket for a little hop-of-my-thumb as you are."

"I think," said Sir Jacquelin —for the boys' voices both rose loud — to the earl, "you had better send that brat home and order him to be whipped."

"Sir count," said the earl, "your manners are insolent, and were we not engaged upon a Crusade, it would please me much to give you a lesson on that score."

Higher and higher the dispute rose, until some angry word caught the ear of the king.

Amid the general buzz of voices King Phillip rose, and speaking a word to King Richard, moved from the table, thus giving the sign for the breaking up of the feast.

Immediately afterwards a page touched the earl and Sir Jacquelin upon the shoulder, and told them that the kings desired to speak with them in the tent of the King of France.

The two nobles strode through the crowd, regarding each other with eyes much like those of two dogs eager to fly at each other's throat.

"My lords, my lords," said King Phillip when they entered, "this is against all law and reason. For shame, to be brawling at my table. I would not say aught openly, but methinks it is early indeed for the knights and nobles engaged in a common work to fall to words."

"Your Majesty," said the Earl of Evesham, "I regret deeply what has happened. But it seemed, from the time we sat down to the meal, that this lord sought to pass a quarrel upon me, and I now beseech your Majesty that you will permit us to settle our differences in the lists."

King Richard gave a sound of assent, but the King of France shook his head gravely.

"Do you forget," he said, "the mission upon which you are assembled here? Has not every knight and noble in these armies taken a solemn oath to put aside private quarrels and feuds until the holy sepulchre is taken? Shall we at this very going off show that the oath is a mere form of words? Shall we show before the face of Christendom that the knights of the cross are unable to avoid flying at each other's throats, even while on their way to wrest the holy sepulchre from the infidel? No, sirs, you must lay aside your feuds, and must promise me and my good brother here that you will keep the peace between you until this war is over. Whose fault it was that the quarrel began I know not. It may be that my Lord of Brabant was discourteous. It may be that the earl here was too hot. But whichever it be, it matters not."

"The quarrel, sire," said Sir Jacquelin, "arose from a dispute between our pages, who were nigh coming to blows in your Majesty's presence. I desired the earl to chide the insolence of his varlet, and instead of so doing he met my remarks with scorn."

"Pooh, pooh," said King Richard, "there are plenty of grounds for quarrel without two nobles interfering in the squabbles of boys. Let them fight; it will harm no one. By-the-bye, your Majesty," he said, turning to the King of France with a laugh, "if the masters may not fight, there is no reason in the world why the varlets should not. We are sorely dull for want of amusement. Let us have a list to-morrow, and let the pages fight it out for the honour of their masters and their nations."

"It were scarce worth while to have the lists set for two boys to fight," said the King of France.

"Oh, we need not have regular lists," said King Richard. "Leave that matter in my hands. I warrant you that if the cockerels are well plucked, they will make us sport. What say you, gentlemen?"

The Brabant noble at once assented, answering that he was sure that his page would be glad to enter the lists; and the earl, gave a similar assent, for he had not noticed how great was the discrepancy between the size of the future combatants.

"That is agreed, then," said King Richard joyously. "I will have a piece of ground marked out on the edge of the camp to-morrow morning. It shall be kept by my men-at-arms, and there shall be a raised place for King Phillip and myself, who will be the judges of the conflict. Will they fight on foot or on horse?"

"On foot, on foot," said the King of France. "It would be a pity that knightly exercises should be brought to scorn by any failure on their part on horseback. On foot at least it will be a fair struggle."

"What arms shall they use?" the Brabant knight asked.

"Oh, swords and battle-axes, of course," said King Richard with a laugh.

"Before you go," King Phillip said, "you must shake hands, and swear to let the quarrel between you drop, at least until after our return. If you still wish to shed each other's blood, I shall offer no hindrance thereto."

The earl and Count Jacquelin touched each other's hands in obedience to the order, went out of the tent together, and strode off without a word in different directions.

"My dear lad," the Earl of Evesham said on entering his tent where his page was waiting him, "this is a serious business. The kings have ordered this little count and myself to put aside our differences till after the Crusade, in accordance with our oath. But as you have in no wise pledged yourself in the same fashion, and as their Majesties feel somewhat dull while waiting here, it is determined that the quarrel between the count and me, and between you and the count's page, shall be settled by a fight between you two in the presence of the kings."

"Well, sir," Cuthbert said, "I am glad that it should be, seeing the varlet insulted me without any cause, and purposely upset the cup over me."

"What is he like?" the earl asked. "Dost think that you are a fair match?"

"I doubt not that we are fair match enough," Cuthbert said. "As you know, sir, I have been well trained to arms of all kinds, both by my father and by the men-at-arms at the castle, and could hold my own against any of your men with light weapons, and have then no fear that this gawky loon, twenty years old though he seems to be, will bring disgrace upon me or discredit upon my nation."

"If thou thinkest so," the earl said, "the matter can go on. But had it been otherwise, I would have gone to the king and protested that the advantage of age was so great that it would be murder to place you in the list together."

"There is," Cuthbert said, "at most no greater difference between us than between a strong man and a weak one, and these, in the ordeal of battle, have to meet in the lists. Indeed I doubt if the difference is so great, for if he be a foot taller than I, methinks that round the shoulders I should have the advantage of him."

"Send hither my armourer," the earl said; "we must choose a proper suit for you. I fear that mine would be of little use; but doubtless there are some smaller suits among my friends."

"The simpler and lighter the better," Cuthbert said. "I'd rather have a light coat of mail and a steel cap, than heavy armour and a helmet which would press me down and a visor through which I could scarce see. The lighter the better, for after all if my sword cannot keep my head, sooner or later the armour would fail to do so too."

The armourer speedily arrived, and the knights and followers of the earl being called in and the case stated, there was soon found a coat of fine linked mail, which fitted Cuthbert well. As to the steel cap, there was no difficulty whatever.

"You must have a plume at least," the earl said, and took some feathers from his own casque and fastened them in.

"Will you want a light sword and battle-axe?"

"No," Cuthbert said, "my arms are pretty well used to those of the men-at-arms. I could wield my father's sword, and that was a heavy one."

The lightest of the earl's weapons were chosen, and it was agreed that all was now ready for the conflict to-morrow.

In the morning there was a slight bustle in the camp.

The news that a fight was to take place between an

English and a Brabant page, by the permission of the Kings of England and France, that their Majesties were to be present, and that all was to be conducted on regular rules, caused a stir of excitement and novelty in the camp.

Nowhere is life duller than among a large body of men kept together for any time under canvas, and the thought of a combat of this novel kind excited general interest.

In a meadow at a short distance from the camp, a body of King Richard's men-at-arms marked off an oval space of about an acre. Upon one side of this a tent was pitched for the kings, and a small tent was placed at each end for the combatants. Round the enclosure the men-at-arms formed the ring, and behind them a dense body of spectators gathered, a place being set aside for nobles, and others of gentle blood.

At the hour fixed the Kings of England and France arrived together. King Richard was evidently in a state of high good humour, for he preferred the clash of arms and the sight of combat to any other pleasure.

The King of France, on the other hand, looked grave. He was a far wiser and more politic king than Richard; and although he had consented to the sudden proposal, yet he felt in his heart that the contest was a foolish one, and that it might create bad feeling among the men of the two nationalities whichever way it went. He had reserved to himself the right of throwing down the baton when the combat was to cease, and he determined to avail himself of this right, to put a stop to the conflict before either party was likely to sustain any deadly injury.

When the monarchs had taken their places the trumpeters sounded their trumpets, and the two combatants advanced on foot from their ends of the lists. A murmur of surprise and dissatisfaction broke from the crowd.

"My Lord of Evesham," the king said angrily to the earl, who with Count Jacquelin was standing by the royal party, "thou shouldst have said that the difference between the two was too great to allow the combat to be possible. The Frenchman appears to be big enough to take your page under his arm and walk off with him."

The difference was indeed very striking. The French champion was arrayed in a full suit of knightly armour—of course without the gold spurs which were the distinguishing mark of that rank—and with his helmet and lofty plume of feathers he appeared to tower above Cuthbert, who, in his close-fitting steel cap and link armour, seemed a very dwarf by the side of a giant.

"It is not size, sire, but muscle and pluck will win in a combat like this. Your Majesty need not be afraid that my page will disgrace me. He is of my blood, though the kinship is not close. He is of mixed Saxon and Norman strain, and will, believe me, do no discredit to either."

The king's brow cleared, for in truth he was very proud of his English nationality, and would have been sorely vexed to see the discomfiture of an English champion, even though that champion were a boy.

"Brother Phillip," he said, turning to the king, "I will wager my gold chain against yours on yonder stripling."

"Methinks that it were robbery to take your wager," the King of France said. "The difference between their bulk is disproportionate. However, I will not baulk your wish. My chain against yours."

The rule of the fight was that they were to commence with swords, but that either could, if he chose, use his battle-axe.

The fight need scarcely be described at length, for the advantage was all one way. Cuthbert was fully a match in strength for his antagonist, although standing nigh a foot shorter. Constant exercise, however, had hardened his muscles into something like steel, while the teaching that he had received had embraced all that was then known of the use of arms.

Science in those days there was but little of; it was a case rather of hard, heavy hitting, than of what we now call swordsmanship.

With the sword Cuthbert gained but slight advantage over his adversary whose superior height enabled him to rain blows down upon the lad, which he was with difficulty enabled to guard; but when the first paroxysm of his adversary's attack had passed, he took to the offensive, and drove his opponent back step by step. With his sword, however, he was unable to cut through the armour of the Frenchman, but in the course of the encounter, guarding a severe blow aimed at him, his sword was struck from his hand, and he then, seizing his axe, made such play with it

that his foe dropped his own sword and took to the same weapon.

In this the superior height and weight of his opponent gave him even a greater advantage than with the sword, and Cuthbert knowing this, used his utmost dexterity and speed to avoid the sweeping blows showered upon him. He himself had been enabled to strike one or two sweeping strokes, always aiming at the same place, the juncture of the visor with the helmet. At last the Frenchman struck him so heavy a blow that it beat down his guard and struck his steel cap from his head, bringing him to the knee. In an instant he was up, and before his foe could be again on guard, he whirled his axe round with all its force, and bringing it just at the point of the visor which he had already weakened with repeated blows, the edge of the axe stove clean through the armour, and the page was struck senseless to the ground.

A great shout broke from the English portion of the soldiery as Cuthbert leant over his prostrate foe, and receiving no answer to the question "Do you yield?" rose to his feet, and signified to the squire who had kept near that his opponent was insensible.

King Richard ordered the pursuivant to lead Cuthbert to the royal enclosure.

"Thou art a brave lad and a lusty," the king said, "and hast borne thee in the fight as well as many a knight would have done. Wert thou older, I would myself dub thee knight; and I doubt not that the occasion will yet come when thou wilt do as good deeds upon the bodies of the Saracens as thou hast upon that long-shanked opponent of thine. Here is a gold chain; take it as a proof that the King of England holds that you have sustained well the honour of his country; and mark me, if at any time you require a boon, bring or send me that chain, and thou shalt have it freely. Sir Walter," he said, turning to the earl, "in this lad thou hast a worthy champion, and I trust me that thou wilt give him every chance of distinguishing himself. So soon as thou thinkst him fit for the knightly rank I myself will administer the accolade."

CHAPTER VII.

REVENGE.

AFTER his interview with the king, Cuthbert was led to his tent amid the hearty plaudits of the English troops.

His own comrades flocked round him; the men of the greenwood headed by Cnut, were especially jubilant over his victory.

"Who would have thought," said the tall forester, "that the lad who but a short time ago was a child, should now have sustained the honour of the country? We feel proud of you, Cuthbert; and trust us some day or other to follow wherever you may lead, and to do some deed which will attain for you honour and glory, and show that the men of Evesham are as doughty as any under King Richard's rule."

"You must be wary, Cuthbert," the earl said to him that evening. "Believe me that you and I have made a foe, who, although he may not have the power, has certainly the will to injure us to the death. I marked the eye of Count Jacquelin during the fight, and again when you were led up to the king. There was hatred and fury in his eye. The page too, I hear, is his own nephew, and he will be the laughing-stock of the French camp at having been conquered by one so much younger than himself. It will be well to keep upon your guard, and not to go out at night unattended. Keep Cnut near you; he is faithful as a watch-dog, and would give his life, I am sure, for you. I will myself be also upon my guard, for it was after all my quarrel, and the fury of this fierce knight will vent itself upon both of us if the opportunity should come. I hear but a poor account of him among his confrères. They say he is one of those disgraces to the name of knight who are but a mixture of robber and soldier; that he harries all the lands in his neighbourhood; and that he has now only joined the Crusade to avoid the vengeance which the cries of the oppressed people had invoked from his liege lord. I am told indeed that the choice was given him to be outlawed, or to join the Crusades with all the strength he could raise. Naturally he adopted the latter alternative; but he has the instincts of the robber still, and will do us an evil turn, if he have the chance."

Two days later the great army broke up its camp and marched south. After a week's journeying they encamped near a town, and halted there two or three days in order to collect provisions for the next advance; for the supplies which they could obtain in the country districts were wholly insufficient for so great a host of men. Here the armies were to separate, the French marching to Genoa, the English to Marseilles, the town at which they were to take ship.

One evening the earl sent Cuthbert with a message to another English lord, staying in the town at the palace of the bishop, who was a friend of his.

Cnut accompanied Cuthbert, for he now made a point of seldom letting him out of his sight. It was light when they reached the bishop's palace, but here they were delayed for some time, and night had fallen when they sallied out.

The town was already quiet, for the inhabitants cared not to show themselves in the streets now that such a large army of fierce men were in the neighborhood.

The orders indeed of the monarchs were stringent, but discipline there was but little of, and the soldiery in those days regarded peaceful citizens as fair game; hence, when they came from the palace the streets of the city were already hushed and quiet, for the orders of the king had been peremptory that no men-at-arms, or others except those on duty, were to be away from their camp after nightfall.

This order had been absolutely necessary, so many were the complaints brought in by country peasants and farmers,

of the doings of bands of soldiers.

Cnut and Cuthbert proceeded along the streets unmolested for some distance. Occasionally a solitary passer-by, with hooded cape, hurried past. The moon was half full, and her light was welcome indeed, for in those days the streets were unlighted, and the pavement so bad that passage through the streets after dark was a matter of difficulty, and even of danger.

Here and there before some roadside shrine a lamp dimly burned; before these they paused and, as good Catholics, Cnut and Cuthbert crossed themselves. Just as they had passed one of these wayside shrines, a sudden shout was heard, and a party of eight or ten men sprang out from a side street and fell upon them.

Cnut and Cuthbert drew their swords and laid about at them heartily, but their assailants were too strong. Cnut was stricken to the ground, and Cuthbert, seeing that defence was hopeless, took to his heels and ran for his life. He was already wounded, but happily not so severely as in any way to disable him.

Seeing that it was speed, and speed alone, which now could save him, he flung aside his belt scabbard and as he ran, and with rapid steps flew along the streets, not knowing whither he went, and striving only to keep ahead of his pursuers. They, more encumbered by arms and armour, were unable to keep up with the flying footsteps of a lad clothed in the light attire of a page; but Cuthbert felt that the blood running from his wound was weakening him fast, and that unless he could gain some refuge his course must speedily come to an end. Happily he saw at some little distance ahead of him a man standing by a door. Just as he arrived the door opened, and a glow of light from within fell on the road, showing that the person entering was a monk.

Without a moment's hesitation Cuthbert rushed through the door, shouting "Sanctuary!" and sank almost fainting on the ground.

The monks, accustomed to wild pursuits and scenes of outrage in those warlike days, hastily closed the door, barring it securely. In a moment there was a rush of men against it from without.

One of the monks opened a lattice above the door.

"What mean you," he said, "by this outrage? Know ye not that this is the Monastery of St. John, and that it is sacrilege to lay a hand of violence even against its postern? Be gone," he said, "or we'll lodge a complaint before the king."

The assailants, nothing daunted, continued to batter at the door; but at this moment the monks, aroused from their beds, hastened to the spot, and seizing bill and sword—for in those days even monks were obliged at times to depend upon carnal weapons—they opened the door, and flung themselves upon the assailants with such force that the latter, surprised and discomfited, were forced to make a hasty retreat.

The doors were then again barred, and Cuthbert was carried up to a cell in the building, where the leech of the monastery speedily examined his wound, and pronounced, that although his life was not in danger by it, he was greatly weakened by the loss of blood, that the wound was a serious one, and that it would be some time before the patient would recover.

It was two days before Cuthbert was sufficiently restored to be able to speak. His first question to the monk was as to his whereabouts, and how long he had been there. Upon being answered, he entreated that a messenger might be despatched to the camp of the Earl of Evesham, to beg that a litter might be sent for him, and to inquire what had become of Cnut, whom he had last seen stricken down.

The monk replied, "My son, I grieve to tell you that your request cannot be complied with. The army moved away yesternoon, and is now some five-and-twenty miles distant. There is nothing for you but patience, and when restored you can follow the army, and rejoin your master before he embarks at Marseilles. But how is it that a lad so young as you can have incurred the enmity of those who sought your life? For it is clear from the pertinacity with which they urged their attack that their object was not plunder, of which indeed they would get but little from you, but to take your life."

Cuthbert recounted the circumstances which had led to the feud of the Count of Brabant against him, for he doubted not that this truculent knight was at the bottom of the attack.

"After what has happened," the monk said, "you will need have caution when you leave here. The place where you have taken refuge is known to them, and should this wild noble persist in his desire for vengeance against you, he will doubtless leave some of his ruffians to watch the monastery. We will keep a look-out, and note if any strangers are to be seen near the gates; if we find that it is so, we shall consider what is best to be done. We could of course appeal to the mayor for protection against them, and could even have the strangers ejected from the town or cast into prison; but it is not likely that we should succeed in capturing more than the fellow who may be placed on the look-out, and the danger would be in no wise lessened to yourself. But there is time to talk over this matter before you leave. It will be another fortnight at least before you will be able to pursue your journey."

Cuthbert gained strength more rapidly than the monk had expected. He was generously fed, and this and his good constitution soon enabled him to recover from the loss of blood; and at the end of five days he expressed his hope that he could on the following day pursue his journey. The monk who attended him shook his head.

"Thou mightst, under ordinary circumstances, quit us to-morrow, for thou art well enough to take part in the ordinary pursuits of a page; but to journey is a different thing. You may have all sorts of hardships to endure; you may have even to trust for your life to your speed and endurance; and it would be madness for you to go until your strength is fully established. I regret to tell you that we have ascertained beyond a doubt that the monastery is closely watched. We have sent some of the acolytes out, dressed in the garbs of monks, and attended by one of our elder brethren; and in each case, a monk who followed at a distance of fifty yards was able to perceive that they were watched. The town is full of rough men, the hangers-on to the army; some, indeed, are followers of laggard knights, but the greater portion are men who merely pursue the army with view to gain by its necessities, to buy plunder from the soldiers, and to rob, and, if necessary, to murder should there be a hope of obtaining gold. Among these men your enemies would have little difficulty in recruiting any number, and no appeal that we could make to the mayor would protect you from them when you have left the walls. We must trust to our ingenuity in smuggling you out. After that, it is upon your own strength and shrewdness that you must rely for an escape from any snares that may be laid for you. You will see, then, that at least another three or four days are needed before you can set forth. Your countrymen are so far away that a matter of a few days will make but little difference. They will in any case be delayed for a long time at Marseilles before they embark; and whether you leave now or a month hence, you would be equally in time to join them before their embarkation—that is, supposing that you make your way through the snares which beset you."

Cuthbert saw the justice of the reason and it was another week before he announced himself as feeling absolutely restored to strength again, and capable of bearing as much exertion as he could have done before his attack.

A long consultation was held with the prior and a monk who had acted as his leech, as to the best plan of getting Cuthbert beyond the walls of the city. Many schemes were proposed and rejected. Every monk who ventured beyond the walls had been closely scrutinized, and one or two of short stature had even been jostled in the streets, so as to throw back their hoods and expose a sight of their faces. It was clear then, that it would be dangerous to trust to a disguise. Cuthbert proposed that he should leave at night, trusting solely to their direction as to the turnings he should take to bring him to the city wall, and that, taking a rope, he should there let himself down, and make the best of his way forward. This, however, the monks would not consent to, assuring him that the watch was so strictly kept round the monastery that he would inevitably be seen.

"No," the prior said, "the method, whatever it is, must be as open as possible; and though I cannot at this moment hit upon a plan, I will think it over to-night, and putting my ideas with those of Father Jerome here, and the sacristan, who has a shrewd head, it will be hard if we cannot between us contrive some plan to evade the watch of those robber villains who beset the convent."

The next morning when the prior came in to see Cuthbert, the latter said, "Good father, I have determined not to endeavour to make off in disguise. I doubt not that your wit could contrive some means by which I should get clear of the walls without observation from the scouts of this villain noble. But once in the country, I should have neither horse nor armour, and should have hard work indeed to make my way down through France, even though none of my enemies were on my track. I will therefore, if it please you, go down boldly to the Mayor, and claim a protection and escort. If he will but grant me a few men-at-arms for one day's ride from the town, I can choose my own route, and riding out in mail can then take my chance of finding my way down to Marseilles."

"I will go down with you, my son," the prior said, "to the mayor. Two of my monks shall accompany us; and assuredly no insult will be offered to you in the street thus accompanied."

Shortly afterwards, Cuthbert started as arranged, and soon arrived at the house of the mayor, Sir John de Cahors.

Upon the prior making known to this knight whom he had brought with him, the mayor exclaimed,—

"Pest! young gentleman; you have caused us no small trouble and concern. We have had ridings to and fro concerning you, and furious messages from your fiery king.

When in the morning a tall, stalwart knave dressed in green was found, slashed about in various places, lying on the pavement, the towns-men, not knowing who he was, but finding that he still breathed, carried him to the English camp, and he was claimed as a follower of the Earl of Evesham. There was great wrath and anger over this; and an hour later the earl himself came down and stated that his page was missing, and that there was reason to believe that he had been foully murdered, as he had accompanied the man found wounded. Fortunately the bulk of the armies had marched away at early dawn, and the earl had only remained behind in consequence of the absence of his followers. I assured the angry Englishman that I would have a thorough search made in the town; and although in no way satisfied, he rode off after his king with all his force, carrying with him the long-limbed man whom we had picked up. Two days after, a message came back from King Richard himself, saying that unless this missing page were discovered, or if, he being killed, his murderers were not brought to justice and punished, he would assuredly on his return from the Holy Land burn the town over our ears. Your king is not a man who minces matters. However, threatened men live long, especially when the person who threatens is starting for a journey, from which, as like or not, he may never return. However, I have had diligent search made for you. All the houses of bad repute have been examined, and their inhabitants questioned. But there are so many camp-followers and other rabble at present in the town that a hundred men might disappear without our being able to obtain a clue. I doubted not indeed that your body had been thrown in the river, and that we should never hear more of you. I am right glad that you have been restored; not indeed from any fear of the threats of the king your master, but because, from what the Earl of Evesham said, you were a lad likely to come to great fame and honour. The earl left in my charge your horse, and the armour which he said you wore at a tournament lately, in case we should hear aught of you."

Cuthbert gave an exclamation of pleasure. His purse contained but a few pieces of silver, and being without arms except for his short dagger, or means of locomotion, the difficulties of the journey down to Marseilles had sorely puzzled him. But with his good horse between his knees, and his suit of Milan armour on his back, he thought that he might make his way through any dangers which threatened him.

The prior now told the knight that circumstances had

occurred, which showed that it was known to the assailants of Cuthbert that he had taken refuge in the convent, over which a strict watch had been kept by Cuthbert's enemies.

"If I could find the varlets, I would hang them over the gates of the town," the knight said wrathfully. "But as at the present moment there are nearly as many rogues as honest men in the place, it would be a wholesale hanging indeed to ensure getting hold of the right people. Moreover, it is not probable that another attempt upon his life will be made inside our walls; and doubtless the main body of this gang are somewhere without, intending to assault him when he continues his journey, and they have left but a spy or two here to inform them as to his movements. I will give you any aid in my power, young sir. The army is by this time nigh Marseilles, and, sooth to say, I have no body of men-at-arms whom I could send as your escort for so long a distance. I have but a small body here, and they are needed, and sorely too, to keep order within the walls."

"I thought, sir," Cuthbert said, "that if you could lend me a party of say four men-at-arms to ride with me for the first day, I could then trust to myself, especially if you could procure me one honest man to act as guide and companion. Doubtless they suppose that I should travel by the main road south; but by going the first day's journey either east or west, and then striking some southward road, I should get a fair start of them, throw all their plans out, and perchance reach Marseilles without interruption."

The knight willingly agreed to furnish four men-at-arms, and a trustworthy guide who would at least take him as far south as Avignon.

"I will," he said, "tell the men-at-arms off to-night. They shall be at the western gate at daybreak with the pass permitting them to ride through. The guide shall be at the convent door half an hour earlier. I will send up to-night your armour and horse. Here is a purse which the Earl of Evesham also left for your use. Is there aught else I can do for you?"

"Nothing, sir," Cuthbert said; "and if I regain the army in safety, I shall have pleasure in reporting to King Richard how kindly and courteously you have treated me."

The arrangements were carried out.

An hour before daybreak Cuthbert was roused, donned his armour and steel casque, drank a flask of wine, and ate a manchet of bread which the prior himself brought him; and then, with a cordial adieu to the kind monks, issued forth.

The guide had just reached the gate, and together they trotted down the narrow streets to the west gate of the city, where four men-at-arms were awaiting them.

The gates were at once opened, and Cuthbert and his little troop sallied forth.

CHAPTER VIII.

THE ATTACK.

ALL day they rode with their faces west, and before nightfall had made a journey of over forty miles. Then bestowing a largess upon the men-at-arms, Cuthbert dismissed them, and took up his abode at a hostelry, his guide looking to the two horses.

Cuthbert was pleased with the appearance of the man who had been placed at his disposal. He was a young fellow of two-or-three-and-twenty, with an honest face. He was, he told Cuthbert, the son of a small farmer near Avignon; but having a fancy for trade, he had been apprenticed to a master smith. Having served his apprenticeship, he found that he had mistaken his vocation, and intended to return to the paternal vineyards.

Cuthbert calculated that he would make at least four days' journey to the south before he could meet with any dangers. Doubtless his exit from the convent had been discovered, and the moment the gates of the city were opened the spy would have proceeded south to warn his comrades, and these would doubtless have taken a road which at a distance would again take them on to that by which Cuthbert would be now travelling. As, however, he rode fast, and made long marches each day, he hoped that he might succeed in distancing them. Unfortunately, upon the third day his horse cast his shoe, and no smith could be met with until the end of the day's journey. Consequently, but a short distance could be done, and this at a slow pace.

Upon the fifth day after their first start they arrived at a small town.

The next morning, Cuthbert on rising found that his guide did not present himself as usual. Making inquiries, he found that the young man had gone out the evening before, and had not returned. Extremely uneasy at the

circumstance, Cuthbert went to the city guard, thinking that perhaps his guide might have got drunk, and been shut up in the cells. No news, however, was to be obtained there, and after waiting some hours, feeling sure that some harm had befallen him, he gave notice to the authorities of his loss, and then, mounting his horse, and leaving some money with the landlord of the hostelry to give to his guide in case the latter should return, he started at mid-day by the southern road.

He felt sure now that he was overtaken, and determined to keep his eyes and faculties thoroughly on watch.

The roads in those days were mere tracks. Here and

there a little village was to be met with; but the country was sparsely cultivated, and travelling lonely work. Cuthbert rode fast, carefully avoiding all copses and small woods through which the road ran, by making a circuit round them and coming on to it again on the other side.

His horse was an excellent one, the gift of the earl, and he had little fear, with his light weight, of being overtaken, if he could once leave his enemies behind him.

At length he approached an extensive forest, which stretched for miles on either side.

Half a mile before he reached it the track divided.

He had for some little time eased his horse down to a walk, as he felt that the wood would be the spot where he would in all probability be attacked, and he needed that his steed should be possessed of its utmost vigour.

At the spot where the track branched, a man in the guise of a mendicant was sitting. He begged for alms, and Cuthbert threw him a small coin.

A sudden thought struck him as he heard a rustling in the bushes near.

"Which is the nearest and best road to Avignon?" he said.

"The right-hand road is the best and shortest," the beggar said. "The other makes a long circuit, and leads through several marshes, which your honour will find it hard to pass."

Cuthbert thanked him, and moved forward, still at a walk, along the right-hand road.

When he had gone about 200 yards, and was hidden from the sight of the man he had left—the country being rough, and scattered with clumps of bushes—he halted, and, as he expected, heard the sound of horses' hoofs coming on at full gallop along the other road.

"Your master must have thought me young indeed," he said, "to try and catch me with such a transparent trick as that. I do not suppose that accursed page has more than ten men with him, and doubtless has placed five on each road. This fellow was placed here to see which track I would follow, and has now gone to give the party on the left hand the news that I have taken this way. Had it not been for him I should have had to run the gauntlet with four or five of my enemies. As it is, the path will doubtless be clear."

So saying, he turned his horse, galloped back to the spot where the tracks separated, and then followed the left-hand route.

As he had hoped, he passed through the wood without incident or interruption, and arrived safely that night at a small town, having seen no signs of his enemies.

The next day he started again early, and rode on until mid-day, when he halted at a large village, at which was the only inn between the place from which he started and his destination. He declined the offer of the servant of the inn to take his horse round to the stable, telling the man to hold him outside the door and give him from a sieve a few handfuls of grain.

Then he entered the inn and ate a hearty meal. As he appeared at the door, he saw several men gathered near. With a single spring he threw himself into the saddle, just as a rush forward was made by those standing round. The man next to him sprang upon him, and endeavoured to drag him from the saddle. Cuthbert drew the little dagger called a Miséricorde from his belt, and plunged it into his throat. Then seizing the short mace which hung at the saddle bow, he hurled it with all his force full in the face of his enemy, the page of Sir Philip, who was rushing upon him sword in hand. The heavy weapon struck him fairly between the eyes, and with a cry he fell back, his face completely smashed in by the blow, the sword which he held uplifted to strike flying far through the air.

Cuthbert struck his spurs into his horse, and the animal dashed forward with a bound, Cuthbert striking with his long sword at one or two men who made a snatch at the reins. In another minute he was cantering out of the village, convinced that he had killed the leader of his foes, and that he was safe now to pursue the rest of his journey on to Marseilles.

So it turned out.

Without further incident, he travelled through the south of France, and arrived at the great seaport. He speedily discovered the quarters in which the Earl of Evesham's contingent were encamped, and made towards this without delay. As he entered a wild shout of joy was heard, and Cnut

ran forward with many gestures of delight.

"My dear Cuthbert, my dear Cuthbert!" he exclaimed. "Can it be true that you have escaped? We all gave you up; and although I did my best, yet had you not survived it I should never have forgiven myself, believing that I might have somehow done better, and have saved you from the cut-throats who attacked us."

"Thanks, thanks, my good Cnut," Cuthbert cried. "I have been through a time of peril, no doubt; but as you see, I am hale and well—better, methinks than you are, for you look pale and ill; and I doubt not that the wound which I received was a mere scratch to that which bore you down. It sounded indeed like the blow of a smith's hammer upon an anvil."

"Fortunately, my steel cap saved my head somewhat," Cnut said, "and the head itself is none of the thinnest; but it tried it sorely, I confess. However, now that you are back I shall, doubt not, soon be as strong as ever I was. I think that fretting for your absence has kept me back more than the inflammation from the wound itself—but there is the Earl at the door of his tent."

Through the foresters and retainers who had at Cnut's shout of joy crowded up, Cuthbert made his way, shaking hands right and left with the men, among whom he was greatly loved, for they regarded him as being in a great degree the cause of their having been freed from outlawry, and restored to civil life again. The earl was really affected. As Cuthbert rode up he held out both arms, and as his page alighted he embraced him as a father.

"My dear Cuthbert!" he exclaimed. "What anxiety have we not suffered. Had you been my own son, I could not have felt more your loss. We did not doubt for an instant that you had fallen into the hands of some of the retainers of that villain Count; and from all we could learn, and from the absence of any dead body by the side of that of Cnut, I imagined that you must have been carried off. It was clear that your chance of life, if you fell into the hands of that evil page, or his equally vile master, was small indeed. The very day that Cnut was brought in, I visited the French camp, and accused him of having been the cause of your disappearance and Cnut's wounds. He affected the greatest astonishment at the charge. He had not, as he said, been out of the camp for two days. My accusation was unfounded and malicious, and I should answer this as well as the previous outrage, when the vow of the Crusaders to keep peace among themselves was at an end. Of course I had no means of proving what I said, or I would have gone direct to the king and charged him with the outrage. As it was I gained nothing by my pains. He has accompanied the French division to Genoa; but when we meet at Sicily, where the two armies are to rendezvous, I will bring the matter before the king, as the fact that his page was certainly concerned in it must be taken as showing that he was the instigator."

"It would, my lord earl, be perhaps better," Cuthbert said, "if I might venture to advise, to leave the matter alone. No doubt the count would say that he had discharged his page after the tournament, and that the latter was only carrying out his private feud with me. We should not be able to disprove the story, and should gain no satisfaction by the matter."

The earl admitted the justice of Cuthbert's reasoning, but reserved to himself the task of punishing the author of the outrage upon the first fitting opportunity.

There was a weary delay at Marseilles before the expedition set sail. This was caused by the fact of the English fleet, which had been ordered to be there upon their arrival, failing to keep the agreement.

The words English fleet badly describe the vessels which were to carry the English contingent to their destination. They were ships belonging to the maritime nations of Italy— the Venetians, Genoese, Pisans, &c.; for England at that time had but few of her own, and these scarcely fitted for the stormy navigation of the Bay of Biscay.

King Richard, impatient as ever of delay, at last lost his temper, and embarked on board a ship with a few of his chosen knights, and set sail by himself for Sicily, the point at which the two armies of the expedition were to re-unite. A few days after his departure, the long-looked-for fleet arrived, and a portion of the English host embarked at once, and set sail for Sicily, where they were to be landed, and the ships were to return to fetch the remaining contingent.

A sea voyage of this kind in those days was a serious matter. Long voyages were rare, and troops were carried very much upon the principle of herrings; that is, were packed as close as they could be, without any reference to their comfort. As the voyages seldom lasted more than twenty-four hours, this did not much matter, but during long voyages the discomforts, or as may be said sufferings, of the troops were considerable. So tightly packed were the galleys in which the English set sail from Marseilles, that there was no walking about. Every man slept where he sat, and considered himself lucky indeed if he could obtain room sufficient to stretch himself at full length. Most slept sitting against bulwarks or other supports. In the cabins, where the knights, their pages and squires, were placed, the crowding was of course less excessive, but even here the amount of space, which a subaltern travelling to India for the first time now-a-days would grumble at, was considered amply sufficient for half-a-dozen knights of distinction. It was a week after sailing, when Cnut touched Cuthbert's arm as he came on deck one morning, and said,—

"Look, look, Cuthbert! that mountain standing up in the water has caught fire on the top. Did you ever see such a thing?"

The soldiers crowded to the side of the vessel, in intense astonishment and no little awe. From the top of a lofty and rugged hill, rising almost straight from the sea, flames were roaring up, smoke hung over the island, and stones were thrown into the air and rattled down the side of the hill, or fell into the sea with a splash.

"That is a fearsome sight," Cnut said, crossing himself.

"It looks as if it was the mouth of purgatory," exclaimed another, standing by.

Cuthbert himself was amazed, for the instruction he had received from Father Francis was of too slight a nature to include the story of volcanoes. A priest, however, who accompanied the ship in the character of leech and confessor, explained the nature of the phenomenon to his astonished listeners, and told them that over on the mainland was a mountain which at times vomited

forth such masses of stones and of liquid rock that it had swallowed up and covered many great cities.

There was also, he told them, another mountain of the same sort, even more vast, on the island of Sicily itself; but that this had seldom, as far back as man could remember, done any great harm.

Sailing on, in another day they arrived off the coast of Sicily itself, and sailing up the straits between it and the mainland, they landed at Messina. Here a considerable portion of the French army had already arrived, having been brought down from Genoa.

There was no news of the King of England; and, as often happens, the saying "the more haste the less speed," had been verified here.

It was some days later before King Richard arrived, having been driven from his course by tempests, well-nigh cast ashore, and having besides gone through many adventures. Three weeks later, the whole of the army of the Crusaders were gathered around Messina, where it was intended to remain some little time before starting. It was a gay time; and the kings vied with each other in entertainments, joustings, and tournaments. The Italian knights also made a brave show, and it might have been thought that this huge army of men were gathered there simply for amusement and feasting. In the tournaments every effort was made to prevent any feeling of national rivalry, and although parties of knights held their own against all comers, these were most carefully selected to represent several nationalities, and therefore victory, on whichsoever side it fell, excited no feelings of bitterness.

Alone, King Richard was undoubtedly the strongest cavalier of the two armies. Against his ponderous strength no knight could keep his seat; and this was so palpable, that after many victories, King Richard was forced to retire from the lists from want of competitors, and to take his place on the daïs with the more peace-loving King of France.

The gaiety of the camp was heightened by the arrival of many nobles and dames from Italy. Here, too, came the Queen of Navarre, bringing with her the beautiful Princess Berengaria.

"Methinks," the Earl of Evesham said to Cuthbert, a fortnight after the arrival of the queen, "that unless my eyes deceive me, the princess is likely to be a cause of trouble."

"In what way?" asked Cuthbert with surprise, for he had been struck with her marvellous beauty, and wondered greatly what mischief so fair a being could do.

"By the way in which our good lord, the king, gazes upon her, methinks that it were like enough that he broke off his engagement with the Princess of France, for the sake of the fair eyes of this damsel."

"That were indeed a misfortune," Cuthbert said gravely, for he saw at once the anger which such a course would excite in the minds of the French king and his knights, who would naturally be indignant in the extreme at the slight put upon their princess. As day after day passed, it became evident to all that the King of England was infatuated by the princess. Again he entered the lists himself, and as some fresh Italian knights and others had arrived, he found fresh opponents, and conspicuously laid the spoils of victory at the feet of the princess, whom he selected as the Queen of Beauty.

All sorts of rumours now became current in camp; violent quarrels between the kings, and bad feeling between the French and English knights, broke out again in consequence, and this more violently than before.

CHAPTER IX.

THE PRINCESS BERENGARIA.

ONE night it chanced that Cuthbert was late in his return to camp, and his road took him through a portion of the French encampment; the night was dark, and Cuthbert presently completely lost all idea as to his bearings. Presently he nearly ran against a tent; he made his way to the entrance in order to crave directions as to his way—for it was a wet night; the rain was pouring in torrents, and few were about of whom he could demand the way—and, as he was about to draw aside the hangings, he heard words said in a passionate voice which caused him to withdraw his hand suddenly.

"I tell you," said a voice, "I would rather drive a dagger myself into her heart, than allow our own princess to be insulted by this hot-headed island dog."

"It is sad indeed," said another, but in a calmer and

smoother tone, "that the success of a great expedition like this, which has for its object the recovery of the holy sepulchre from the infidels, should be wrecked by the headstrong fancies of one man. It is even, as is told by the old Grecian poet, as when Helen caused a great war between peoples of that nation."

"I know nothing," another voice said, "either of Helen or the Greeks, or of their poets. They are a shifty race, and I can believe aught that is bad of them. But touching this princess of Navarre, I agree with our friend, it would be a righteous deed to poniard her, and so to remove the cause of dispute between the two kings, and, indeed, the two nations. This insult laid upon our princess is more than we, as French knights and gentlemen, can brook; and if the king says the word, there is not a gentleman in the army but will be ready to turn his sword against the islanders."

Then the smooth voice spoke again.

"It would, my brethren, be wrong and useless to shed blood; but methinks, that if this apple of discord could be removed, a good work would be done; not, as our friend the count has suggested, by a stab of the dagger; that indeed would be worse than useless. But surely there are scores of religious houses, where this bird might be placed in a cage without a soul knowing where she was, and where she might pass her life in prayer that she may be pardoned for having caused grave hazards of the failure of an enterprise in which all the Christian world is concerned."

The voices of the speakers now fell, and Cuthbert was straining his ear to listen, when he heard footsteps approaching the tent, and he glided away into the darkness.

With great difficulty he recovered the road to the camp, and when he reached his tent he confided to the Earl of Evesham what he had heard.

"This is serious indeed," the earl said, "and bodes no little trouble and danger. It is true that the passion which King Richard has conceived for Berengaria bids fair to wreck the Crusade, by the anger which it has excited in the French king and his nobles; but the disappearance of the princess would no less fatally interfere with it, for the king would be like a raging lion deprived of his whelps, and would certainly move no foot eastward until he had exhausted all the means in his power of tracing his lost lady love. You could not, I suppose, Cuthbert, point out the tent where this conversation took place?"

"I could not," Cuthbert answered; "in the darkness one tent is like another. I think I should recognize the voices of the speakers did I hear them again; indeed, one voice I did recognize, it was that of the Count of Brabant, with whom we had trouble before."

"That is good," the earl said, "because we have at least an object to watch. It would never do to tell the king what you have heard. In the first place, his anger would be so great that it would burst all bounds, and would cause, likely enough, a battle at once between the two armies; nor would it have any good effect, for he of Brabant would of course deny the truth of your assertions, and would declare it was merely a got-up story to discredit him with the king, and so to wipe out the old score now standing between us. No, if we are to succeed, alike in preventing harm happening to the princess, and an open break between the two monarchs, it must be done by keeping a guard over the princess, unsuspected by all, and ourselves frustrating any attempt which may be made."

Cuthbert expressed his willingness to carry out the instructions which the earl might give him; and, much disturbed by the events of the day, both earl and page retired to rest, to think over what plan had best be adopted.

The princess was staying at the palace of the bishop of the town; this he, having another residence a short distance outside the walls, had placed at the disposal of the queen of Navarre and her suite; and the first step of Cuthbert in the morning was to go into the town, to reconnoitre the position and appearance of the building. It was a large and irregular pile, and communicated with the two monasteries lying alongside of it. It would therefore clearly be a most difficult thing to keep up a complete watch on the exterior of so large a building. There were so many ways in which the princess might be captured and carried off by unscrupulous men, that Cuthbert in vain thought over every plan by which it could be possible to safeguard her. She might be seized upon returning from a tournament or entertainment; but this was improbable, as the queen would always have an escort of knights with her, and no attempt could be successful except at the cost of a public fraças and much loss of blood. Cuthbert regarded as out of the question that an outrage of this kind would be attempted.

The fact that one of the speakers in the tent had used the words "my sons," showed that one priest or monk, at least, was connected with the plot. It was possible that this man might have power in one of the monasteries, or he might be an agent of the bishop himself; and Cuthbert saw that it would be easy enough in the night for a party from one or other of the monasteries to enter by the door of communication with the palace, and carry off the princess without the slightest alarm being given. Once within the walls of the convent, she could be either hidden in the dungeons or secret places, which buildings of that kind were sure to possess, or could be at once carried out by some quiet entrance, and taken into the country, or transferred to some other building in the town.

When Cuthbert joined the earl he told him the observations that he had made, and Sir Walter praised the judgment which he had shown in his conclusions. The earl was of opinion that it would be absolutely necessary to get some clue as to the course which the abductors purposed to take; indeed it was possible that on after-consideration they might drop their plan altogether, for the words which Cuthbert had overheard scarcely betokened a plan completely formed and finally decided upon.

The great point he considered, therefore, was that the tent of his old enemy should be carefully watched, and that an endeavour should be made to hear something of what passed within, which might give a clue to the plan fixed upon. They did not, of course, know whether the tent in which the conversation had been heard by Cuthbert was that of Sir de Jacquelin Barras, or of one of the other persons who had spoken; and Cuthbert suggested that the first thing would be to find out whether the count, after nightfall, was in the habit of going to some other tent, or whether, on the other hand, he remained within, and was visited by others.

It was easy, of course, to discover which was his tent; and Cuthbert soon got its position, and then took Cnut into his counsels.

"The matter is difficult," Cnut said, "and I see no way by which a watch can be kept up by day; but after dark—I have several men in my band who can track a deer, and surely could manage to follow the steps of this baron without being observed. There is little Jack, who is no bigger than a boy of twelve, although he can shoot, and run, and play with the quarter-staff, or, if need be, with the bill, against the best man in the troop. I warrant me that if you show him the tent, he will keep such sharp watch that no one shall enter or depart without his knowing where they go to. On a dark night he will be able to slip among the tents, and to move here and there without being seen. He can creep on his stomach without moving leaf, and trust me the eyes of these French men-at-arms will look in vain for a glimpse of him."

"You understand, Cnut, all that I want to know is whether the other conspirators in this matter visit his tent, or whether he goes to theirs."

"I understand," Cnut said. "That is the first point to be arrived at."

Three days later Cnut brought news that each night after dark a party of five men met in the tent that was watched;

that one of the five always came out when all had assembled, and took his station before the entrance of the tent, so as to be sure that no eavesdropper was near.

Cuthbert smiled,—

"It is a case of locking the door after the horse has gone."

"What is to be done now?" Cnut asked.

"I will talk with the earl before I tell you, Cnut. This matter is too serious for me to take a step without consulting Sir Walter."

That night there was a long talk between the earl and his page as to the best course to be pursued. It was clear that their old enemy was the leading person in the plot, and that the only plan to baffle it with any fair chances of success was to keep a constant eye upon his movements, and also to have three or four of the sturdiest men of the band told off to watch, without being perceived, each time that the princess was in her palace.

The Earl of Evesham left the arrangements entirely in the hands of his page, of whose good sense and sagacity he had a very high opinion.

His own first impulse had been to go before the king and denounce the Count of Brabant. But the ill-will between them was already well known; for not only was there the original dispute at the banquet, but when the two armies had joined at Sicily, King Richard, who had heard from the earl of the attempt at the assassination of Cuthbert, had laid a complaint before King Phillip of the conduct of his subject.

Sir de Jacquelin Barras, however, had denied that he had any finger in the matter.

"He had," he said, "discharged his page after the encounter with Cuthbert, and knew nothing further whatever of his movements."

Although it was morally certain that the page could not have purchased the services of the men who assisted him, from his own purse, or gain them by any means of persuasion, but that they were either the followers of the Count of Brabant, or ruffians hired with his money, as no proof could be obtained, the matter was allowed to drop.

The earl felt, however, that an accusation against the count by him of an intention to commit a high crime, and this merely on the evidence of his page, would appear like an attempt to injure the fair fame of his rival.

Feeling, therefore, that nothing could be done save to watch, he left the matter entirely in the hands of his page, telling him that he could take as many men-at-arms or archers as he might choose and use them in his name.

Cnut entered warmly into Cuthbert's plans; and finally it was arranged between them that six of the archers should nightly keep watch opposite the various entrances of the bishop's palace and of the two monasteries joining. Of course they could not patrol up and down without attracting attention, but they were to take up posts where they could closely observe the entrances, and were either to lie down and feign drunken sleep, or to conceal themselves within the shadow of an arch or other hiding-place.

Down on the sea-shore, Cuthbert made an arrangement with one of the owners of small craft lying there that ten of his men should sleep on board every night, together with some fisher-men accustomed to the use of the oar.

Cuthbert himself determined to be always with this party.

Night after night passed, and so long a time went by that Cuthbert began to think the design must have been given up.

However, he resolved to relax none of his watchfulness during the remaining time that the expedition might stop in Sicily. It was in January, three weeks after the first watch had been set, when one of the men who had been placed to watch the entrance to one of the monasteries, leapt on board the craft and shook Cuthbert by the shoulder.

"A party of some five men," he said, "have just issued out from the monastery. They are bearing a burden—what, I cannot see. They were making in the direction of the water. I whistled to Dick, who was next to me in the lane. He is following them, and I came on to tell you to prepare."

The night was pitch dark, and it was difficult in the extreme to see any one moving at a short distance off.

There were two or three streets that led from the monastery, which stood at the top of the town, towards the sea; and a party coming down might take any of these, according to the position in which the boat they were seeking was placed.

Cuthbert now instantly sent five or six of his men, with instructions to avoid all noise, along the line of the port, with orders to bring in word should any one come down and take boat, or should they hear any noise in the town.

He himself with the sailors loosed the ropes which

fastened the boat to shore, got out the oars, and prepared to put off at a moment's notice.

He was of course ignorant whether the abductors would try to carry the princess off by water, or would hide her in one of the convents of the town; but he was inclined to think that the former would be the course adopted; for the king in his wrath would be ready to lay the town in flames, and to search every convent from top to bottom for the princess. Besides, there would be too many aware of the secret.

Cuthbert was not wrong in his supposition.

Soon the man he had sent to the extreme right came running up with the news that a boat had embarked at the farther end, with a party of some ten men on board. As he came along he had warned the others, and in five minutes the whole party were collected in the craft, numbering in all twelve of Cuthbert's men and six sailors. They instantly put out, and rowed in the direction in which the boat would have gone, the boatmen expressing their opinion that probably the party would make for a vessel which was lying anchored at some little distance from shore. The bearings of the position of this ship was known to the boatmen, but the night was so dark that they were quite unable to find it. Orders had been given that no sound or whisper was to be heard on board the boat; and after rowing as far as they could, the boatmen said they were in the direction of the ship.

The boatmen all lay on their oars, and all listened intently. Presently the creaking of a pulley was heard in the still night, at a distance of a few hundred yards. This was enough. It was clear that the vessel was getting up sail. The boat's head was turned in that direction; the crew rowed steadily but noiselessly, and in a few minutes the tall mast of a vessel could be seen faintly against the sky. Just as they perceived the situation, a hail from on board showed that their approach was now observed.

"Stretch to your oars," Cuthbert said, "we must make a

dash for it now."

The rowers bent to their work and in a minute the boat ran alongside the craft.

As Cuthbert and his followers scrambled upon the deck, they were attacked by those of the crew and passengers who were standing near; but it was evident at once that the chiefs of the expedition had not heard the hail, and that there was no general plan of defence against them.

It was not until the last of them had gained a footing, and

were beginning to fight their way along the vessel, that from below three or four men-at-arms ran up, and one in a tone of authority demanded what was the matter. When he heard the clash of swords and the shouts of the combatants, he put himself at once at the head of the party, and a fierce and obstinate fight now took place.

The assailants had, however, the advantage.

Cuthbert and his men were all lightly clad, and this on the deck of a ship lumbered with ropes and gear, and in the dark, was a great advantage, for the mailed men-at-arms frequently stumbled and fell. The fight lasted for several minutes. Cnut who was armed with a heavy mace, did great service, for with each of his sweeping blows he broke down the guard of an opponent, and generally levelled him to the deck.

The numbers at the beginning of the fight were not unequal, but the men to whom the vessel belonged made but a faint resistance when they perceived that the day was going against them. The men-at-arms, however, consisting of three, who appeared to be the leaders, and of eight pikemen, fought stubbornly and well.

Cuthbert was not long in detecting in the tones of the man who was clearly at the head of affairs the voice of Sir de Jacquelin Barras. To do him justice he fought with extreme bravery, and when almost all his followers were cut down or beaten overboard, he resisted staunchly and well. With a heavy two-handed sword he cleaved a space at the end of the boat, and kept the whole of Cuthbert's party at bay.

At last Cnut, who had been engaged elsewhere, came to the front, and a tough fight ensued between them.

It might have ended badly for the brave forester, for his lack of armour gave an enormous advantage to his opponent. Soon, however, the count's foot slipped on the boards of the deck, and before he could recover himself the mace of Cnut descended with tremendous force upon his head, which was unprotected as he had taken off his casque on arriving at the ship. Without a word or a cry the count fell forward on the deck, killed as a bullock by a blow of a pole-axe.

While this conflict had been going on, occasionally the loud screams of a woman had been heard below.

Cuthbert, attended by Cnut and two of his followers, now descended.

At the bottom of the steps they found a man-at-arms placed at the door of a cabin. He challenged them as they approached, but being speedily convinced that the vessel was in their hands, and that his employer and party were all conquered, he made a virtue of necessity, and laid down his arms.

"You had better go in alone," Cnut said, "Master Cuthbert. The lady is less likely to be frightened by your appearance then by us, for she must wonder indeed what is going on."

On entering the cabin, which had evidently been fitted up for the use of a lady, Cuthbert saw standing at the other end the princess, whom of course he knew well by sight. A lamp was burning in the cabin, and by its light he could see that her face was deadly pale. Her robes were torn and disarranged, and she wore a look at once of grave alarm and surprise upon seeing a handsomely dressed page enter with a deep reverence.

"What means this outrage, young sir? Whoever you be, I

warn you that the King of England will revenge this indignity."

"Your Highness," Cuthbert said, "you have no further reason for alarm; the knaves who carried you off from the bishop's palace and conveyed you to this ship are all either killed or in our power. I am the page of the Earl of Evesham, a devoted follower of King Richard. Some of the designs of the bold men came to the ears of my lord, and he ordered me and a band of his followers to keep good guard over the palace and buildings adjoining. We were unable to gather our strength in time to prevent your being taken on board, but we lost no time in putting forth when we found that your abductors had taken boat, and by good fortune arrived here in time; a few minutes later, and the knaves would have succeeded in their object, for the sails were already being hoisted, and the vessel making way, when we arrived. Your abductors are all either killed or thrown overboard, and the vessel's head is now turned towards the shore, and I hope in a few minutes to have the honour of escorting you to the palace."

The princess, with a sigh of much satisfaction and relief, sank on to a couch.

"I am indeed indebted to you, young sir," she said. "Believe me, the Princess Berengaria is not ungrateful, and should it be ever in her power to do aught for your lord, or for yourself, or for those who have accompanied you to rescue her, believe me that she will do it."

"May I be so bold as to ask a boon?" Cuthbert said, dropping on one knee before her.

"It is granted at once, whatever it be, if in my power."

"My boon is, lady," he said, "that you will do your best to assuage the natural anger which the King of England will feel at this bold and most violent attempt. That he should be told, is of course necessary; but, lady, much depends upon the telling, and I am sure that at your request the king would restrain his anger. Were it not for that, I fear that such quarrels and disputes might arise as would bring the two armies to blows, and destroy for ever all hope of the successful termination of our joint enterprise."

"You are a wise and good youth," the princess said, holding out her hand to Cuthbert, which, as in duty bound, he placed to his lips. "Your request is wise and most thoughtful. I will use any poor influence which I may possess"—and Cuthbert could see that the blood came back now to the white face—"to induce King Richard to allow this matter to pass over. There is no reason why he should take up the case. I am no more under his protection than under that of the King of France, and it is to the latter I should appeal, for as I believe the men who abducted me were his subjects."

"The leader of them, madam, was a certain Sir de Jacquelin Barras, a Count of Brabant, with whom my master has had an old feud, and who has been just killed by the leader of our men-at-arms. The others, who have had the most active hand in the matter, have also perished; and it would, I think, be doubtful whether any clue could be obtained to those who were in league with them. The only man in the party who is alive, was placed as a sentry at your door, and as he is but a man-at-arms, we may be sure that he knows nought of the enterprise, but has merely carried out the orders of his master."

The vessel had by this time brought up close to the port. The princess determined to wait on board until the first dawn was seen in the skies, and then under the escort of her deliverers to go back to the palace, before the town was moving. This plan was carried out, and soon after dawn the princess was safe in the palace from which she had been carried a few hours previously.

CHAPTER X.

PIRATES.

IT was not possible that a matter of this sort could be entirely hushed up. Not many hours passed before rumours were current of events which had taken place, though none knew what those events were.

There were reports that the tire-woman of the Princess Berengaria had in the night discovered that her mistress's couch was unoccupied, that she had found signs of a struggle, and had picked up a dagger on the floor, where it had evidently fallen from the sheath; also it was said, that the princess had returned at daylight escorted by an armed party, and that she was unable to obtain entrance to the palace until one of the ladies of the queen had been fetched down to order the sentries at the gate to allow her to enter.

This was the news which rumour carried through the camp. Few, however, believed it, and none who could have enlightened them opened their lips upon the subject.

It was known, however, that a messenger had come to King Richard early, and that he had at once mounted, and ridden off to the bishop's palace. What had happened there none could say, but there were rumours that his voice had been heard in furious outbursts of passion. He remained there until the afternoon, when he sent for a number of his principal nobles.

When these arrived, they found him standing on a dais in

the principal hall of the palace, and he there formally introduced to them the Princess Berengaria as his affianced wife. The ceremony of the marriage, he told them, would shortly take place.

This announcement caused a tremendous stir in both armies. The English, who had never been favourable to the alliance with the French princess, were glad to hear that this was broken off; and were well content that the Princess Berengaria should be their future queen for her beauty, high spirit, and kindness had won all hearts.

On the part of the French, on the other hand, there was great indignation, and for some time it was feared that the armies would come to open blows.

King Phillip, however, although much angered, was politic enough to deprecate any open outbreak. He knew that a dispute now began, would not only at once put a stop

to the Crusade, but that it might lead to more serious consequences at home. The fiery bravery of the English king, backed as it would be by the whole strength of his subjects, might render him a very formidable opponent; and the king felt that private grievances must be laid aside where the good of France was concerned.

Still the coldness between the armies increased, their camps were moved further apart, and during the time that they remained in Sicily, there was but little commerce between the two forces.

As soon as the winter had broken, the French monarch broke up his camp, and in March sailed for the Holy Land.

The English had expected that the marriage ceremony of the king and Princess Berengaria would be celebrated before they left Sicily, but this was not the case. There were high joustings and fétes in honour of the princess, but the marriage was delayed. A fortnight after the French had sailed, the English embarked in the 200 ships, which had been prepared, and sailed also on their way to Acre.

It must not be supposed that the attempted abduction of the Princess Berengaria was unimportant in its results to

Cuthbert.

After returning from the palace the king, who had heard from her the details of what had taken place, and the names of her rescuers, sent for the Earl of Evesham. The latter had of course learned from Cuthbert all that had happened, and had expressed his high approval of his conduct, and his gratification at the result.

"I learn, Sir Earl," said King Richard, "that it is to you that I am indebted for the rescue of the princess. She tells me, that suspecting some plot, you placed a guard around the bishop's palace, with a strong body on the shore ready to rescue her from the hands of any who might attempt to take her to sea."

"It is as you say, sire," replied the earl; "but the whole merit of the affair rests upon my page, the lad whom you may remember as having fought with and conquered the French page, and of whose conduct you then approved highly. You may also remember that he escaped by some display of bravery and shrewdness the further attempts to assassinate him, and your Majesty was good enough to make a complaint to King Phillip of the conduct of one of his nobles on that head. It seems that some two months since, the lad in coming through the French camp at night missed his way, and accidentally overheard a few words spoken in a voice which he recognized as that of his enemy. The name of your Majesty being mentioned, he deemed it his duty to listen, and thus discovered that a plot was on foot for carrying off the princess. After consultation with me, we agreed upon the course to be adopted, namely, to place sentries round the bishop's palace and the buildings adjoining, who should follow and bring word should she be taken to another place in town, while a band was placed on the shore in readiness to interfere at once to prevent her being carried away by sea. He undertook the management of all details, having with him a trusty squire who commands my Saxon bowmen."

"For your own part I thank you, my lord," the king said, "and, believe me, you shall not find Richard ungrateful. As to your page, he appears brave and wise beyond his years. Were it not that I think that it would not be good for him, and might attract some envy upon the part of others, I would at once make him a knight. He already has my promise that I will do so on the first occasion when he can show his prowess upon the infidels. Bring him to me to-morrow, when the princess will be here with the Queen of Navarre at a banquet. I would fain thank him before her; and, although I have agreed—at the princess's earnest solicitation—to take no further notice of the matter, and to allow it to pass as if it had not been, yet I cannot forgive the treachery which has been used, and, without letting all know exactly what has occurred, would fain by my reception of your page, let men see that something of great import has happened, of the nature of which I doubt not that rumour will give some notion."

Upon the following day, therefore, Cuthbert to his confusion found himself the centre of the royal circle. The king expressed himself to him in the most gracious manner patting him on the shoulder, and said that he would be one day one of the best and bravest of his knights. The

princess and the Queen of Navarre gave him their hands to kiss; and somewhat overwhelmed, he withdrew from the royal presence, the centre of attention, and, in some minds, of envy.

Cnut too did not pass unrewarded.

His Majesty, finding that Cnut was of gentle Saxon blood, gave him a gold chain in token of his favour, and distributed a heavy purse among the men who had followed him.

When the British fleet, numbering 200 ships, set sail from Sicily, it was a grand and martial sight. From the masts were the colours of England and those of the nobles who commanded; while the pennons of the knights, the bright plumes and mantles, the flash of armour and arms, made the decks alive with light and colour.

The king's ship advanced in the van, and round him were the vessels containing his principal followers. The Queen of Navarre and the Princess Berengaria were with the fleet. Strains of music rose from the waters, and never were the circumstances of war exhibited in a more picturesque form.

For two days the expedition sailed on, and then a change of a sudden and disastrous kind took place.

"What is all this bustle about?" Cuthbert said to Cnut. "The sailors are running up the ladders, and all seems confusion."

"Methinks," said Cnut, "that we are about to have a storm. A few minutes ago scarce a cloud was to be seen; now that bank over there has risen half-way up the sky. The sailors are accustomed to these treacherous seas, and the warnings which we have not noticed have no doubt been clear enough to them."

With great rapidity the sails of the fleet came down, and in five minutes its whole aspect was changed; but quickly as the sailors had done their work, the storm was even more rapid in its progress. Some of the ships whose crews were slower or less skilful than the others, were caught by the gale before they could get their sails snug, and the great sheets of white canvas were blown from the bolt ropes as if made of paper, and a blackness which could almost be felt, covered the sea, the only light being that given by the frothing waters. There was no longer any thought of order. Each ship had to shift for herself; and each captain to do his best to save those under his charge, without thought of what might befall the others.

In the ship which carried the Earl of Evesham's contingent, order and discipline prevailed. The earl's voice had been heard at the first puff of wind, shouting to the men to go below, save a few who might be of use to haul at ropes. His standard was lowered, the bright flags removed from the sides of the ship, the shields which were hanging over the bulwarks were hurriedly taken below, and when the gale smote them, the ship was trim, and in readiness to receive it. A few square yards of sail alone were all that the captain had thought it prudent to keep spread, and in a minute from the time she was struck the lofty hulk was tearing along through the waters at a tremendous speed. Four of the best hands were placed at the helm; and here the captain took his post.

The danger was now that in the darkness they might run against one of their consorts. Even in the war of the elements they could hear from time to time crashes as of vessels striking against each other, with shouts and cries. Once or twice from the darkness ships emerged, close on one hand or the other; but the steadiness of the captain in each case saved the ship from collision.

As the storm continued, these glimpses of other vessels became more and more rare, and the ship being a very fast sailer, the captain indulged the hope that he was now clear of the rest of the fleet.

He now attempted to lie-to to the storm, but the wind was too strong. The ships in those days too, were so high out of the water, and offered in themselves such a target to the wind, that it was useless to adopt any other maneuver than to run before it.

For two days and nights the tempest raged.

"What think you," the earl said to the captain, "of our position? Where are we, and where will the course upon which we are running take us?"

"I cannot say with certainty," the captain said, "for the wind has shifted several times. I had hoped to gain the shelter of Rhodes but a shift of wind bore us away from there, and I much fear that from the direction in which we have been running we must be very nigh on the coast of Africa."

"Pest!" the earl said. "That would indeed be a speedy end to our Crusade. These Moors are pirates and cutthroats to a man; and even should we avoid the risk of being dashed to pieces, we should end our lives as slaves to one of these black infidels."

Three hours later, the captain's prophecies turned out right. Breakers were seen in various points in front, and with the greatest difficulty the vessel was steered through an opening between them; but in another few minutes she struck heavily, one of her masts went over the side, and she lay fast and immovable. Fortunately, the outside bank of sand acted as a sort of breakwater; had she struck upon this, the good ship would have gone to pieces instantly; but although the waves still struck her with considerable force, the captain had good hope that she would not break up. Darkness came on; the tempest seemed to lull. As there was no immediate danger, and all were exhausted by the tossing which they had received during the last forty-eight hours, the crew of the "Rose" slept soundly.

In the morning the sun rose brilliantly, and there was no sign of the great storm which had scattered the fleet of England. The shore was to be seen at a distance of some four miles. It was low and sandy, with lofty mountains in the distance. Far inland a white town with minaret and dome could be seen.

"Know you where we are?" the earl asked.

"As far as I can tell," the captain said, "we have been driven up the bay called the Little Syrtis—a place full of shoals and shallows, and abounding with pirates of the worst kind."

"Think you that the ship has suffered injury?"

"Whether she has done so or not," the captain said, "I fear greatly that she is fast in the sand, and even the lightening of all her cargo will scarce get her off; but we must try at least."

"It is little time that we shall have to try, Master Captain," Cuthbert, who was standing close, said. "Methinks those two long ships which are putting out from that town will have something to say to that."

"It is too true," the captain said. "Those are the galleys of the Moorish corsairs. They are thirty or forty oars, draw but little water, and will be here like the wind."

"What do you advise?" asked the earl. "The balistas which you have upon the poop can make but a poor resistance to boats that can row around us, and are no doubt furnished with heavy machines. They will quickly perceive that we are aground and defenceless, and will be able to plump their bolts into us until they have knocked the good ship to pieces. However, we will fight to the last. It shall not be said that the Earl of Evesham was taken by infidel dogs and sold as a slave, without striking a blow in his defence."

Cuthbert stood watching the corsairs, which were now rowing towards them at all speed.

"Methinks, my lord," he said, presently, "if I might venture to give an opinion, that we might yet trick the infidel."

"As how, Cuthbert?" the earl said. "Speak out; you know that I have great faith in your sagacity."

"I think, sir," the page said, "that did we send all your men below, leaving only the crew of the vessel on deck, they would take us for a merchant ship which has been wrecked here, and exercise but little care how they approach us. The men on deck might make a show of shooting once or twice with the balistas. The pirates, disdaining such a foe, would row alongside. Once there, we might fasten one or both to our side with grapnels, and then, methinks, that English bill and bow will render us more than a match for Moorish pirates, and one of these craft can scarcely carry more men than we have. I should propose to take one of them by force, and drive the pirates overboard; take possession of, if possible, or beat off, her consort; and then take the most valuable stores from the ship, and make our way as best we can to the north."

"Well thought of!" exclaimed the earl, cordially. "You have indeed imagined a plan which promises well. What think you, captain?"

"I think, my lord," the Genoese said, "that the plan is an excellent one, and promises every success. If your men will all go below, holding their arms in readiness for the signal, mine shall prepare grapnels and ropes, and the first of these craft which comes alongside they will lash so securely to the "Rose" that I warrant me she gets not away."

These preparations were soon made.

The soldiers, who at first had been filled with apprehension at the thought of slavery among the infidels, were now delighted at the prospect of a struggle ending in escape.

The archers prepared their bows and arrows, and stood behind the port-holes in readiness to pour a volley into the enemy; the men-at-arms grasped their pikes and swords; while above, the sailors moved hither and thither as if making preparations for defence, but in reality preparing the grapnels and ropes.

One of the pirates was faster than the other, and soon coming within reach, poured flights of javelins and stones upon the "Rose" from powerful machines, which she carried in her bow.

The crew of the "Rose" replied with their crossbows and arrows from the poop.

The corsair at first did not keep her course direct for the ship, but rowed round her, shooting arrows and casting javelins. Then, apparently satisfied that no great precaution need be observed with a feebly-manned ship in so great a strait as the "Rose," they set up a wild cry of "Allah!" and rowed towards her.

In two minutes the corsair was alongside of the "Rose," and the fierce crew were climbing up her sides. As she came alongside the sailors cast grapnels into her rigging, and fastened her to the "Rose," and then a loud shout of "Hurrah for England!" was heard; the ports opened, and a volley of arrows was poured upon the astonished corsair; and from the deck above the assailants were thrown back into the galley, and a swarm of heavily armed men leapt down from the ship upon them.

Taken by surprise, and indeed outnumbered, the resistance of the corsairs was but slight. In a close fierce mêlée like this the light-armed Moors had but little chance with the mail-clad English, whose heavy swords and axes clove their defences at a blow. The fight lasted but three minutes, and then the last of the corsairs was overboard.

The men who rowed the galley had uttered the most piercing cries while this conflict had been raging. They were unable to take any part in it, had they been disposed to do so, for they were all slaves chained to the oars.

Scarcely had the conflict ended when the other galley arrived upon the scene; but seeing what had happened, and that her consort had fallen into the hands of the English, she at once turned her head, and rowed back rapidly to the town from which she had come.

Among the slaves who rowed the galley were many white men, and their cries of joy at their liberation greatly affected those who had thus unexpectedly rescued them. Hammers were soon brought into requisition, the shackles struck off them, and a scene of affecting joy took place. The slaves were of all nationalities, but Italians and Spaniards, French and Greeks, formed the principal part. There was no time, however, to be lost; the arms and munitions of war were hastily removed from the "Rose," together with the most valuable of the stores.

The galley-slaves again took their places, and this time willingly, at the oars, the places of the weakest being supplied by the English, whose want of skill was made up by the alacrity with which they threw their strength into the work; and in an hour from the time that the galley had arrived alongside of the "Rose," her head was turned north, and with sixty oars she was rowing at all speed for the mouth of the bay.

CHAPTER XI.

IN THE HOLY LAND.

As soon as the galley which had escaped reached the town from which it had started, it with three others at once set out in pursuit; while from a narrow creek two other galleys made their appearance.

There were a few words of question among the English whether to stop and give battle to these opponents, or to make their way with all speed. The latter counsel prevailed; the earl pointing out that their lives were now scarcely their own, and that they had no right on their way to the holy sepulchre to risk them unnecessarily.

Fortunately they had it in their hands to fight or escape, as they chose; for doubly banked as the oars now were, there was little chance of the enemy's galleys overtaking them. Gradually as they rowed to sea the pursuing vessels became smaller and smaller to view, until at last they were seen to turn about and make again for land.

After some consultation between the earl and the captain of the lost ship, it was determined to make for Rhodes. This had been settled as a halting-point for the fleet, and the earl thought it probable that the greater portion of those scattered by the storm would rendezvous there.

So it proved; after a voyage, which although not very long was tedious, owing to the number of men cramped up in so small a craft, they came within sight of the port of Rhodes, and were greatly pleased at seeing a perfect forest of masts there, showing that at least the greater portion of the fleet had survived the storm.

This was indeed the fact, and a number of other single ships dropped in during the next day or two.

There was great astonishment on the part of the fleet when the long swift galley was seen approaching, and numerous conjectures were offered as to what message the pirates could be bringing—for there was no mistaking the appearance of the long, dangerous-looking craft.

When, upon her approach, the standard of the Earl of Evesham was seen flying on the bow, a great shout of welcome arose from the fleet; and King Richard himself, who happened to be on the deck of the royal ship, shouted to the earl to come on board and tell him what masquerading he was doing there. The earl of course obeyed the order, anchoring near the royal vessel, and going on board in a small boat, taking with him his page and squire.

The king heard with great interest the tale of the adventures of the "Rose;" and when the Earl of Evesham said that it was to Cuthbert that was due the thought of the stratagem by which the galley was captured, and its crew saved from being carried away into hopeless slavery, the king patted the boy on the shoulder with such hearty force as nearly to throw Cuthbert off his feet.

"By St. George!" said the monarch, "you are fated to be a very pink of knights. You seem as thoughtful as you are brave; and whatever your age may be, I declare that the next time your name is brought before me I will call a chapter of knights, and they shall agree that exception shall be made in your favour, and that you shall at once be admitted to the honourable post. You will miss your page, Sir Walter; but I am sure you will not grudge him that."

"No, no, sire," said the earl. "The lad, as I have told your Majesty, is a connexion of mine—distant, it is true, but one of the nearest I have—and it will give me the greatest pleasure to see him rising so rapidly, and on a fair way to distinguish himself highly. I feel already as proud of him as if he were my own son."

The fleet remained some two or three weeks at Rhodes, for many of the vessels were sorely buffeted and injured, masts were carried away as well as bulwarks battered in, and the efforts of the crews and of those of the whole of the artificers of Rhodes were called into requisition. Light sailing craft were sent off in all directions, for the king was in a fever of anxiety. Among the vessels still missing was that which bore the Queen of Navarre and the fair Berengaria.

One day a solitary vessel was seen approaching.

"Another of our lost sheep," the earl said, looking out over the poop.

She proved, however, to be a merchant ship of Greece, and newly come from Cyprus.

Her captain went on board the royal ship, and delivered a message to the king, to the effect that two of the vessels had been cast upon the coast of Cyprus, that they had been plundered by the people, the crews ill-treated and made prisoners by the king, and that the Queen of Navarre and the princess were in their hands.

This roused King Richard into one of his furies.

"Before I move a step towards the Holy Land," he said, "I will avenge these injuries upon this faithless and insolent king. I swear that I will make him pay dearly for having laid a hand upon these ladies."

At once the signal was hoisted for all the vessels in a condition to sail to take on board water and provisions, and to prepare to sail for Cyprus; and the next morning at daybreak the fleet sailed out, and made their way towards that island, casting anchor off the harbour of Famagosta.

King Richard sent a messenger on shore to the king, ordering him at once to release the prisoners; to make the most ample compensation to them; to place ships at their service equal to those which had been destroyed; and to pay a handsome sum of money as indemnity.

The King of Cyprus, however, an insolent and haughty despot, sent back a message of defiance. King Richard at once ordered the anchors to be raised, and all to follow the royal ship.

The fleet entered the harbour of Famagosta; the English archers began the fight by sending a flight of arrows into the town. This was answered from the walls by a shower of stones and darts from the machines.

There was no time wasted. The vessels were headed towards the shore, and as the water was deep, many of them were able to run close alongside the rocky wharves. In an instant, regardless of the storm of weapons poured down by the defenders, the English leapt ashore.

The archers kept up so terrible a rain of missiles against the battlements that the defenders could scarcely show themselves for an instant there, and the men-at-arms, placing ladders against them, speedily mounted, and putting aside all opposition, poured into the town. The effeminate Greek soldiers of the monarch could offer no effectual resistance whatever, and he himself fled from the palace and gained the open country, followed by a few adherents. The English gained a considerable booty, for in those days a town taken by assault was always looked upon as the property of the captors. The Queen of Navarre and the princess were rescued.

King Richard, however, was not satisfied with the success he had gained, and was determined to punish this insolent little king. Accordingly the English were set in motion into the interior, and town after town speedily fell, or opened their gates to him. The king, deserted by his troops, and detested by his people for having brought so terrible a scourge upon them by his reckless conduct, now sued for peace; but King Richard would give him no terms except dethronement, and this he was forced to accept. He was deprived of his crown, and banished from the island.

The king now, to the surprise of his barons, announced

his intention of at once marrying the Princess Berengaria.

Popular as he was, there was yet some quiet grumbling among his troops; as they said, with justice, they had been waiting nearly six months in the island of Sicily, and the king might well have married there, instead of a fresh delay being caused when so near their place of destination.

However, the king as usual had his own way, and the marriage was solemnized amidst great rejoicing and solemnity.

It was a brilliant scene indeed in the cathedral of

Limasol. There were assembled all the principal barons of England, together with a great number of the nobles of Cyprus.

Certainly no better matched pair ever stood at the altar together, for as King Richard was one of the strongest and bravest men of his own or any other time, so Berengaria is admitted to have been one of the loveliest maidens.

The air was rent with the acclamations of the assembled English host and of the numerous inhabitants of Limasol as they emerged from the cathedral. For a fortnight the town was given up to festivity; tournaments, joustings, banquets succeeded each other day after day, and the islanders, who were fond of pleasure, and indeed very wealthy, vied with the English in the entertainments which they gave in honour of the occason.

The festivities over, the king gave the welcome order to proceed on their voyage. They had now been joined by all the vessels left behind at Rhodes, and it was found that only a few were missing, and that the great storm, terrible as it had been, had inflicted less damage upon the fleet than was at first feared.

Two days' sail brought them within sight of the white walls of Acre, and it was on the 8th of June, 1191, that the fleet sailed into the port of that town. Tremendous acclamations greeted the arrival of the English army by the host assembled on the shores.

Acre had been besieged for two years, but in vain; and even the arrival of the French army under Phillip Augustus had failed to turn the scale. The inhabitants defended themselves with desperate bravery; every assault upon the walls had been repulsed with immense slaughter; and at no great distance off the Sultan Saladin, with a large army, was watching the progress of the siege.

The fame of King Richard and the English was so great, however, that the besiegers had little doubt that his arrival would change the position of things; and even the French, in spite of the bad feeling which had existed in Sicily, joined with the knights and army of the King of Jerusalem in acclaiming the arrival of the English.

Phillip Augustus, the French King, was of a somewhat weak and wavering disposition. It would have been thought that after his dispute with King Richard he would have gladly done all in his power to carry Acre before the arrival of his great rival. To the great disappointment of the French, however, he declared that he would take no step in the general assault until the arrival of Richard; and although the French had given some assistance to the besiegers, the army had really remained passive for many weeks.

Now, however, that the English had arrived, little time was lost; for the moment the dissensions and jealousies between the monarchs were patched up, the two hosts naturally imitated the example of their sovereigns, and French and English worked side by side in throwing up trenches against the walls, in building movable towers for the attack, and in preparing for the great onslaught.

The French were the first to finish their preparations, and they delivered a tremendous assault upon the walls. The besieged, however, did not lose heart, and with the greatest bravery repulsed every attempt. The scaling ladders were hurled backwards, the towers were destroyed by Greek fire; boiling oil was hurled down upon the men who advanced under the shelter of machines to undermine the walls; and after desperate fighting the French fell back, baffled and beaten.

There was some quiet exultation in the English lines at the defeat of the French, for they believed that a better fortune would crown their own efforts. Such, however, to their surprise and mortification, was not the case. When their preparations were completed, they attacked with splendid bravery. They were fighting under the eyes of their king, and in sight of the French army, who had a few days before been baffled; and if bravery and devotion could have carried the walls of Acre, assuredly King Richard's army would have accomplished the task.

It was, however, too great for them, and with vast loss the army fell back to its camp, King Richard raging like a wounded lion. Many of his barons had been killed in the assault, and the pikemen and men-at-arms had suffered heavily. The Earl of Evesham had been wounded; Cuthbert had taken no part in the assault, for the earl, knowing his bravery, had forbidden his doing so, as he foresaw the struggle would be of the most desperate character; and as it was not usual for pages to accompany their lords on the

battle-field, Cuthbert could not complain of his being forbidden to take part in the fight.

The earl, however, permitted him to accompany Cnut and the bowmen, who did great service by the accuracy of their aim, preventing by their storm of arrows the men on the battlements from taking steady aim and working their machines, and so saved the Earl of Evesham's troop and those fighting near him from suffering nearly as heavy loss as some of those engaged in other quarters.

But while successful in beating off all assaults, the defenders of Acre were now nearly at the end of their resources. The Emperor Saladin, although he had collected an army of 200,000 men, yet feared to advance and give battle to the crusaders in their own lines—for they had thrown up round their camp strong entrenchments, to prevent the progress of the siege being disturbed by forces from without.

The people of Acre seeing the time pass and no sign of a rescuing force, their provisions being utterly exhausted, and pestilence and fever making frightful ravages in the city, at last determined to surrender.

For over two years they had made a resistance of the most valiant description, and now, despairing of success or rescue, and seeing the hosts of their besiegers increasing day by day, they hoisted a flag upon the walls, and sent a deputation to the kings, asking for terms if they submitted. They would have done well had they submitted upon the arrival of the French and English reinforcements. For the monarchs, annoyed by the defeat of their forces and by the heavy losses they had sustained, and knowing that the besieged were now at their last crust, were not disposed to be merciful.

However, the horrors which then attended the capture of cities in a war in which so little quarter was given on either side, were avoided. The city was to be surrendered; the much-prized relic contained within its walls—said to be a piece of the true Cross which had been captured by the Saracens at the battle of Tiberias, in which they had almost annihilated the Christian armies a few years before—was to be surrendered; the Christian prisoners in their hands were to be given up unharmed, and the inhabitants undertook to pay 200,000 pieces of gold to the kings within forty days, under the condition that the fighting men now taken prisoners were to be put to death should this ransom not be paid.

The conquest of Acre was hailed throughout Christendom as a triumph of the highest importance. It opened again the gates of the Holy Land; and so tremendous was the strength of the fortress, that it was deemed that if this stronghold were unable to resist effectually the arms of the crusaders, and that if Saladin with so great an army did not dare to advance to its rescue, then the rest of the Holy Land would speedily fall under the hands of the invading army.

With the fall of Acre, however, the dissensions between the two kings, which had for a while been allowed to rest while the common work was to be done, broke out again with renewed intensity. The jealousy of Phillip Augustus was raised to the highest point by the general enthusiasm of the combined armies for the valiant King of England, and by the authority which that monarch exercised in the councils.

He therefore suddenly announced his intention of returning to France.

This decision at first occasioned the greatest consternation in the ranks of the crusaders; but this feeling was lessened when the king announced that he should leave a large portion of the French army behind, under the command of the Duke of Burgundy. The wiser councillors were satisfied with the change. Although there was a reduction of the total fighting force, yet the fact that it was now centred under one head, and that King Richard would now be in supreme command, was deemed to more than counterbalance the loss of a portion of the French army.

Before starting on the march for Jerusalem, King Richard sullied his reputation by causing all the defenders of Acre to be put to death, their ransom not having arrived at the stipulated time.

Then the allied army set out upon their journey. The fleet cruised along near them, and from it they obtained all that was requisite for their wants, and yet, notwithstanding these advantages, the toil and fatigue were terrible. Roads scarcely existed, and the army marched across the rough and broken country. There was no straggling, but each kept his place; and if unable to do so, fell and died. The blazing sun poured down upon them with an appalling force; the dust which rose when they left the rocks and came upon flat sandy ground, almost smothered them. Water was only obtainable at the halts, and then was frequently altogether insufficient for the wants of the army; while in front, on flank, and in rear hovered clouds of the cavalry of Saladin.

At times King Richard would allow parties of his knights to detach themselves from the force to drive off these enemies. But it was the chase of a lion after a hare. The knights in their heavy armour and powerful steeds were left behind as if standing still, by the fleet Bedouins on their desert coursers; and the pursuers, exhausted and worn out, were always glad to regain the ranks of the army.

These clouds of cavalry belonging to the enemy did not content themselves with merely menacing and cutting off stragglers. At times, when they thought they saw an opening, they would dash in and attack the column desperately, sometimes gaining temporary advantages, killing and wounding many, then fleeing away again into the desert.

Finding that it was impossible to catch these wary horsemen, King Richard ordered his bowmen to march outside his cavalry, so that when the enemy's horse approached within bowshot they should open upon them with arrows; then, should the horsemen persist in charging, the archers were at once to take refuge behind the lines of the knights.

Day after day passed in harassing conflicts. The distance passed over each day was very small, and the sufferings of the men from thirst, heat, and fatigue enormous. Cuthbert could well understand now what he had heard of great armies melting away, for already men began to succumb in large numbers to the terrible heat, and the path traversed by the army was scattered with corpses of those who had fallen victims to sunstroke. Not even at night did the attacks of the enemy cease, and a portion of the harassed force was obliged to keep under arms to repel assaults.

So passed the time until the army arrived at Azotus, and there, to the delight of the crusaders, who only longed to get at their foes, they beheld the whole force of Saladin, 200,000 strong, barring their way. Had it not been for the stern discipline enforced by King Richard, the knights of England and France would have repeated the mistake which had caused the extermination of the Christian force at Tiberias, and would have levelled their lances and charged recklessly into the mass of their enemies. But the king, riding round the flanks and front of the force, gave his orders in the sternest way, with the threat that any man who moved from the ranks should die by his hand.

The army was halted, the leaders gathered round the

king, and a hasty consultation was held. Richard insisted upon the fight being conducted upon the same principles as the march—that the line of archers should stand outside the knights, and should gall the advancing force with arrows till the last moment, and then retire among the cavalry, only to sally out again as the Bedouins fell back from the steel wall of horsemen.

Cuthbert had now for the first time donned full armour, and rode behind the Earl of Evesham as his esquire, for the fomer esquire had been left behind, ill with fever, at Acre.

CHAPTER XII.

THE ACCOLADE..

IT was now a year since they had left England, and Cuthbert had much grown and widened out in the interval, and had never neglected an opportunity of practising with arms; and the earl was well aware that he should obtain an efficient assistance from him in time of need as he could desire.

This was the first time that Cuthbert, and indeed the great proportion of those present in the Christian host, had seen the enemy in force, and they eagerly watched the vast array. It was picturesque in the extreme, with a variety and brightness of colour rivalling that of the Christian host. In banners and pennons the latter made a braver show; but the floating robes of the infidel showed a far brighter mass of colour than the steel armour of the Christians.

Here were people drawn from widely separated parts of Saladin's dominions. Here were Nubians from the Nile, tall and powerful men, jet black in skin, with lines of red and white paint on their faces, giving a ghastly and wild appearance to them. On their shoulders were skins of lions and other wild animals. They carried short bows, and heavy clubs studded with iron. By them were the Bedouin cavalry, light, sinewy men, brown as berries, with white turbans and garments. Near these were the cavalry from Syria and the plains of Assyria—wild horsemen with semi-barbarous armour and scarlet trappings. Here were the solid lines of the Egyptian infantry, steady troops, upon whom Saladin much relied. Here were other tribes, gathered from afar, each distinguished by its own particular marks. In silence did this vast array view awhile the solid mass of the Christians. Suddenly a strange din of discordant music from thousands of musical instruments—conches and horns, cymbals and drums, arose in wild confusion. Shouts of defiance in a dozen tongues and from 200,000 throats rose wild and shrill upon the air, while clear above all the din were heard the strange vibratory cries of the warriors from the Egyptian highlands.

"One would think," said Cnut grimly to Cuthbert, "that the infidels imagine we are a flock of antelopes to be frightened by an outcry. They would do far better to save their wind for future use. They will want it, methinks, when we get fairly among them. Who would have thought that a number of men, heathen and infidel though they be, could have made so foul an outcry?"

Cuthbert laughed.

"Every one fights according to his own method, Cnut; and I am not sure that there is not something to be said for this outcry, for it is really so wild and fearful that it makes my blood almost curdle in my veins; and were it not that I know the proved valour of our knights and footmen, I should feel shaken by this terrible introduction to the fight."

"I heed it no more," said Cnut, "than the outcry of wild fowl, when one comes upon them suddenly on a lake in winter. It means no more than that; and I reckon that they are trying to encourage themselves fully as much as to frighten us. However, we shall soon see. If they can fight as well as they can scream, they certainly will get no answering shouts from us. The English bulldog fights silently, and bite as hard as he will, you will hear little beyond a low growl. Now, my men," he said, turning to his archers, "methinks the heathen are about to begin in earnest. Keep steady; do not fire until you are sure that they are within range. Draw your bows well to your ears, and straightly and steadily let fly. Never heed the outcry or the rush, keep steady to the last moment. There is shelter behind you, and fierce as the attack may be, you can find a sure refuge behind the line of the knights."

Cnut with his archers formed part of the line outside the array of English knights, and the arrows of the English bowmen fell fast as bands of the Bedouin horse circled round them in the endeavour to draw the Christians on to the attack. For some time Saladin persisted in these tactics. With his immense superiority of force he reckoned that if the Christian chivalry would but charge him, the victory of Tiberias would be repeated. Hemmed in by numbers, borne down by the weight of armour and the effects of the blazing sun, the knights would succumb as much to fatigue

as to the force of their foes. King Richard's orders, however, were well obeyed, and at last the Moslem chief, urged by the entreaties of his leading emirs, who felt ashamed that so large a force should hesitate to attack one so vastly inferior in numbers, determined upon taking the initiative, and forming his troops in a semicircle round the Christian army, launched his horsemen to the attack. The instant they came within range, a cloud of arrows from the English archers fell among them, but the speed at which the desert horses covered the ground rendered it impossible for the archers to discharge more than one or two shafts before the enemy were upon them. Quickly as they now slipped back and sought refuge under the lances of the knights, many of them were unable to get back in time, and were cut down by the

Saracens. The rest crept between the horses or under their bellies into the rear, and there prepared to sally out again as soon as the enemy retired. The Christian knights sat like a wall of steel upon their horses, their lances were levelled, and, brave as the Bedouin horsemen were, they felt to break this massive line was impossible. The front line, however, charged well up to the points of the lances, against which they hewed with their sharp scimitars, frequently severing the steel top from the ashpole, and then breaking through and engaging in hand-to-hand conflict with the knights. Behind the latter sat their squires, with extra spears and arms ready to hand to their masters; and in close combat, the heavy maces with their spike ends were weapons before which the light clad horsemen went down like reeds before a storm.

Hour after hour the Arab horsemen persisted in their attack, suffering heavily, but determined to conquer if possible. Then Saladin suddenly ordered a retreat, and at seeing their enemy fly, the impetuosity of the crusaders at last broke out. With a shout they dashed after the foe. King Richard, knowing that his followers had already shown a patience far beyond what he could have expected, now headed the onslaught, performing prodigies of valour with his single arm, and riding from point to point to see that all was well.

The early resistance of the infidel host was comparatively slight. The heavy mass of the Christian cavalry, with their levelled lances, swept through the ranks of the light horsemen, and trampled them down like grass beneath their feet; but every moment the resistance became more stubborn.

Saladin, knowing the Christians would sooner or later assume the offensive, had gathered his troops line in line behind the front ranks, and as the force of the crusaders' charge abated, so did the number of foes in their front multiply. Not only this, but upon either side chosen bands swept down, and ere long the Christians were brought to a stand, and all were fighting hand to hand with their enemies. The lances were thrown away now, and with axe and mace each fought for himself.

The Earl of Evesham was one of a group of knights whom King Richard had that day ordered to keep close to his person, and around this group the fight raged most furiously.

Saladin, aware of the extreme personal valour and warlike qualities of King Richard, set the greatest value upon his death or capture, and had ordered a large number of his best troops to devote their whole attention to attacking the King of England. The royal standard carried behind the king was a guide to their onslaught, and great as was the strength and valour of King Richard, he with difficulty was able to keep at bay the hosts that swept around him.

Now that the lance had been abandoned for battle-axe, Cuthbert was able to take an active part in the struggle, his duties consisting mainly in guarding the rear of his master, and preventing his being overthrown by any sudden attack on the flank or from behind.

King Richard was bent not only on defending himself from the attacks of his foes, but on directing the general course of the battle; and from time to time he burst, with his own trusty knights, through the ring of foes, and rode from point to point of the field, calling the knights together, exhorting them to steadiness, and restoring the fight where its fortunes seemed doubtful. At one time the impetuosity of the king led him into extreme danger. He had burst through the enemy surrounding him, and these, by order of their captain, allowed him to pass through their ranks, and then threw themselves together in his rear, to cut him off from the knights who rode behind. The maneuver was successful. The rush of horsemen fairly carried away the Christian

knights, and one
or two alone
were able to
make their way
through.

Amid the wild confusion that raged, where each man was
fighting for his own life, and but little view of what was
passing could be obtained through the barred visor, the fact
that the king was separated from them was known to but
few. Sir Walter himself was engaged fiercely in a hand-to-
hand fight with four Bedouins who surrounded him, when
Cuthbert shouted,—

"The king, Sir Walter! the king! He is cut off and
surrounded! For heaven's sake ride to him. See! the royal
standard is down."

With a shout the earl turned, brained one of his foes with
a sweep of his heavy axe, and, followed by Cuthbert, dashed
to the assistance of the king. The weight of his horse and
armour cleft through the crowd, and in a brief space he

penetrated to the side of King Richard, who was borne upon by a host of foes. Just as they reached them a Bedouin who had been struck from his horse crawled beneath the noble charger of King Richard, and drove his scimitar deep into its bowels. The animal reared high in its sudden pain, and then fell on the ground, carrying the king, who was unable to disengage himself quickly enough.

In an instant the Earl of Evesham had leapt from his horse and with his broad triangular shield extended sought to cover him from the press of enemies. Cuthbert imitated his lord, and strove to defend the latter from attacks from the rear. For a moment or two the sweep of the earl's heavy axe and Cuthbert's circling sword kept back the foe, but this could not last. King Richard in vain strove to extricate his leg from beneath his fallen steed. Cuthbert saw at a glance that the horse still lived, and with a sudden slash of his sword he struck it on the hind quarter. Goaded by the pain the noble animal made a last effort to rise, but only to fall back dead. The momentary action was, however, sufficient for King Richard, who drew his leg from under it, and with his heavy battle-axe in hand, rose with a shout, and stood by the side of the earl.

In vain did the Bedouins strive to cut down and overpower the two champions; in vain did they urge their horses to ride over them. With each sweep of his axe the king either dismounted a foe or clove in the head of his steed, and a wall of slain around them testified to the tremendous power of their arms. Still, even such warriors as these could not long sustain the conflict. The earl had already received several desperate wounds, and the king himself was bleeding from some severe gashes with the keen-edged scimitars. Cuthbert was already down, when a shout of "St. George!" was heard, and a body of English knights clove through the throng of Saracens and reached the side of King Richard. Close behind these in a mass pressed the British footmen with bill and pike, the enemy giving way foot by foot before their steady discipline.

The king was soon on horseback again, and rallying his troops on, led them for one more great and final charge upon the enemy. The effect was irresistible. Appalled by the slaughter which they had suffered, and by the tremendous strength and energy of the Christian knights, the Saracens broke and fled; and the last reserves of Saladin gave way as the king, shouting his war-cry of "God help the holy sepulchre!" fell upon them. Once, indeed, the battle still seemed doubtful, for a fresh band of the enemy at that moment arrived and joined in the fray. The crusaders were now, however, inspired with such courage and confidence that they readily obeyed the king's war-cry, gathered in a firm body, and hurled themselves upon this new foe. Then the Saracens finally turned and fled, and the Christian victory was complete.

It was one of the features of this war that however thorough the victories of the Christians, the Saracens very speedily recovered from their effects. A Christian defeat was crushing and entire; the knights died as they stood, and defeat meant annihilation. Upon the other hand, the Saracens and Bedouins when they felt that their efforts to win the battle were unsuccessful, felt no shame or humiliation in scattering like sheep. On their fleet horses and in their light attire they could easily distance the Christians, who never, indeed, dreamt of pursuing them. The day after the fight, the enemy would collect again under their chiefs, and be as ready as before to renew their harassing warfare.

On his return from the field, the king assembled many of his principal knights and leaders, and summoned the Earl of Evesham, with the message that he was to bring his esquire with him. When they reached the tent, the king said,—

"My lords, as some of you may be aware, I have this day had a narrow escape from death. Separated from you in the battle, and attended only by my standard-bearer, I was surrounded by the Saracens. I should doubtless have cleft my way through the infidel dogs, but a foul peasant stabbed my charger from below, and the poor brute fell with me. My standard-bearer was killed, and in another moment my nephew Arthur would have been your king, had it not been that my good lord here, attended by this brave lad, appeared. I have seen a good deal of fighting, but never did I see a braver stand than they made above my body. The Earl of Evesham, as you all know, is one of my bravest knights, and to him I can simply say, 'Thanks; King Richard does not forget a benefit like this.' But such aid as I might well look for from so stout a knight as the Earl of Evesham, I could hardly have expected on the part of a mere boy like this. It is not the first time that I have been under a debt of

gratitude to him; for it was his watchfulness and bravery which saved Queen Berengaria from being carried off by the French in Sicily. I deemed him too young then for the order of knighthood—although indeed bravery has no age; still for a private benefit, and that performed against allies, in name at least, I did not wish so far to fly in the face of usage as to make him a knight. I promised him then, however, that the first time he distinguished himself against the infidel he should win his spurs. I think that you will agree with me, my lords, that he has done so. Not only did he stand over me, and with great bravery defend Sir Walter from attacks from behind, but his ready wit saved me, when even his sword and that of Sir Walter would have failed to do so. Penned down under poor Robin, I was powerless to move until our young esquire, in an interval of slashing at his assailants, found time to give a sharp blow together with a shout to Robin. The poor beast tried to rise, and the movement, short as it was, enabled me to draw my leg from under him, and then with my mace I was enabled to take a stand until you arrived at my side. I think, my lords, that you will agree with me that Cuthbert, the son of Sir William de Lance, is fit for the honour of knighthood."

A general chorus of approval arose from the assembly, and the king, bidding Cuthbert kneel before him, drew his sword and laid it across his shoulders, dubbing him Sir Cuthbert de Lance. When he had risen, the great barons of England pressed round to shake his hand, and Cuthbert, who was a modest young fellow, felt almost ashamed at the honours which were bestowed upon him. The usual ceremonies and penances which young knights had to undergo before admission into the body—and which in those days were extremely punctilious, and indeed severe, consisting, among other things, in fasting, in watching the armour at night, in seclusion and religious services—were omitted when the accolade was bestowed for bravery in the field.

The king ordered his armourer at once to make for Cuthbert a suit of the finest armour, and authorized him to carry on his shield a sword raising a royal crown from the ground, in token of the deed for which the honour of knighthood had been bestowed upon him.

Upon his return to the earl's camp the news of his new dignity spread at once among the followers of Sir Walter, and many and hearty were the cheers that went up from the throats of the Saxon foresters, led by Cnut. These humble friends were indeed delighted at his success, for they felt that to him they owed very much; and his kindness of manner and the gaiety of heart which he had shown during the hardships they had undergone since their start, had greatly endeared him to them.

Cuthbert was now to take rank among the knights who followed the banner of the earl. A tent was erected for him, an esquire assigned to him, and the lad as he entered his new abode felt almost bewildered at the change which had taken place in one short day—that he, at the age of sixteen, should have earned the honour of knighthood, and the approval of the King of England, expressed before all the great barons of the realm, was indeed an honour such as he could never have hoped for; and the thought of what his mother would say should the news reach her in her quiet Saxon home, brought the tears into his eyes. He had not gone through the usual religious ceremonies, but he knelt in his tent alone, and prayed that he might be made worthy of the honours bestowed upon him; that he might fulfil the duties of a Christian knight fearlessly and honourably; that his sword might never be raised but for the right; that he might devote himself to the protection of the oppressed, and the honour of God; that his heart might be kept from evil; and that he might carry through life, unstained his new escutcheon.

If the English had thought that their victory would have gained them immunity from the Saracen attacks, they were speedily undeceived. The host, indeed, which had barred their way had broken up; but its fragments were around them, and the harassing attacks began again with a violence and persistency even greater than before. The crusaders, indeed, occupied only the ground upon which they stood. It was death to venture 100 yards from the camp, unless in a strong body; and the smallest efforts to bring in food from the country round were instantly met and repelled. Only in very strong bodies could the knights venture from camp even to forage for their horses, and the fatigues and sufferings of all were in no way relieved by the great victory of Azotus.

CHAPTER XIII.

IN THE HANDS OF THE SARACENS.

THE English had hoped that after one pitched battle they should be able to advance upon Jerusalem, but they had reckoned without the climate and illness.

Although unconquered in the fray, the Christian army was weakened by its sufferings to such an extent that it was virtually brought to a standstill. Even King Richard, with all his impetuosity, dared not venture to cut adrift from the seashore, and to march direct upon Jerusalem; that city was certainly not to be taken without a long siege, and this could only be undertaken by an army strong enough, not only to carry out so great a task, but to meet and defeat the armies which Saladin would bring up to the rescue, and to keep open the line down to Joppa, by which alone provisions, and the engines necessary for the siege, could be brought up. Hence the war resolved itself into a series of expeditions and detached fights.

The British camp was thoroughly fortified, and thence parties of the knights sallied out and engaged in conflicts with the Saracens, with varying success. On several of these expeditions Cuthbert attended the earl, and behaved with a bravery which showed him well worthy of the honours which he had received.

Upon one occasion the news reached camp that a party of knights, who had gone out to guard a number of footmen cutting forage and bringing it into camp, had been surrounded and had taken refuge in a small town, whose gates they had battered in when they saw the approach of an overwhelming host of the enemy. King Richard himself headed a strong force and advanced to their assistance. Their approach was not seen until within a short distance of the enemy, upon whom the crusaders fell with the force of a thunderbolt, and cleft their way through their lines. After a short pause in the little town, they prepared to again cut their way through, joined by the party who had there been besieged. The task was now however, far more difficult; for the footmen would be unable to keep up with the rapid charge of the knights, and it was necessary not only to clear the way, but to keep it open for their exit. King Richard himself and the greater portion of his knights were to lead the charge; another party were to follow behind the footmen, who were ordered to advance at the greatest speed of which they were capable, while their rearguard by charges upon the enemy, kept them at bay. To this latter party Cuthbert was attached.

The Saracens followed their usual tactics, and this time with great success. Dividing as the king with his knights charged them, they suffered these to pass through with but slight resistance, and then closed in upon their track, while another and still more numerous body fell upon the footmen and their guard. Again and again did the knights charge through the ranks of the Moslems, while the billmen stoutly kept together and resisted the onslaughts of the enemy's cavalry. In spite of their bravery, however, the storm of arrows shot by the desert horsemen thinned their ranks with terrible rapidity. Charging up to the very point of the spears, these wild horsemen fired their arrows into the faces of their foe, and although numbers of them fell beneath the more formidable missiles sent by the English archers, their numbers were so overwhelming that the little band melted away. The small party of knights, too, were rapidly thinned, although performing prodigious deeds of valour. The Saracens when dismounted or wounded still fought on foot, their object being always to stab or hough the horses, and so dismount the riders. King Richard and his force, though making the most desperate efforts to return to the assistance of the rearguard, were baffled by the sturdy resistance of the Saracens, and the position of those in the rear was fast becoming hopeless.

One by one the gallant little band of knights fell, and a sea of turbans closed over the fluttering plumes. Cuthbert, after defending himself with extreme bravery for a long time, was at last separated from the small remainder of his comrades by a rush of the enemy's horse, and when fighting desperately he received a heavy blow at the back of the head from the mace of a huge Nubian soldier, and fell senseless to the ground.

When he recovered his consciousness, the first impression upon his mind was the stillness which had succeeded to the din of battle; the shouts and war-cries of the crusaders, the wild yells of the Moslems, were hushed, and in their place was a quiet chatter in many unknown tongues, and the sound of laughter and feasting. Raising his head and looking round, Cuthbert saw that he and some ten of his comrades were lying together in the midst of a Saracen camp, and that he was a prisoner to the infidels. The sun streamed down with tremendous force upon them; there was no shelter; and though all were wounded and parched with thirst, the Saracens of whom they besought water, pointing to their mouths and making signs of their extreme thirst, laughed in their faces, and signified by a gesture that it was scarcely worth the trouble to drink when they were likely so soon to be put to death.

It was late in the afternoon before any change was manifest. Then Cuthbert observed a stir in the camp; the men ran to their horses, leapt on their backs, and with wild cries of "Welcome!" started off at full speed. Evidently some personage was about to arrive, and the fate of the prisoners would be solved. A few words were from time to time exchanged between these, each urging the other to keep up his heart and defy the infidel. One or two had succumbed to their wounds during the afternoon, and only six were able to stand erect when summoned to do so by some of their guard, who made signs to them that a great personage was coming. Soon the shouts of the horsemen and other sounds announced that the great chief was near at hand, and the captives gathered from the swelling shouts of the Arabs that the new arrival was Sultan Suleiman—or Saladin, for he was called by both names—surrounded by a body-guard of splendidly-dressed attendants. The emir, who was himself plainly attired, reined up his horse in front of the captives.

"You are English," he said, in the lingua-franca which was the medium of communication between the Eastern and Western peoples in those days. "You are brave warriors,

and I hear that before you were taken you slaughtered numbers of my people. They did wrong to capture you and bring you here to be killed. Your cruel king gives no mercy to those who fall into his hands. You must not expect it here, you who without a pretence of right invade my country, slaughter my people, and defeat my armies. The murder of the prisoners of Acre has closed my heart to all mercy. There, your king put 10,000 prisoners to death in cold blood, a month after the capture of the place, because the money at which he had placed their ransom had not arrived. We Arabs do not carry huge masses of gold about with us; and although I could have had it brought from Egypt, I did not think that so brave a monarch as Richard of England could have committed so cruel an action in cold blood. When we are fresh from battle, and our wounds are warm, and our hearts are full of rage and fury, we kill our prisoners; but to do so weeks after a battle is contrary to the laws alike of your religion and of ours. However, it is King Richard who has sealed your doom, not I. You are knights, and I do not insult you with the offer of turning from your religion and joining me. Should one of you wish to save his life on these conditions, I will, however, promise him a place of position and authority among us."

None of the knights moved to accept the offer, but each, as the eye of the emir ran along the line, answered with an imprecation of contempt and hatred. Saladin waved his hand, and one by one the captives were led aside, walking as proudly to their doom as if they had been going to a feast. Each wrung the hand of the one next to him as he turned, and then without a word followed his captors. There was a dull sound heard, and one by one the heads of the knights rolled in the sand. Cuthbert happened to be last in the line, and as the executioners laid hands upon him and removed his helmet, the eye of the sultan fell upon him, and he almost started at perceiving the extreme youth of his captive. He held his hand aloft to arrest the movements of the executioners, and signalled for Cuthbert to be brought before him again.

"You are but a boy," he said. "All the knights who have hitherto fallen into my hands have been men of strength and power; how is it that I see a mere youth among their ranks, and wearing the golden spurs of knighthood?"

"King Richard himself made me a knight," Cuthbert said proudly, "after having stood across him when his steed had been foully stabbed at the battle of Azotus, and the whole

Moslem host were around him."

"Ah!" said the emir, "were you one of the two who, as I have heard, defended the king for some time against all assaults? It were hard indeed to kill so brave a youth. I doubt me not that at present you are as firmly determined to die a Christian knight as those who have gone before you?

But time may change you. At any rate for the present your doom is postponed."

He turned to a gorgeously-dressed noble next to him, and said,—

"Your brother, Ben Abin, is Governor of Jerusalem, and the gardens of the palace are fair. Take this youth to him as a present, and set him to work in his gardens. His life I have spared, in all else Ben Abin will be his master."

Cuthbert heard without emotion the words which changed his fate from death to slavery. Many, he knew, who were captured in these wars were carried away as slaves to different parts of Asia, and it did not seem to him that the change was in any way a boon. However, life is dear, and it was but natural that a thought should leap into his heart that soon either the crusaders might force a way into Jerusalem and there rescue him, or that he himself might in some way escape.

The sultan having thus concluded the subject, turned

away, and galloped off surrounded by his body-guard.

Those who had captured the Christians now stripped off the armour of Cuthbert; then he was mounted on a bare-backed steed, and with four Bedouins, with their long lances, riding beside him, started for Jerusalem. After a day of long and rapid riding, the Arabs stopped suddenly, on the crest of a hill, with a shout of joy, and throwing themselves from their horses, bent with their foreheads to the earth at the sight of their holy city. Cuthbert, as he gazed at the stately walls of Jerusalem, and the noble buildings within, felt bitterly that it was not thus that he had hoped to see the holy city. He had dreamt of arriving before it with his comrades, proud and delighted at their success so far, and confident in their power soon to wrest the town before them from the hands of the Moslems. Instead of this he was a slave—a slave to the infidel, perhaps never more to see a white face, save that of some other unfortunate like himself.

Even now in its fallen state no city is so impressive at first sight as Jerusalem; the walls, magnificent in height and strength, and picturesque in their deep embattlements, rising on the edge of a deep valley. Every building has its name and history. Here is the church built by the first crusaders; there the mighty mosque of Suleiman on the site of the Temple; far away on a projecting ridge the great building known as the Tomb of Moses; on the right beyond the houses rise the towers on the Roman walls; the Pool of Bethsaida lies in the hollow; the centre are the cupolas of the Church of the Holy Sepulchre. Among all the fairest cities of the world, there are none which can compare in stately beauty with Jerusalem. Doubtless it was a fairer city in those days, for long centuries of Turkish possession have reduced many of the former stately palaces to ruins. Then, as now, the banner of the Prophet floated over the high places; but whereas at present the population is poor and squalid, the city in those days contained a far larger number of inhabitants, irrespective of the great garrison collected for its defence.

The place from which Cuthbert had his first sight of Jerusalem is that from which the best view is to be obtained—the crest of the Mount of Olives. After a minute or two spent in looking at the city, the Arabs with a shout continued their way down into the valley. Crossing this they ascended the steep road to the walls, brandishing their lances and giving yells of triumph; then riding two upon each side of their prisoner, to protect him from any fanatic who might lay a hand upon him, they passed under the gate known as the Gate of Suleiman into the city.

The populace thronged the streets; and the news brought by the horsemen that a considerable portion of the Christian host had been defeated and slain, passed from mouth to mouth, and was received with yells of exultation. Execrations were heaped upon Cuthbert, who rode along with an air as quiet and composed as if he were the centre of an ovation instead of that of an outburst of hatred.

He would, indeed, speedily have been torn from his guards, had not these shouted that he was placed in their hands by Saladin himself for conduct to the governor. As the emir was as sharp and as ruthless with his own people as with the prisoners who fell into his hands, the name acted as a talisman, and Cuthbert and his escort rode forward without molestation until they reached the entrance to the palace.

Dismounting, Cuthbert was now led before the governor himself, a stern and grave-looking man, sitting cross-legged on a divan surrounded by officers and attendants. He heard in silence the account given him by the escort, bowed his head at the commands of Suleiman, and, without addressing a word to Cuthbert, indicated to two attendants that he was to be removed into the interior of the house. Here the young knight was led to a small dungeon-like room; bread and dates with a cruse of water were placed before him; the door was then closed and locked without, and he found himself alone with his thoughts.

No one came near him that night, and he slept as soundly as he would have done in his tent in the midst of the Christian host. He was resolved to give no cause for ill-treatment or complaint to his captors, to work as willingly, as cheerfully, as was in his power, and to seize the first opportunity to make his escape, regardless of any risk of his life which he might incur in doing so.

In the morning the door opened, and a black slave led him into the garden, which was surrounded by a very high and lofty wall. It was large, and full of trees and flowers, and far more beautiful than any garden that Cuthbert had seen in his native land. There were various other slaves at work; and an Arab, who appeared to be the head of the gardeners, at once appointed to Cuthbert the work assigned to him. A guard of Arabs with bow and spear watched the doings of the slaves.

With one glance round, Cuthbert was assured that escape from this garden, at least, was not to be thought of, and that for the present, patience alone was possible. Dismissing all ideas of that kind from his mind, he set to work with a steady attention to his task. He was very fond of flowers, and soon he became so absorbed in his work as almost to forget that he was a slave. It was not laborious—digging, planting, pruning and training the flowers, and giving them copious draughts of water from a large fountain in the centre of the garden.

The slaves were not permitted to exchange a word with each other. At the end of the day's work they were marched off to separate chambers, or, as they might be called, dungeons. Their food consisted of water, dried dates, and bread, and they had little to complain of in this respect; indeed, the slaves in the gardens of the governor's house at Jerusalem enjoyed an exceptionally favoured existence. The governor himself was absorbed in the cares of the city. The head gardener happened to be a man of unusual humanity, and it was really in his hands that the comfort of the prisoners was placed.

Sometimes in the course of the day, veiled ladies would issue in groups from the palace, attended by black slaves with drawn scimitars. They passed without unveiling across the point where the slaves were at work, and all were forbidden on pain of death to look up, or even to approach the konak or pavilion, where the ladies threw aside their veils, and enjoyed the scent and sight of the flowers, the splash of murmuring waters, and the strains of music touched by skilful hands.

Although Cuthbert wondered in his heart what these strange wrapped-up figures might look like when the veils were thrown back, he certainly did not care enough about the matter to run any risk of drawing the anger of his guards upon himself by raising his eyes towards them; nor did he ever glance up at the palace, which was also interdicted to the slaves. From the lattice casements during the day the strains of music and merry laughter often came down to the captives; but this, if anything, only added to the bitterness of their position, by reminding them that they were shut off for life from ever hearing the laughter of the loved ones they had left behind.

For upwards of a month Cuthbert remained steadily at work, and during that time no possible plan of escape had occurred to him, and he had indeed resigned himself to wait, either until, as he hoped, the city would be taken by the Christians or until, he himself might be removed from his present post and sent into the country, where, although his lot would doubtless be far harder, some chance of escape might open before him.

One night, long after slumber had fallen upon the city, Cuthbert was startled by hearing his door open. Rising to his feet, he saw a black slave, and an old woman beside him. The latter spoke first in the lingua-franca,—

"My mistress, the wife of the governor, has sent me to ask your story. How is it that, although but a youth, you are already a knight? How is it that you come to be a slave to our people? The sultan himself sent you to her lord. She would fain hear through me how it has happened. She is the kindest of ladies, and the sight of your youth has touched her heart."

With thanks to the unknown lady who had felt an interest in him, Cuthbert briefly related the events which had led to his captivity. The old woman placed on the ground a basket containing some choice fruit and white bread, and then departed with the negro as quietly as she had come, leaving Cuthbert greatly pleased at what had taken place.

"Doubtless," he said to himself, "I shall hear again; and it may be, that through the pity of this lady some means of escape may open to me."

Although for some little time no such prospect appeared, yet the visits of the old woman, which were frequently repeated, were of interest to him, and seemed to form a link between him and the world.

After coming regularly every night for a week, she bade the young knight follow her, holding her finger to her lips in sign that caution must be observed. Passing through several passages, he was at length led into a room where a lady of some forty years of age, surrounded by several slaves and younger women, was sitting. Cuthbert felt no scruple in making a deep obeisance to her; the respect shown to women in the days of chivalry was very great, and Cuthbert in bowing almost to the ground before the lady who was really his mistress, did not feel that he was humiliating himself.

"Young slave," she said, "your story has interested us. We have frequently watched from the windows, and have seen how willingly and patiently you have worked; and it seems strange indeed that one so young should have performed such feats of bravery as to win the honour of knighthood from the hand of that greatest of warriors, Richard of England. What is it, we would fain learn from your lips, that stirs up the heart of the Christian world that they should launch their armies against us, who wish but to be left alone, and who have no grudge against them? This city is as holy to us as it is to you; and as we live around it, and all the country for thousands of miles is ours, is it likely that we should allow it to be wrested from us by strangers from a distance?"

This was spoken in some Eastern language of which Cuthbert understood no word, but its purport was translated to him by the old woman who had hitherto acted as his mistress's messenger.

Cuthbert reported the circumstances of the fight at Azotus, and endeavoured to explain the feelings which had given rise to the Crusade. He then, at the orders of the lady, related the incidents of his voyage out, and something of his life at home, which was more interesting even than the tale of his adventures to his hearers, as to them the home-life of these fierce Christian warriors was entirely unknown.

After an audience of two hours Cuthbert was conducted back to his cell, his mistress assuring him of her good-will, and promising to do all in her power to make his captivity as light as possible.

CHAPTER XIV.

AN EFFORT FOR FREEDOM.

TWO or three nights afterwards the old woman again came to Cuthbert, and asked him, in her mistress's name, if in any way he could suggest a method of lightening his captivity, as his extreme youth, and bravery of demeanour, had greatly pleased her.

Cuthbert replied that nothing but freedom could satisfy his longings; that he was comfortable and not overworked, but that he pined to be back again with his friends.

The old woman brought him on the following night a message to the effect that his mistress would willingly grant him his liberty, but as he was sent to her husband by the sultan, it would be impossible to free him openly.

"From what she said," the old woman continued, "if you could see some plan of making your escape, she would in no way throw difficulties in your path; but it must not be known that the harem in any way connived at your escape, for my lord's wrath would be terrible, and he is not a man to be trifled with."

Looking round at the high walls that surrounded the garden, Cuthbert said that he could think of no plan whatever for escaping from such a place; that he had often thought it over, but that it appeared to him to be hopeless. Even should he manage to scale these walls, he would only find himself in the town beyond, and his escape from that would be altogether hopeless.

"Only," he said, "if I were transported to some country

palace of the governor could I ever hope to make my escape." The next night the messenger brought him the news that his mistress was disposed to favour his escape in the way he had pointed out, and that she would in two or three days ask the governor for permission to pay a visit to their palace beyond the walls, and that with her she would take a number of gardeners—among them Cuthbert—to beautify the place. Cuthbert returned the most lively and

hearty thanks to his patroness for her kind intentions, and hope began to rise rapidly in his heart.

It is probable, however, that the black guards of the harem heard something of the intentions of their mistress, and that they feared the anger of the governor should Cuthbert make his escape, and should it be discovered that this was the result of her connivance. Either through this or through some other source the governor obtained an inkling that the white slave sent by the sultan was receiving unusual kindness from the ladies of the harem.

Two nights after Cuthbert had begun to entertain bright

hopes of his liberty, the door of the cell was softly opened. He was seized by four slaves, gagged, tied hand and foot, covered with a thick burnous, and carried out from his cell. By the sound of their feet he heard that they were passing into the open air, and guessed that he was being carried through the garden; then a door opened and was closed after them; he was flung across a horse like a bale of goods, a rope or two were placed around him to keep him in that position, and then he felt the animal put in motion, and heard by the trampling of feet that a considerable number of horsemen were around him. For some time they passed over the rough, uneven streets of the city; then there was a pause and exchange of watchword and countersign, a creaking of doors, and a lowering of a drawbridge, and the party issued out into the open country. Not for very long did they continue their way; a halt was called, and Cuthbert was taken off his horse.

On looking round, he found that he was in the middle of a considerable group of men. Those who had brought him were a party of the governor's guards; but he was now delivered over to a large band of Arabs, all of whom were mounted on camels. One of these creatures he was ordered to mount, the bonds being loosed from his arms and feet. An Arab driver, with lance, bows, and arrows, and other weapons, took his seat on the neck of the animal, and then with scarcely a word the caravan marched off, with noiseless step, and with their faces turned southwards.

It seemed to Cuthbert almost as a dream. A few hours before he had been exalted with the hope of freedom; now he was being taken away to a slavery which would probably end but with his life. Although he could not understand any of his captors, the repetition of a name led him to believe that he was being sent to Egypt as a present to some man in high authority there; and he doubted not that the Governor of Jerusalem, fearing that he might escape, and dreading the wrath of the sultan, should he do so, had determined to transfer the troublesome captive to a more secure position and to safer hands.

For three days the journey continued; they had now left the fertile lowlands of Palestine, and their faces were turned west. They were entering upon that sandy waste which stretches between the southern corner of Palestine and the land of Egypt, a distance which can be travelled by camels in three days, but which occupied the Children of Israel forty years.

At first the watch had been very sharply kept over the captive; but now that they had entered the desert the Arabs appeared to consider that there was no chance of an attempt to escape. Cuthbert had in every way endeavoured to ingratiate himself with his guard. He had most willingly obeyed their smallest orders, had shown himself pleased and grateful for the dates which formed the staple of their repasts. He had assumed so innocent and quiet an appearance that the Arabs had marvelled much among themselves, and had concluded that there must have been some mistake in the assertion of the governor's guard who had handed the prisoner over to them, that he was one of the terrible knights of King Richard's army.

Cuthbert's heart had not fallen for a moment. He knew well that if he once reached Cairo all hope of escape was at an end; and it was before reaching that point that he determined if possible to make an effort for freedom. He had noticed particularly the camel which appeared to be the fleetest of the band; it was of lighter build than the rest, and it was with difficulty that its rider had compelled it to accommodate itself to the pace of the others. It was clear from the pains he took with it, by the constant patting and the care bestowed upon its watering and feeding, that its rider was extremely proud of it; and Cuthbert concluded that if an escape was to be made, this was the animal on which he must accomplish it.

Upon arriving at the end of each day's journey the

camels were allowed to browse at will, a short cord being tied between one of their hind and one of their fore feet. The Arabs then set to work to collect sticks and to make a fire—not for cooking, for their only food was dried dates and some black bread, which they brought with them—but for warmth, as the nights were damp and somewhat chilly, as they sat round the fire, talked, and told stories. Before finally going off to rest, each went out into the bushes and brought in his camel; these were then arranged in a circle around the Arabs, one of the latter being mounted as sentry to prevent any sudden surprise—not indeed that they had the smallest fear of the Christians, who were far distant; but then, as now, the Arabs of the desert were a plundering race, and were ever ready to drive off each other's camels or horses. Cuthbert determined that if flight was possible, it must be undertaken during the interval after the arrival at the halting-place and before the bringing in of the camels. Therefore, each day upon the halt he had pretended great fatigue from the rough motion of the camel, and had, after hastily eating the dates handed to him, thrown himself down, covered himself with his Arab robe, and feigned instant sleep. Thus they had in the three days from starting come to look upon his presence sleeping close to them as a matter of course.

The second day after entering the desert, however, Cuthbert threw himself down by the side of an uprooted shrub of small size and about his own length. He covered himself as usual with his long, dark-blue robe, and pretended to go to sleep. He kept his eyes, however, on the alert through an aperture beneath his cloth, and observed particularly the direction in which the camel upon which he had set his mind wandered into the bushes. The darkness came on a very few minutes after they had halted, and when the Arabs had once settled round their fire, Cuthbert, very quietly shifted the robe from himself to the long low bush near him, and then crawled stealthily off into the darkness.

He had no fear of his footfall being heard upon the soft sand, and was soon on his feet, looking for the camels. He was not long in finding them, or in picking out the one which he had selected. The bushes were succulent, and close to the camping-ground; indeed, it was for this that the halting-places were always chosen. It was not so easy, however, to climb into the high wooden saddle, and Cuthbert tried several times in vain. Then he repeated in a sharp tone the words which he had heard the Arabs use to order their camels to kneel, striking the animal at the same moment behind the fore-legs with a small switch. The camel immediately obeyed the order to which he was accustomed, and knelt down, making, however, as he did so, the angry grumble which those creatures appear to consider it indispensable to raise when ordered to do anything. Fortunately this noise is so frequently made, and the camels are so given to quarrel among themselves, that although in the still air it might have been heard by the Arabs sitting a short hundred yards away, it attracted no notice, and Cuthbert, climbing into the seat, shook the cord that served as a rein, and the animal, rising, set off at a smooth, steady swing in the direction in which his head was turned—that from which they had that day arrived.

Once fairly away from the camping-ground, Cuthbert, with blows of his stick, increased the speed of the camel to a long shuffling trot, and the fire in the distance soon faded out into the darkness.

Cuthbert trusted to the stars as guides. He was not unarmed, for as he crawled away from his resting-place, he had picked up one of the Arabs' spears and bow and arrows, and a large bag of dates from the spot where they had been placed when their owner dismounted. He was already clad in Eastern garb, and was so sun-burnt and tanned that he had no fear whatever of any one at a distance detecting that he was a white man.

Steering his course by the stars, he rode all night without

stopping. He doubted not that he would have at least three hours' start, for the Arabs were sure to have sat that time round the fires before going out to bring in their camels. Even then they would suppose for some time that the animal upon which he was seated had strayed, and no pursuit would be attempted until it was discovered that he himself had made his escape, which might not be for a long time, as the Arabs would not think of looking under the cloth to see if he were there. He hoped, therefore, that he would reach the cultivated land long before he was overtaken. He had little fear but that he should then be able to journey onward without attracting attention.

A solitary Arab when travelling rides straight, and his communications to those whom he meets are confined to the set form of two or three words, "May Allah protect you!" the regular greeting of Moslems when they meet.

When morning broke Cuthbert, even when ascending to the top of a somewhat lofty mound, could see no signs of pursuers in the vast stretch of desert behind him. In front, the ground was already becoming dotted here and there with vegetation, and he doubted not that after a few hours' ride he should be fairly in the confines of cultivated country. He gave his camel a meal of dates, and having eaten some himself, again set the creature in motion. These camels, especially those of good breed, will go on for three or four days with scarcely a halt; and there was no fear of that on which he rode breaking down from fatigue, for the journeys hitherto had been comparatively short.

By mid-day Cuthbert had reached the cultivated lands of Palestine. Here and there over the plain, villages were dotted, and parties of men and camels were to be seen. Cuthbert now arranged his robes carefully in Arab fashion, slung the long spear across his shoulders, and went boldly forward at a slinging trot, having little fear that a passer-by would have any suspicion whatever as to his being other than an Arab bent upon some rapid journey. He soon found that his hopes were justified. Several times he came upon parties of men whom he passed with the salute, and who scarcely raised their eyes as he trotted by them. The plain was an open one, and though cultivated here and there, there were large tracts lying unworked. There was no occasion therefore to keep to the road; so riding across country, and avoiding the villages as far as possible, stopping only at a stream to give his camel water, Cuthbert rode without ceasing until nightfall. Then he halted his camel near a wood, turned it in to feed on the young foliage, and wrapping himself in his burnous was soon asleep, for he ached from head to foot with the jolting motion which had now been continued for so many hours without an interval. He had little fear of being overtaken by the party he had left behind; they would, he was convinced, be many hours behind, and it was extremely improbable that they would hit upon the exact line which he had followed, so that even if they succeeded in coming up to him, they would probably pass him a few miles either to the right or left.

So fatigued was he with his long journey, that the next day he slept until after the sun had risen. He was awakened suddenly by being seized by a party of Arabs, who, roughly shaking him, questioned him

as to where he came from, and what he was doing there. He saw at a glance that they were not with the party from which he had escaped, and he pointed to his lips to make signs that he was dumb. The Arabs evidently suspected that something was wrong. They examined the camel, and then the person of their captive. The whiteness of his skin at once showed them that he was a Frank in disguise, and without more ado or questioning, they tied him hand and foot, flung him across the camel, and, mounting their own animals, rode rapidly away.

From the position of the sun, Cuthbert saw that they were making their course nearly due east, and therefore that it could not be their intention to take him to Jerusalem, which was to the north of the line they were following. A long day's journeying, which to Cuthbert seemed interminable, found them on the low spit of sand which runs along by the side of the Dead Sea.

Behind, lofty rocks rose almost precipitously, but through a cleft in these the Arabs had made their way. Cuthbert saw at once that they belonged to some desert tribe over whom the authority of Suleiman was but nominal. When summoned for any great effort, these children of the desert would rally to his armies and fight for a short time; but at the first disaster, or whenever they became tired of the discipline and regularity of the army, they would mount their camels and return to the desert, generally managing on the way to abstract from the farms of those on their route either a horse, cattle, or some other objects which would pay them for the labours they had undergone.

They were now near the confines of their own country, and apparently had no fear whatever of pursuit. They soon gathered some of the dead wood cast on the shores of the sea, and with these a fire was speedily lighted, and an earthenware pot was taken down from among their baggage: it was filled with water from a skin, and then grain having been placed in it, it was put among the wood ashes.

Cuthbert, who was weary and aching in every limb from the position in which he had been placed on the camel, asked them by signs for permission to bathe in the lake. This was given, principally apparently from curiosity, for but very few Arabs were able to swim; indeed, as a people they object so utterly to water, that the idea of any one bathing for his amusement was to them a matter of ridicule.

Cuthbert, who had never heard of the properties of the Dead Sea, was perfectly astonished upon entering the water to find that instead of wading in it up to the neck before starting to swim, as he was accustomed to do at home, the water soon after he got waist-deep took him off his feet, and a cry of astonishment burst from him as he found himself on rather than in the fluid. The position was so strange and unnatural that with a cry of alarm he scrambled over on to his feet, and made the best of his way to shore, the Arabs indulging in shouts of laughter at his astonishment and alarm. Cuthbert was utterly unable to account for the strange sensations he had experienced; he perceived that the water was horribly salty, and that which had got into his mouth almost choked him. He was, however, unaware that saltness adds to the weight of water, and so to the buoyancy of objects cast into it. The saltness of the fluid he was moreover painfully conscious of by the smarting of the places on his wrists and ankles where the cords had been bound that fastened him to the camel. Goaded, however, by the laughter of the Arabs, he determined once more to try the experiment of entering this strange sheet of water, which from some unaccountable cause appeared to him to refuse to allow anybody to sink in it. This time he swam about for some time, and felt a little refreshed. When he returned to the shore he soon re-attired himself in his Bedouin dress, and seated himself a little distance from his captors, who were now engaged in discussing the materials prepared by themselves. They made signs to Cuthbert that he might partake of their leavings, for which he was not a little grateful, for he felt utterly exhausted and worn out with his cruel ride and prolonged fasting.

The Arabs soon wrapped themselves in their burnouses, and feeling confident that their captive would not attempt to escape from them, in a place where subsistence would be impossible, paid no further attention to him beyond motioning to him to lie down at their side.

Cuthbert, however, determined to make another effort to escape; for although he was utterly ignorant of the place in which he found himself, or of the way back, he thought that anything would be better than to be carried into helpless slavery into the savage country beyond the Jordan. An hour, therefore, after his captors were asleep he stole to his feet, and fearing to arouse them by exciting the wrath of one of the camels by attempting to mount him, he struck up into the hills on foot. All night he wandered, and in the morning found himself at the edge of a strange precipice falling abruptly down to a river, which, some fifty feet wide, ran at its foot. Upon the opposite side the bank rose with equal rapidity, and to Cuthbert's astonishment he saw that the cliffs were honeycombed by caves.

Keeping along the edge for a considerable distance, he came to a spot where it was passable, and made his way down to the river bank. Here he indulged in a long drink of fresh water, and then began to examine the caves which perforated the rocks. These caves Cuthburt knew, had formerly been the abode of hermits. It was supposed to be an essentially sacred locality, and between the third and fourth centuries of Christianity some 20,000 monks had lived solitary lives on the banks of that river. Far away he saw the ruins of a great monastery, called Mar Saba, which had for a long time been the abode of a religious community, and which at the present day is still tenanted by a body of monks. Cuthbert made up his mind at once to take refuge in these caves. He speedily picked out one some fifty feet up the face of the rock, and approachable only with the greatest difficulty and by a sure foot. First he made the ascent to discover the size of the grotto, and found that although the entrance was but four feet high and two feet wide, it opened into an area of considerable dimensions. Far in the corner, when his eyes became accustomed to the light, he discovered a circle of ashes, and his conjectures that these caves had been the abode of men were therefore verified. He again descended, and collected a large bundle of grass and rushes for his bed. He discovered growing among the rocks many edible plants, whose seeds were probably sown there centuries before, and gathering some of these he made his way back to the cavern. The grass furnished him with an excellent bed, and he was soon asleep.

CHAPTER XV.

A HERMIT'S TALE.

THE next day he discovered on his excursions plenty of eatable berries on the bushes; and now that he had no longer fear of hunger he resolved to stay for some little time, until his wounds, which had festered badly, had recovered, before making an attempt to rejoin the Christian army.

One day when employed in gathering berries he was surprised by meeting a wild-looking figure, who appeared suddenly from one of the caves. It was that of a very old man, with an extremely long white beard flowing to his waist; his hair, which was utterly unkempt, fell to the same point. He was thin to an extraordinary extent, and Cuthbert wondered how a man could have been reduced to such a state of starvation, with so plentiful a supply of fruit and berries at hand.

The old man looked at Cuthbert attentively, and then made the sign of the cross. Cuthbert gave a cry of joy, and repeated the sign.

The old man at once came down from his cavern, and looked at him with surprise and astonishment, and then addressed him in the French language.

"Are you a Christian truly; and if so, whence do you come?"

Cuthbert at once explained that he had been taken prisoner when with King Richard's army, and had effected his escape. He also told the old man that he had been remaining for the last four days in a cave higher up the stream. The hermit—for he was one—beckoned him to follow him, and Cuthbert found himself in a cave precisely similar to that which he himself inhabited. There were no signs of comfort of any kind; a bed-place made of great stones stood in one corner, and Cuthbert, remembering the comforts of his own grassy couch, shuddered at the thought of the intense discomfort of such a sleeping-place. In another corner was an altar, upon which stood a rough crucifix before which the hermit knelt at once in prayer, Cuthbert following his example. Rising again, the hermit motioned to him to sit down, and then began a conversation with him.

It was so long since the hermit had spoken to any living being, that he had almost lost the use of his tongue, and his sentences were slow and ill-formed. However, Cuthbert was able to understand him, and he was able to gather the drift of what Cuthbert told him.

The old man then showed him, that by touching a stone in the corner of his cave the apparently solid rock opened, and revealed an entrance into an inner cave, which was lit by a ray of light, which penetrated from above.

"This," he said, "was made centuries ago, and was intended as a refuge from the persecutors of that day. The caves were then almost all inhabited by hermits, and although many recked not of their lives, and were quite ready to meet death through the knife of the infidel, others clung to existence, and preferred to pass many years of penance on earth for the sake of atoning for their sins before called upon to appear before their Maker.

'If you are pursued, it will be safer for you to take up your abode here. I am known to all the inhabitants of this country, who look upon me as mad, and respect me accordingly. None ever interfere with me, or with the two or three other hermits, the remains of what was once almost an army, who now alone survive. I can offer you no hospitality beyond that of a refuge; but there is water in the river below, fruits and berries in abundance on the shrubs. What would you have more?"

Cuthbert accepted the invitation with thanks; for he thought that even at the worst the presence of this holy man would be a protection to him from any Arabs who might discover him.

For three or four days he resided with the hermit, who, although he stretched his long lean body upon the hard stones of his bed, and passed many hours of the night kneeling on the stone floor in front of his altar, yet had no objection to Cuthbert making himself as comfortable as he could under the circumstances.

At the end of the fourth day Cuthbert asked him how long he had been there, and how he came to take up his abode in so desolate and fearsome a place. The hermit was silent for a time, and then said,—

"It is long indeed since my thoughts have gone back to

the day when I was of the world. I know not whether it would not be a sin to recall them; but I will think the matter over to-night, and if it appears to me that you may derive good from my narrative, I will relate it to you to-morrow."

The next day Cuthbert did not renew the request, leaving it to the hermit to speak should he think fit. It was not until the evening that he alluded to the subject; and then taking his seat on a bank near the edge of the river, he motioned to Cuthbert to sit beside him, and began,—

"My father was a peer of France, and I was brought up at the court. Although it may seem strange to you, looking upon this withered frame, sixty-five years back I was as bold and comely a knight as rode in the train of the king, for I am now past ninety, and for sixty years I have resided here. I was a favourite of the king's, and he loaded me with wealth and honour. He, too, was young, and I joined with him in the mad carousals and feastings of the court. My father resided for the most part at one of his castles in the country, and I, an only son, was left much to myself. I need not tell you that I was as wild and as wicked as all those around me; that I thought little of God, and feared neither Him nor man.

"It chanced that one of the nobles—I need not mention his name—whose castle lay in the same province as that of my father, had a lovely daughter, who, being an only child, would be his heiress. She was considered one of the best matches in France, and reports of her exceeding beauty had reached the court. Although my allowance from my father, and from the estates which the king had given me personally, should have been more than enough for my utmost wants, gambling and riotous living swallowed up my revenue faster than it came in, and I was constantly harassed by debt.

"Talking one night at supper with a number of bold companions, as to the means we should take for restoring our wasted fortunes, some said in jest that the best plan would be for one of us to marry the beauty of Dauphiny. I at once said that I would be the man to do it; the idea was a wild one, and a roar of laughter greeted my words. Her father was known to be a stern and rigid man, and it was certain that he would not consent to give his daughter to a spendthrift young noble like myself. When the laughter had subsided I repeated my intention gravely, and offered to wager large sums with all around the table that I would succeed.

"On the morrow I packed up a few of my belongings, put in my valise the dress of a wandering troubadour, and taking with me only a trusty servant, started for Dauphiny. It would be tedious to tell you the means I resorted to to obtain the affections of the heiress. I had been well instructed in music and could play on the lute, and knew by heart large numbers of ballads, and could myself, in case of necessity, string verses together with tolerable ease. As a troubadour I arrived at the castle gate, and craved permission to enter to amuse its occupants. Troubadours then, as now, were in high esteem in the south, and I was at once made a welcome guest.

"Days passed, and weeks; still I lingered at the castle, my heart being now as much interested as my pride in the wager which I had undertaken. Suffice it to say, that my songs, and perhaps my appearance—for I cannot be accused of vanity now in saying nature had been bountiful to me—won my way to her heart. Troubadours were licensed folk, and even in her father's presence there was nought unseemly in my singing songs of love.

"While he took them as the mere compliments of a troubadour, the lady, I saw, read them as serious effusions of my heart.

"It was only occasionally that we met alone; but ere long she confessed that she loved me. Without telling her my real name, I disclosed to her that I was of her own rank, and that I had entered upon the disguise I wore in order to win her

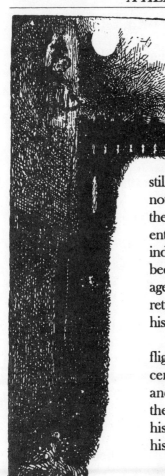

love. She was romantic, and was flattered by my devotion. I owned to her that hitherto I had been wild and reckless; and she told me at once that her father destined her for the son of an old friend of his, to whom it appeared she had been affianced while still a baby. She was positive that nothing would move her father. For the man she was to marry she entertained no kind of affection, and indeed had never seen him, as she had been brought up in a convent to the age of fifteen; and just before she had returned thence, he had gone to finish his education at Padua.

"She trembled when I proposed flight; but I assured her that I was certain of the protection of the king, and that he would, I was sure, when the marriage was once celebrated, use his influence with her father to obtain his forgiveness.

"The preparations for her flight were not long in making. I purchased a fleet horse in addition to my own, and ordered my servant to bring it to a point a short distance from the castle gate. I had procured a long rope with which to lower her down from her lattice to the moat below, which was at present dry, intending myself to slide after her. The night chosen was one when I knew that the count was to have guests, and I thought that they would probably, as is the custom, drink heavily, and that there would be less fear of any watch being kept.

"The guests arrived just at night-fall. I had feigned illness, and kept my room. From time to time I heard through the windows of the banqueting hall bursts of laughter. These gradually ceased; and at last, when all was still, I, after waiting some time, stole from my room with a rope in my hand to the apartment occupied by her. A slight tap at the door, as arranged, was at once answered, and I found her ready cloaked and prepared for the enterprise. She trembled from head to foot, but I cheered her to the best of my power, and at last she was in readiness to be lowered. The window was at a considerable height from the ground; but the rope was a long one, and I had no fear of its reaching the bottom. Fastening it round her waist, I began to lower her from the window.

"The night was a windy one, and she swung backwards and forwards as she went down. By what chance it was I know not,—for I had examined the rope and found it secure—but methinks in swaying backwards and forwards it may have caught a sharp stone, maybe it was a punishment from Heaven upon me for robbing a father of his child—but suddenly I felt there was no longer a weight on my arms. A fearful shriek rang through the air, and, looking out, I saw far below a white figure stretched senseless in the mud!

"For a minute I stood paralyzed. But the cry had aroused others, and, turning round, I saw a man at the door with a drawn sword. Wild with grief and despair, and thinking, not of making my escape, or of concealing my part in what had happened, but rushing without an instant's delay to the body of her I loved so well, I drew my sword, and like a madman rushed upon him who barred the door. The combat was brief but furious, and nerved by the madness of despair I broke down his guard and ran him through the body. As he fell back, his face came in the full light of the moon, which streamed through the open door on the passage, and to my utter horror and bewilderment I saw that I had slain my father.

"What happened after that night I know not. I believe that I made my escape from the castle and rushed round to the body of her whose life I had destroyed, and that there finding her dead, I ran wildly across the country. When I came to my senses months had passed, and I was the inmate of an asylum for men bereaved of their senses, kept by noble monks. Here for two years I remained, the world believing that I was dead. None knew that the troubadour whose love had cost the lady her life, who had slain the guest of her father, and had then disappeared, was the unhappy son of that guest. My friends in Paris when they heard of the tragedy of course associated it with me, but they all kept silent. The monks, to whom I confessed the whole story, were shocked indeed, but consoled me in my grief and despair by the assurance that however greatly I had sinned, the death of the lady had been accidental, and that if I were a parricide it was at least unintentionally.

"My repentance was deep and sincere; and after a while, under another name, I joined the army of the crusaders, to expiate my sin by warring for the holy sepulchre. I fought as men fight who have no wish to live; but while all around me fell by sword and disease, death kept aloof from me. When the crusade had failed I determined to turn for ever from the world, and to devote my life to prayer and penance; and so casting aside my armour, I made my way here, and took up my abode in a cave in this valley, where at that time were many thousands of other hermits—for the Saracens, while they gained much money from fines and exactions from pilgrims who came to Jerusalem, and fought stoutly against those who sought to capture that city, were in the main tolerant, and offered no hindrance to the community of men whom they looked upon as mad.

"Here, my son, for more than sixty years have I prayed, with much fasting and penance. I trust now that the end is nearly at hand, and that my long life of mortification may be deemed to have obliterated the evil deeds which I did in my youth. Let my fate be a warning to you. Walk steadily in the right way; indulge not in feasting and evil companionship; and above all, do not enter upon evil deeds, the end of which no man can see."

The hermit was silent, and Cuthbert, seeing that his thoughts had again referred to the past, wandered away, and left him sitting by the river side. Some hours later he returned, and found the hermit kneeling before the altar;

and the next morning the latter said,—

"I presume, my son, you do not wish to remain here as a hermit, as I have done? Methinks it were well that we made our arrangements for your return to the Christian host, who will, I hope, ere long be at the gates of Jerusalem."

"I should like nothing better," Cuthbert said. "But ignorant as I am of the nature of the country, it seems to be nigh impossible to penetrate through the hosts of the Saracens to reach the camp of King Richard."

"The matter is difficult and not without danger," the hermit said. "As to the nature of the country, I myself know but little, for my dealings with the natives have been few and simple. There are, however, several Christian communities dwelling among the heathen. They are poor, and are forced to live in little-frequented localities. Their Christianity may be suspected by their neighbours, but as they do no man harm, and carry on their worship in secret, they are little interfered with. There is one community among the hills between this and Jerusalem, and I can give you instructions for reaching this, together with a token which will secure you hospitality there, and they will no doubt do their best to forward you to another station. When you approach the flat country where the armies are maneuvering you must doubtless trust to yourself; but as far as the slopes extend, methinks that our friends will be able to pass you without great difficulty."

Cuthbert's heart rose greatly at the prospect of once again entering upon an active life, and the next evening, with many thanks for his kindness, he knelt before the aged hermit to receive his blessing.

With the instructions given him he had no difficulty in making his way through the mountains, until after some five hours' walk he found himself at a little village situated in a narrow valley.

Going to the door of the principal hut, he knocked, and upon entering showed the owner—who opened the door—a rosette of peculiar beads, and repeated the name of Father Anselm. The peasant at once recognized it, and bade Cuthbert welcome. He knew but a few words of French, although doubtless his ancestors had been of European extraction. In the morning he furnished Cuthbert with the sheepskin and short tunic which formed the dress of a shepherd, and dyeing his limbs and face a deep brown, he himself started with Cuthbert on his journey to the next Christian community.

This was a small one, consisting of two huts only, built almost on the summit of a mountain, the inhabitants living partly on the milk and cheese of their goats, and partly upon the scanty vegetables which grew around the huts.

His welcome was as cordial as that of the night before; and the next morning, his former guide taking leave of him, the peasant in whose house he had slept, again conducted him forward to another community. This was the last station, and stood in a narrow gorge on the face of the hills looking down over the plain, beyond which in the far distance a faint line of blue sea was visible.

This community was far more prosperous and well-to-do than those at which the previous nights had been passed. The head of the village appeared to be a personage of some importance; and although clinging in secret to his Christian faith, he and his belongings had so far adopted the usages of the Mussulmen that apparently no thought of their Christianity entered into the minds of the authorities. He was the owner of two or three horses, and of some extensive vineyards and olive grounds. He was also able to speak French with some degree of fluency.

At considerable length he explained to Cuthbert the exact position of the Christian army, which had moved some distance along the coast since Cuthbert had left it. It was, he said, exposed to constant attacks by the Saracens, who harassed it in every way, and permitted it no repose. He said that the high hopes which had been raised by the defeat of the Saracens at Azotus, had now fallen, and that it was feared the Christians would not be able to force their way forward to Jerusalem. The great portion of their animals had died, and the country was so eaten up by the Saracen hosts, that an advance upon Jerusalem without a large baggage train was next to impossible; and indeed if the Christians were to arrive before that city, they could effect nothing without the aid of the heavy machines necessary for battering the walls or effecting an escalade.

Cuthbert was vastly grieved when he heard of the probable failure of the expedition, and he burned with eagerness to take his part again in the dangers and difficulties which beset the Christian army. His host pointed out to him the extreme difficulty and danger of his crossing the enemy's lines, but at the same time offered to do all in his power to assist him. After two days' stay at the village, and discussing the pros and cons of all possible plans, it was decided that the best chance lay in a bold effort. The host placed at his disposal one of his horses, together with such clothes as would enable him to ride as an Arab chief of rank and station; a long lance was furnished him, a short and heavy mace, and scimitar; a bag of dates was hung at the saddle-bow; and with the sincerest thanks to his protector, and with a promise that should the Christian host win their way to Jerusalem the steed should be returned with ample payment, Cuthbert started on his journey.

CHAPTER XVI.

A FIGHT OF HEROES.

THE horse was a good and spirited one, and when he had once descended to the plains, Cuthbert rode gaily along, exulting in his freedom, and in once again possessing arms to defend himself should it be needed. His appearance was so exactly that of the horsemen who were continually passing and repassing that no observation whatever was attracted by it. Through villages, and even through camps, Cuthbert rode fearlessly, and arrived, without having once been accosted, near the main camp of the Saracens, which extended for miles parallel to the sea. But at a distance of some three leagues beyond, could be seen the white tents of the Christian host, and Cuthbert felt that the time of trial was now at hand.

He dismounted for an hour to allow his steed to rest itself, fed it with dates from his wallet, and gave it a drink of water at the stream. Then, when he felt that it had thoroughly recovered its strength and freshness, he re-mounted, and rode briskly on as before. He passed unchallenged, attracting no more notice than a person now-a-days would do in walking along a crowded street. Without hesitation he passed through the tents and started across the open country. Bands of horsemen were seen here and there, some going, and some coming from the direction of the Christian camp. As it was doubtless supposed that he was on his way to join some band that had gone on in advance, the passage of the solitary horseman excited no comment until he approached within about two miles of the

Christian camp. There were now, so far as he could see, no enemies between him and the point he so longed to gain. But at this minute a group of Arab horsemen, gathered, apparently on the look-out against any movement of the Christians, shouted to him "Halt!" demanding whither he was going.

Up to this point Cuthbert had ridden at a gentle canter; but at the challenge he put spurs into his steed and made across the plain at full speed. With a wild yell the Arabs started in pursuit. They lay at first some 200 yards on his right, and he had therefore a considerable start of them. His horse was fairly fresh, for the journey that he had made had only been about fifteen miles—an inconsiderable distance to an Arab steed. For half a mile he did not think that his pursuers gained much upon him, riding as they had done sideways. They had now gathered in his rear, and the nearest was some 150 yards behind him. A quarter of a mile farther he again looked round, and found that two of the Arabs, far better mounted than the others, had come within half the distance which separated them from him when he last glanced back. His horse was straining to the utmost, and he felt that it could do no more; he therefore prepared himself for a desperate fight should his pursuers overtake him. In another quarter of a mile they were but a short distance behind, and an arrow whizzing by Cuthbert's ear told him they had betaken themselves to their bows.

Half a mile ahead he saw riding towards him a group of Christian knights; but he felt that it was too late for him to hope to reach them, and that his only chance now was to boldly encounter his pursuers. The main body of the Arabs was fully 200 yards behind—a short distance when going at a gallop which left him but little time to shake off the pursuit of the two immediately behind him.

A sharp stinging pain in his leg told him that it was time to make his effort; and checking his horse, he wheeled suddenly round. The two Arabs with a yell rode at him with

pointed lance. With his right hand Cuthbert grasped the
short heavy mace which hung at his saddle-bow, and being
well practised in the hurling of this weapon—which formed
part of the education of a good knight—he cast it with all his
force at the chest of the Arab approaching on that side.The
point of the spear was within a few yards of his breast as he
flung the mace; but his aim was true, for it smote the
Saracen full on the chest, and hurled him from his horse as

if struck with a thunderbolt. At the same instant Cuthbert
threw himself flat on the neck of his steed and the lance of
the Arab who came up on the other side passed harmlessly
between his shoulders, tearing his clothes as it went. In an
instant Cuthbert had wheeled his horse, and, before the
Arab could turn his steed Cuthbert, coming up from

behind, had run him through the body.

Short as the delay had been, the main body of the pursuers were scarcely fifty yards away; but Cuthbert now continued his flight towards the knights, who were galloping forward at full speed; and a moment afterwards glancing back, he saw that his pursuers had turned and were in full flight.

With a shout of joy he rode forward to the party who had viewed with astonishment this conflict between what appeared to be three of the infidels. Even louder than his first shout of exultation was the cry of joy which he raised at seeing among the party to whom he rode up, the Earl of Evesham, who reined in his horse in astonishment, and drew his sword as the supposed enemy galloped towards him.

"My lord, my lord! "Cuthbert said. "Thank heaven I am safe with you again."

The earl lowered his sword in astonishment.

"Am I mad," he said, "or dreaming, or is this really Sir Cuthbert?"

"It is I sure enough," Cuthbert exclaimed, "although truly I look more like a Bedouin soldier than a Christian knight."

"My dear boy!" exclaimed the earl, galloping forward and throwing his arms around Cuthbert's neck, "we thought you were dead. But by what wonderful fortune have you succeeded in escaping?"

In a few words Cuthbert related the principal incidents of his adventures, and he was heartily congratulated by the assembled knights.

There was, however, no time for long explanations. Large bodies of the Saracen horse were already sweeping down, to capture, if possible, this small band of knights who had ventured so far from the camp; and as King Richard's orders were that none should venture upon conflicts except by his orders, the party reluctantly turned their horses and galloped back to the camp. Great as had been the earl's joy, it was, if possible, exceeded by that of Cnut on discovering in the Arab chief who rode up alongside the earl, the lad he loved so well. Loud and hearty were the cheers which rang out from the earl's camp as the news spread, and Cuthbert was compelled to shake hands with the whole party before entering the earl's tent, to refresh himself and give the narrative of what had happened.

Cuthbert, retiring to his tent with the Earl of Evesham, inquired of him what had taken place during his absence.

"For," he said, "although but a short three days' march from here, I have been as one of the dead, and have heard nothing whatever of what has taken place."

"Nothing could have gone worse," the earl said. "We have had nothing but dissensions and quarrels. First, the king fell out with the Archduke of Austria."

"On what ground did this happen?" Cuthbert asked.

"For once," the earl said, "the king our master was wholly in the wrong, which is not generally the case. We had just taken Ascalon, and were hard at work fortifying the place. King Richard with his usual zeal, in order to encourage the army, seized heavy stones and himself bore them into their place. The Archduke stood near with some of his knights: and it may be that the haughty Austrian looked somewhat superciliously at our king, thus labouring.

"'Why do you not make a show of helping?' King Richard said, going up to him. 'It would encourage the men, and show that the labour upon which we are engaged can be undertaken by all without derogation.'

"To this the Archduke replied,—

" 'I am not the son of a mason!'

"Whereupon Richard, whose blood no doubt had been excited by the air of the Austrian, struck him with his hand a fierce blow across the face. We nearly betook ourselves to our swords on both sides; but King Richard himself could have scattered half the Austrians, and these, knowing that against his impetuous valour they could do nothing, simply withdrew from our camp, and sailed the next day for home. Then the king, in order to conciliate some at least of his allies, conferred the crown of Jerusalem upon Conrad of Montferrat. No sooner had he done this than Conrad was mysteriously wounded. By whom it was done none knew. Some say that it was by emissaries of the Old Man of the Mountain. Others affirm that it was the jealousy of some of the knights of the holy orders. But be that as it may, he died. Some of the French, ever jealous of the valour of our king, ascribed it to his orders. This monstrous accusation coming to the ears of King Richard, he had hot words with the Duke of Burgundy. In this I blame him not, for it is beyond all reason that a man like the king, whose faults, such as they are, arise from too much openness, and from the want of concealment of such dislikes as he may have, should resort to poison to free himself of a man whom he himself had but a day or two before appointed King of Jerusalem. However it be, the consequences were most unfortunate, for the result of the quarrel was that the Duke of Burgundy and his Frenchmen followed the example of the Austrians, and we were left alone. Before this we had marched upon Jerusalem. But the weather had been so bad, and our train was so insufficient to carry the engines of war, that we had been forced to fall back again. King Richard again advanced, and with much toil we went as far as the village of Bethany."

"Why," Cuthbert exclaimed, "I passed through that village, and it is but three miles from the holy city."

"That is so," the earl said; "and many of us, ascending the hill in front, saw Jerusalem. But even then it was certain that we must again retrace our steps; and when we asked King Richard to come to the crest of the hill to see the holy city, he refused to do so, saying, 'No; those who are not worthy of conquering Jerusalem should not look at it!' This was but a short time since, and we are now retracing our steps to Acre, and are treating with Saladin for a peace."

"Then," Cuthbert said sadly, "all our hopes and efforts

are thrown away; all this blood has been shed for nothing; and after the three great powers of Europe have engaged themselves solemnly in the war, we are baffled, and have to fall back before the hordes of the infidels."

"Partly before them," the earl said, "partly as the result of our own jealousies and passions. Had King Richard been a lesser man than he is, we might have conquered Jerusalem. But he is so extraordinary a warrior that his glory throws all others into the shade. He is a good general, perhaps the best in Europe; and had he done nothing but lead, assuredly we should have carried out our purpose. See how ably he maneuvered the army at the fight of Azotus. Never was a more complete defeat than that which he inflicted there upon the Saracens; and although the fact that his generalship achieved this, might have caused some jealousy to the other commanders, this might have died away could he between the battles have been a general, and nothing more. But alas! he is in addition a knight-errant—and such a knight-errant as Europe has never seen before. Wherever there is danger, Richard will plunge into the midst. There are brave men in all the three armies; but the strongest and bravest are as children to King Richard. Alone he can dart into ranks of the infidels, and cut a lane for himself by the strength of his right arm. More than this, when danger has threatened he has snatched up his battle-axe and dashed into the fray without helm or cuirass, performing such prodigies of valour and strength that it has been to his prowess alone that victory was to be ascribed. Hence he is the idol of all the soldiers, whatever their nationality; for he is as ready to rush to the rescue of a French or Austrian knight when pressed as to that of his own men. But the devotion which the whole army felt for him was as gall and wormwood to the haughty Austrian and the indolent Frenchman; and the retirement of the King of France, which left Richard in supreme command, was in every way unfortunate."

Upon the following day the army again marched, and

Cuthbert could not but notice the difference, not only in number but in demeanour, from the splendid array which had left Acre a few months before. There was little now of the glory of pennon and banner; the bright helms and cuirasses were rusted and dinted, and none seemed to care aught for bravery of show. The knights and men-at-arms were sunburnt and thin, and seemed but half the weight that they had been when they landed. Fatigue, hardship, and the heat had done their work; disease had swept off vast numbers. But the remains of the army were so formidable in their fighting powers that the Saracens, although following them at a distance in vast numbers, did not venture an attack upon them.

A few days after their arrival at Acre, the king gave orders for the embarcation of the troops. Just as they were preparing to enter the ships a small vessel was seen entering the harbour. It drew up to the shore, and a knight leaped from it, and, inquiring where King Richard was to be found, made his way to the king, who was standing superintending the embarcation of some of the horses.

"The Saracens, sire!" he exclaimed. "The Saracens are besieging Jaffa, and the place must be lost unless assistance arrives in a day or two."

The king leaped on board the nearest ship, shouted to his leading officers to follow him, and gave orders to others to bring down the troops with all possible speed, to waste not a moment, and to see that all was done, and then, in five minutes after the receipt of the news he started for Jaffa. The Earl of Evesham and Cuthbert had been standing near the king when the order was given, and followed him at once on board the boat which he had chosen.

"Ah, my gallant young knight," the king exclaimed, "I am right glad to see you with me. We shall have more fighting before we have done, and I know that that suits your mood as well as my own."

The king's vessel was far in advance of any of the others,

when early the following morning it arrived at Jaffa.

"Your eyes are better than mine," the king said to Cuthbert. "Tell me what is that flag flying on the top of the town."

Cuthbert looked at it earnestly.

"I fear, sire, that it is the crescent. We have arrived too late."

"By the holy cross," said King Richard, "that shall not be so; for if the place be taken, we will retake it."

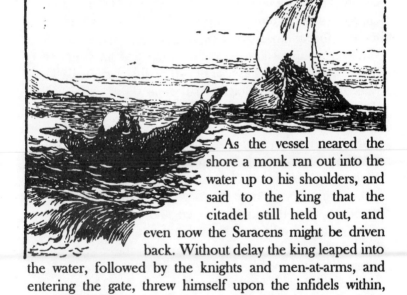

As the vessel neared the shore a monk ran out into the water up to his shoulders, and said to the king that the citadel still held out, and even now the Saracens might be driven back. Without delay the king leaped into the water, followed by the knights and men-at-arms, and entering the gate, threw himself upon the infidels within, who, busy plundering, had not noticed the arrival of the ship.

The war cry of "St. George! St. George!" which the king always shouted in battle, struck panic among the infidels; and although the king was followed but by five knights and a few men-at-arms, the Saracens, to the number of 3000, fled before him, and all who tarried were smitten down. The king followed them out upon the plain, driving them before him as a lion would drive a flock of sheep, and then returned triumphant into the city.

The next day, some more ships having arrived, King Richard found that in all, including the garrison, he could muster 2000 combatants. The enemy renewed the attack in great numbers, and the assaults upon the walls were continuous and desperate. King Richard, who loved fighting in the plain rather than behind walls, was impatient at this, and at one time so fierce was the attack that he resolved to sally out. Only ten horses remained in the town, and King Richard, mounting one, called upon nine of the knights to mount and sally out with him. The little band of ten warriors charged down upon the host of the Saracens and swept them before them. It was a marvellous sight indeed to see so small a group of horsemen dashing through a crowd of Saracen warriors. These, although at first beaten back, yet rallied, and the ten knights had great difficulty in fighting their way back to the town. When near the walls the Christians again made a stand, and a few knights sallied out from the town on foot and joined them. Among these was Cuthbert, the Earl of Evesham having accompanied King Richard in his charge. In all, seventeen knights were now rallied round the king. So fierce was the charge of the Saracens that the king ordered those on horseback to dismount, and with their horses in the centre, the little body knelt with their lances opposed to the Saracens. Again and again the wild cavalry swept down upon this little force, but in vain did they attempt to break their ranks. The scene was indeed an extraordinary one. At last the king, seeing that the enemy were losing heart, again ordered the knights to mount, and these dashing among the enemy, completed their defeat.

While this had been going on, news came to the king that the Saracens from another side had made their way into Jaffa, and were massacring the Christians. Without an instant's delay he flew to their succour, followed only by two knights, and a few archers, the rest being so worn by their exertions as to be unable to move. The Mamelukes, the chosen guard of Saladin, had headed the attack; but even these were driven out from the town, and Richard dashed out from the city in their pursuit. One Saracen emir, distinguished for his stature and strength, ventured to match himself against the king, and rode boldly at him. But with one blow Richard severed his head, and his right shoulder and arm, from his body. Then having, by his single arm, put to rout the Saracens at this point, he dashed through them to the aid of the little band of knights who had remained on the defensive when he left them at the alarm of the city being entered. These were almost sinking with fatigue and wounds; but King Richard opened a way around them by slaying numbers of the enemy, and then charged again alone into the midst of the Mussulman host, and was lost to the sight of his companions. All thought that they would never see him again. But he soon reappeared, his horse covered with blood, but himself unwounded; and the attack of the enemy ceased.

From the hour of daybreak, it is said, Richard had not ceased for a moment to deal out his blows, and the skin of his hand adhered to the handle of his battle-axe. This narration would appear almost fabulous, were it not that it is attested in the chronicles of several eye-witnesses, and for centuries afterwards the Saracen women hushed their babes when fractious by threatening them with Malek-Rik, the name which they gave to King Richard.

Glorious as was the success, it was a sad one, for several of the most devoted of the followers of King Richard were wounded badly, some few to death. Among these last, to the terrible grief of Cuthbert, was his friend and patron, the Earl of Evesham. The king, on taking off his armour, hurried to his tent.

"The glory of this day is marred indeed," he said to the wounded knight, "if I am to lose you, Sir Walter."

"I fear that it must even be so, my lord," the dying earl said. "I am glad that I have seen this day, for never did I think to witness such feats as those which your Majesty has performed; and though the crusade has failed, and the Holy City remains in the hands of the infidel, yet assuredly no shadow of disgrace has fallen upon the English arms, and, indeed, great glory has accrued to us. Whatever may be said

of the Great Crusade, it will, at least, be allowed by all men, and for all time, that had the princes and soldiers of other nations done as your Majesty and your followers have done, the holy city would have fallen into our hands within a month of our putting foot upon the soil. Your Majesty, I have a boon to ask."

"You have but to name it, Sir Walter, and it is yours."

"Sir Cuthbert, here," he said, pointing to the young knight, who was sorrowfully kneeling by his bedside, "is as a son to me. The relationship by blood is but slight, but by affection it is as close as though he were mine own. I have, as your Majesty knows, no male heirs, and my daughter is but young, and will now be a royal ward. I beseech your Majesty to bestow her in marriage, when the time comes, upon Sir Cuthbert. They have known each other as children, and the union will bring happiness, methinks, to both, as well as strength and protection to her; and further, if it might be, I would fain that you should bestow upon him my title and dignity."

"It shall be so," the king said. "When your eyes are closed, Sir Walter, Sir Cuthbert shall be Earl of Evesham, and, when the time comes, the husband of your daughter."

Cuthbert was too overwhelmed with grief to feel a shadow of exaltation at the gracious intimation of the king; although, even then, a thought of future happiness in the care of the fair young lady Marguerite passed before his mind. For the last time the king gave his hand to his faithful servant, who pressed it to his lips, and a few minutes afterwards breathed his last.

CHAPTER XVII.

AN ALPINE STORM.

THE tremendous exertions which King Richard had made told upon him, and attacks of fever succeeded each other at short intervals. This, however, mattered the less, since negotiations were now proceeding between him and Saladin. It was impossible, with the slight means at his disposal, for Richard further to carry on the crusade alone. Moreover, pressing news had arrived from his mother in England, urging him to return, as his brother John was intriguing against him, and had already assumed all but the kingly title. Saladin was equally desirous of peace. His wild troops were, for the most part, eager to return to their homes, and the defeats which they had suffered, and the, to them, miraculous power of King Richard's arm, had lowered their spirit and made them eager to be away. Therefore he consented without difficulty to the terms proposed. By these, the Christians were to surrender Ascalon, but were to keep Jaffa, Tyre, and the fortresses along the coast. All hostilities were to be suspended on both sides for the space of three years, three months, three weeks, three days, and three hours, when Richard hoped to return again and to recommence the struggle.

Between the sultan and King Richard a feeling approaching that of friendship had sprung up during the campaign. Saladin was himself brave in the extreme, and exposed his life as fearlessly as did his Christian rival, and the two valiant leaders recognized the great qualities of each other. Several times during the campaign, when Richard had been ill, the emir had sent him presents of fruit and other matters, to which Richard had responded in the same spirit. An interview had taken place between them which further cemented their friendship; and when Richard promised to return again at the end of the truce with a far larger army, and to accomplish the rescue of the holy city, the sultan smiled, and said that it appeared that valour alone was not sufficient to conquer in the Holy Land, but that if Jerusalem were to fall into the hands of the Christians, it could fall into no worthier hands than those of Malek-Rik.

So, with many mutual courtesies, the great rivals separated, and, soon after, King Richard and the little remnant of his army embarked on board ship, and set sail for England.

It was on the 11th of October, 1192, that Richard Cœur de Lion left Palestine. Soon after they started, a storm suddenly burst upon them, and dispersed them in various directions. The ship in which Queen Berengaria was carried, arrived safely in Sicily; but that in which King Richard was borne was missing, and none of his fellow-voyagers knew what had become of him.

Sir Cuthbert was in the same vessel as the king, and the boat was driven upon the Island of Corfu. All reached shore in safety, and King Richard then hired three small vessels, in which he sailed to the port of Zara, whence he hoped to reach the domains of his nephew, Otho of Saxony, the son of his sister Matilda. The king had with him now but two of his knights, Baldwin of Béthune, and Cuthbert of Evesham. Cnut was with his feudal chief—for such Cuthbert had now, by his accession to the rank of Earl of Evesham, become—and three or four English archers.

"I fear, my lords," the king said to his knights as he sat in a little room in an inn at Zara, "that my plight is a bad one. I am surrounded by enemies, and, alas! I can no longer mount my steed and ride out as at Jaffa to do battle with them. My brother, John Lackland, is scheming to take my place upon the throne of England. Philip of France, whose mind is far better at such matters than at setting armies in the field, is in league with him. The Emperor Henry has laid claim to the throne of Sicily. Leopold of Austria has not forgiven me the blow I struck him in the face at Ascalon, and the friends of Conrad of Montferat are spreading far and wide the lie that I was the instigator of his murder.

"Sure never had a poor king so many enemies, and few have ever had so small a following as I have now. What think you, my lords? What course would you advise that I should adopt? If I can reach Saxony, doubtless Otho will aid me. But hence to Dresden is a long journey indeed. I have neither credit nor funds to hire a ship to take us by sea. Nor would such a voyage be a safe one, when so many of my enemies' ships are on the main. I must needs, I think, go in disguise, for my way lies wholly through the country of my enemies."

"Surely," Cuthbert said, "no potentate could for very shame venture to detain your Majesty on your way from the Holy Land, where you have wrought such great deeds. Were I in your place, I would at once proclaim myself, mount my horse, have my banner carried before me, and ride openly on. You have, too, another claim, namely, that of being shipwrecked, and even in war-time nations respect those whom the force of God has thrown upon their shores."

"I fear me, Sir Cuthbert," Sir Baldwin said, "that you overrate the chivalry of our master's enemies. Had we been thrown on the shores of France, Philip perhaps would hesitate to lay hands upon the king; but these petty German princelings have no idea of the observances of true chivalry. They are coarse and brutal in their ways; and though in outward form following the usages of knighthood, they have never been penetrated with its spirit. If the friends of Conrad of Montferat lay hands upon King Richard, I fear that no scruples will prevent them from using their advantage to the utmost. Even their emperor I would not trust. The course which you advise would no doubt be in accordance with the spirit of King Richard; but it would be madness for him to judge other people's spirit by his own, and it would be rushing into the lion's den to proclaim himself here. I should recommend, if I might venture to do so, that his Majesty should assume a false name, and that we should travel in small parties so as to attract no attention, each making his way to Saxony as best he may."

There was silence for a minute or two, and then the king with a sigh, said,—

"I fear that you are right, Sir Baldwin, and that there is no chivalry among these swinish German lords. You shall accompany me. Not, Sir Cuthbert," he observed kindly, noticing a look of disappointment upon the face of the young knight, "that I estimate your fidelity one whit lower than that of my brave friend; but he is the elder and the more versed in European travel, and may manage to bring matters through better than you would do. You will have dangers enough to encounter yourself, more even than I

shall, for your brave follower, Cnut, can speak no language but his own, and your archers will be hard to pass as any other than what they are. You

must be my messenger to England, should you arrive there
without me. Tell my mother and wife where you left me,
and that, if I do not come home I have fallen into the hands
of one or other of my bitter foes. Bid them bestir themselves
to hold England for me against my brother John, and, if
needs be, to move the sovereigns of Europe to free me from
the hands of my enemies. Should a ransom be needed, I
think that my people of England will not grudge their goods
for their king."

The following day the king bade farewell to his faithful
followers, giving his hand to kiss, not only to Sir Cuthbert,
but to Cnut and his archers.

"You have done me brave service," he said, "and I trust
may yet have occasion to do it again. These are bad times
when Richard of England has nought wherewith to reward
his friends. But," he said, taking a gold chain from his neck
and breaking it with his strong fingers into five fragments,
"that is for you, Cnut, and for your four archers, in
remembrance of King Richard."

The men, albeit hardened by many scenes of warfare, yet
shed tears plenteously at parting with the king.

"We had better," Cuthbert said to them when they were
alone, "delay here for a few days. If we are taken, the news
that some Englishmen have been captured making their way
north from Zara will spread rapidly, and may cause the
enemies of Richard to be on the look-out for him,
suspecting that the ship which bore us may also have carried
him; for the news that he is missing will spread rapidly
through Europe, and will set all his enemies on the alert."

In accordance with this plan, they delayed for another ten
days at Zara, and then, hiring a small boat, were landed
some thirty miles further along the coast. Cuthbert had
obtained for Cnut the dress of a palmer, as in this he would
pass almost unquestioned, and his silence might be
accounted for on the ground that he had taken a vow of
silence. He himself had placed on his coat and armour a

red cross, instead of the white cross borne by the English knights, and would now pass as a French knight. Similar changes were made in the dress of his followers, and he determined to pass as a French noble who had been wrecked on his way home, and who was returning through Germany to France. The difficulties in his own case would not be serious, as his French would pass muster anywhere in Germany. The greatest difficulty would be with his attendants; but he saw no way of avoiding this.

Cuthbert's object, when with his little party he separated from King Richard, was to make his way to Verona, thence cross by Trent into Bavaria, and so to journey to Saxony. Fortunately he had, at the storming of Acre, become possessed of a valuable jewel, and this he now sold, and purchased a charger for himself. He had little fear of any trouble in passing through the north of Italy, for this was neutral ground, where knights of all nations met, and where, neither as an English nor a French crusader would he attract either comment or attention.

It was a slow journey across the northern plains, as of course he had to accommodate his pace to that of his men. Cnut and the archers had grumbled much at the change in the colour of the cross upon their jerkins; and, as Cnut said, would have been willing to run greater perils under their true colours than to affect to belong to any other nationality. On their way they passed through Padua, and there stopped a few days, Cuthbert could but feel, in looking at the splendour of this Italian city, the courteous manner of its people, and the university which was even then famous, how far in advance were those stately cities of Italy to Western Europe. His followers were as much surprised as himself at the splendour of the city. Here they experienced no trouble or annoyance whatever, for to the cities of Italy knights of all nations resorted, learned men came to study, philosophers to dispute, and as these brought their attendants with them, you might in the streets of Padua and its sister cities hear every language in Europe spoken.

From Padua they journeyed to Verona, marvelling greatly at the richness of the country. The footmen, however, grumbled at the flatness of the plain, and said that it was as bad as marching in the Holy Land. On their right, however, the slopes of the Alps, thickly clad with forests, reached down nearly to the road, and Cuthbert assured them that they would have plenty of climbing before they had done. At Verona they tarried again, and wondered much at the great amphitheatre, then almost perfect. Cuthbert related to Cnut and the archers, how men had there been set to fight, while the great stone benches round were thronged with men and women looking on at their death struggles, and said that not unfrequently British captives were brought hither and made to contend in the arena. The honest fellows were full of indignation and horror at the thought of men killing themselves to give sport to others. They were used to hard knocks, and thought but little of their life, and would have betaken themselves to their bows and bills without hesitation in case of a quarrel. But to fight in cold blood for amusement seemed to them very terrible.

Cuthbert would then have travelled on to Milan at that time next to Rome the richest city in Europe, but he longed to be back in England, and was the more anxious as he knew that King Richard would he passing through great dangers, and he hoped to meet him at the Court of Saxony. His money, too, was fast running out, and he found that it would be beyond his slender means to extend his journey so far. At Verona, then, they turned their back on the broad plains of Lombardy, and entered the valley of the Trent.

So far no observation whatever had been excited by the passage of the English knight. So many crusaders were upon their way home, many in grievous plight, that the somewhat shabby retinue passed unnoticed. But they were now leaving Italy, and entering a country where German was spoken. Trent, in those days an important city, was then, and is still, the meeting place of Italy and Germany. Both tongues are here spoken; but while the Italian perhaps preponderates, the customs, manners, and mode of thought of the people belong to those of the mountaineers of the Tyrol, rather than of the dwellers on the plains.

"You are choosing a stormy time," the landlord of the hostelry where they put up said to Cuthbert. "The winter is now at hand, and storms sweep across the passes with terrible violence. You had better, at the last village you come to in the valley, obtain the services of a guide, for should a snowstorm come on when you are crossing, the path will be lost, and nothing will remain but a miserable death. By daylight the road is good. It has been cut with much trouble, and loaded mules can pass over without difficulty. Poles have been erected at short distances to mark the way when the snow covers it. But when the snowstorms sweep across the mountains, it is impossible to see ten paces before you, and if the traveller leaves the path he is lost."

"But I suppose," Cuthbert said, "that even in winter travellers pass over?"

"They do," the host said. "The road is as open in winter as in summer, although, of course, the dangers are greater. Still, there is nothing to prevent vigorous men from crossing over when the storms come on. Now, too, with the snow already lying in the upper forests, the wolves are abroad, and should you be attacked by one of those herds, you will find it hard work to defend your lives. Much has been done to render the road safe. At the distance of every league stone houses have been erected, where travellers can find shelter either from the storm or from the attacks of wolves or bears, for these, too, abound in the forests, and in summer there is fine hunting among them. You are, as I see, returning from the Holy Land, and are therefore used to heat rather than cold, so I should advise you before you leave this city to buy some rough cloaks to shield you from the cold. You can obtain them for your followers very cheaply, made of the mountain goat or of sheepskins, and even those of bearskin well dressed are by no means dear."

Obtaining the address of a merchant who kept these things, Cuthbert proceeded thither; and purchased five cloaks of goat-skin with hoods to pull over their heads for his followers, while for himself he obtained one of rather finer material.

Another two days' journey brought them to the foot of the steep ascent, and here they hired the services of a guide. The ascent was long and difficult, and in spite of the praises

which the host had bestowed upon the road, it was so steep that Cuthbert was, for the most part, obliged to walk, leading his steed, whose feet slipped on the smooth rock, and as in many places a false step would have thrown them down many hundreds of feet into the valley below. Cuthbert judged it safer to trust himself to his own feet. He disencumbered himself of his helmet and gorget and placed these upon the horse's back. At nightfall they had attained a very considerable height, and stopped at one of the small refuges of which the landlord had spoken.

"I like not the look of the weather," the guide said in the morning—at least that was what Cuthbert judged him to say, for he could speak no word of the man's language. His actions, however, as he looked towards the sky, and shook his head, spoke for themselves, and Cuthbert, feeling his own powerlessness in a situation so novel to him, felt serious misgivings at the prospect.

The scenery was now very wild. On all sides crags and mountain tops covered with snow glistened in the sun. The woods near the path were free of snow; but higher up they rose black above the white ground. The wind blew keenly, and all rejoiced in the warm cloaks which they had obtained; for even with the protection of these they had found the cold bitter during the night.

"I like not this country," Cnut said. "We grumbled at the heat of Palestine, but I had rather march across the sand there than in this inhospitable frozen region. The woods look as if they might contain spectres. There is a silence which seems to be unnatural, and my courage, like the warmth of my body, is methinks oozing out from my fingers."

Cuthbert laughed.

"I have no doubt that your courage would come again much quicker than the warmth, Cnut, if there were any occasion for it. A brisk walk will set you all right again, and banish these uneasy fancies. To-night we shall be at the highest point, and to-morrow begin to descend towards Germany."

All day the men kept steadily on. The guide from time to time looked apprehensively at the sky; and although in the earlier part of the day Cuthbert's inexperienced eye saw nothing to cause the slightest uneasiness, towards the afternoon the scene changed. Light clouds began to gather on the top of all the hills and to shut the mountain peaks entirely from view. The wind moaned between the gorges and occasionally swept along in such sudden gusts that they could with difficulty retain their feet. The sky became gradually overcast, and frequently light specks of snow, so small as to be scarcely perceptible, were driven along on the blast, making their faces smart by the force with which they struck them.

"It scarcely needs our guide's face," Cuthbert said, "to tell us that a storm is at hand, and that our position is a dangerous one. As for me, I own that I feel better pleased now that the wind is blowing, and the silence is broken, than at the dead stillness which prevailed this morning. After all, methinks that a snowstorm cannot be more dreaded than a sandstorm, and we have faced those before now."

Faster and faster the snow came down, until at last the whole air seemed full of it, and it was with difficulty that they could stagger forward. Where the path led across open places the wind swept away the snow as fast as it fell, but in the hollows the track was already covered; and feeling the difficulty of facing the blinding gale, Cuthbert now understood the urgency with which his host had insisted upon the danger of losing the track. Not a word was spoken among the party as they plodded along. The guide kept ahead, using the greatest caution wherever the path was obliterated by the snow, sometimes even sounding with his iron-shod staff to be sure that they were upon the level rock. In spite of his warm cloak Cuthbert felt that he was becoming chilled to the bone. His horse could with difficulty keep his feet; and Cnut and the archers lagged behind.

"You must keep together, lads," he shouted. "I have heard that in these mountains when sleepiness overpowers the traveller, death is at hand. Therefore, come what may, we must struggle on."

Many times the gale was so violent that they were obliged to pause, and take shelter under the side of a rock or precipice, until the fury of the blast had passed; and Cuthbert eagerly looked out for the next refuge. At last they reached it, and the guide at once entered. It was not that in which he had intended to pass the night, for this lay still higher; but it would have been madness to attempt to go further in the face of such a gale. He signed to Cuthbert that it was necessary at once to collect firewood, and he himself proceeded to light some brands which had been left by previous travellers. Cuthbert gave directions to Cnut and the archers; and these, feeling that life depended upon a good fire being kept up, set to with a will, cutting down shrubs and branches growing in the vicinity of the hut. In half an hour a huge fire blazed in the refuge; and as the warmth thawed their limbs, their tongues were unloosened, and a feeling of comfort again prevailed.

"If this be mountaineering, my lord," Cnut said, "I trust that never again may it be my fortune to venture among the hills. How long, I wonder, do the storms last here? I was grumbling all the way up the hill at the load of provisions which the guide insisted that each of us should bring with him. As it was to be but a three days' journey before we reached a village on the other side, I wondered why he insisted upon our taking food enough to last us at least for a week. But I understand now, and thank him for his foresight; for if this storm goes on, we are assuredly prisoners here for so long as it may continue."

The horse had to be brought into the hut, for it would have been death for it to have remained outside.

"What is that?" Cnut said presently, as a distant howl was heard between the lulls of the storm. The guide muttered some word, which Cuthbert did not understand. But he said to Cnut, "I doubt not that it is wolves. Thank God that we are safe within this refuge, for here not even the most ravenous beasts could make their way."

"Pooh!" Cnut said contemptuously. "Wolves are no bigger than dogs. I have heard my grandfather say that he shot one in the forest, and that it was no bigger than a hound. We should make short work of them."

"I know not," Cuthbert said. "I have heard tales of these animals which show that they must be formidable opponents. They hunt in great packs, and are so furious that they will attack parties of travellers; many of these have perished miserably, horses and men, and nothing but their swords and portions of their saddles have remained to tell where the battle was fought."

CHAPTER XVIII.

SENTENCED TO DEATH.

JUST before arriving at the refuge, they had passed along a very steep and dangerous path. On one side the rock rose precipitously, ten feet above their heads. On the other, was a fall into the valley below. The road at this point was far wider than usual.

Presently, the howl of a wolf was heard near, and soon the solitary call was succeeded by the howling of great numbers of animals. These speedily surrounded the hut, and so fierce were their cries, that Cnut changed his opinion as to the ease with which they could be defeated, and allowed that he would rather face an army of Saracens than a troop of these ill-conditioned animals. The horse trembled in every limb at the sound of the howling of the wolves; and cold as was the night, in spite of the great fire that blazed on the hearth, his coat became covered with the lather of fear. Even upon the roof above the trampling of the animals could be heard; and through the open slits of the windows which some travellers before them had stuffed with straw, they could hear the fierce breathing and snorting of the savage beasts, who scratched and tore to make an entrance.

"Methinks," Cuthbert said, "that we might launch a few arrows through these loopholes. The roof appears not to be over strong; and should some of them force an entrance, the whole pack might follow."

Dark as was the night, the black bodies were visible against the white snow, and the archers shot several arrows forth, each stretching a wolf dead on the ground. Those killed were at once pounced upon by their comrades, and torn to pieces; and this mark of savageness added to the horror which those within felt of the ferocious animals. Suddenly there was a pause in the howling around the hut, and then Cnut, looking forth from the loophole, declared that the whole body had gone off at full speed along the path by which they had reached the refuge. Almost immediately afterwards a loud shout for help was heard, followed by the renewed howling and yelping of the wolves.

"Good heavens!" Cuthbert exclaimed. "Some traveller coming after us is attacked by these horrible beasts. Let us

sally out, Cnut. We cannot hear a Christian torn to pieces by these beasts, without lending him a hand."

In spite of the angry shouts and entreaties of the guide, the door was thrust open, and the party, armed with their axes and bows, at once rushed out into the night. The storm had for the moment abated and they had no difficulty in making their way along the track. In fifty yards they came to a bend of the path, and saw, a little distance before them, a black mass of animals, covering the road, and congregated round a figure who stood with his back to the rock. With a shout of encouragement they sprang forward, and in a few moments were in the midst of the savage animals, who turned their rage against them at once. They had fired two or three arrows apiece, as they approached, into them; and now, throwing down their bows, the archers betook themselves to their swords, while Cuthbert with his heavy battle-axe hewed and cut at the wolves as they sprang towards him. In a minute they had cleared their way to the figure, which was that of a knight in complete armour. He leant against the rocks completely exhausted, and could only mutter a word of thanks through his closed visor. At a short distance off a number of the wolves were gathered, rending and tearing the horse of the knight; but the rest soon recovering from their surprise, attacked with fury the little party. The thick cloaks of the archers stood them in good stead against the animals' teeth, and standing in a group with their backs to the rock, they hewed and cut vigorously at their assailants. The numbers of these, however, appeared almost innumerable, and fresh stragglers continued to come along the road, and swell their body. As fast as those in front fell, their heads cleft with the axes of the party, fresh ones sprang forward; and Cuthbert saw that in spite of the valour and strength of his men, the situation was well nigh desperate. He himself had been saved from injury by his harness, for he still had on his greaves and leg pieces.

"Keep together," he shouted to his men, "and each lend aid to the other if he sees him pulled down. Strike lustily for life, and hurry not your blows, but let each tell." This latter order he gave perceiving that some of the archers, terrified by this furious army of assailants with gaping mouths and glistening teeth, were striking wildly, and losing their presence of mind.

The combat, although it might have been prolonged, could yet have had but one termination, and the whole party would have fallen. At this moment, however, a gust of wind, more furious than any which they had before experienced, swept along the gorge, and the very wolves had to crouch on their stomachs to prevent themselves being hurled by its fury into the ravine below. Then even above the storm a deep roar was heard. It grew louder and louder. The wolves, as if struck with terror, leaped to their feet, and scattered on either way along the path at full speed.

"What sound can this be?" Cnut exclaimed in an awestruck voice. "It sounds like thunder; but it is regular and unbroken; and, my lord, surely the earth quakes under our feet!"

Louder and louder grew the roar.

"Throw yourselves down against the wall of rock," Cuthbert shouted, himself setting the example.

A moment afterwards, from above, a mighty mass of rock and snow poured over like a cascade, with a roar and sound which nigh stunned them. For minutes—it seemed for hours to them—the deluge of snow and rock continued. Then, as suddenly as it had begun, it ceased, and a silence as of death reigned over the place.

"Arise," Cuthbert said; "the danger, methinks, is past. It was what men call an avalanche—a torrent of snow slipping down from the higher peaks. We have had a narrow escape indeed."

By this time the knight whom they had rescued was able to speak, and raising his visor, he returned his deepest thanks to those who had come so opportunely to his aid.

"I was well nigh exhausted," he said, "and it was only my armour which saved me from being torn to pieces. A score of them had hold of me; but, fortunately, my mail was of

Milan proof, and even the jaws and teeth of these enormous beasts were unable to pierce it."

"The refuge is near at hand," Cuthbert said. "It is but a few yards round yonder point. It is well that we heard your voice. I fear that your horse has fallen a victim."

Assisting the knight, who, in spite of his armour, was sorely bruised and exhausted, they made their way back to the refuge. Cnut and the archers were all bleeding freely from various wounds inflicted upon them in the struggle, breathless and exhausted from their exertions, and thoroughly awe-struck by the tremendous phenomenon of which they had been witnesses, and which they had only escaped from their good fortune in happening to be in a place so formed that the force of the avalanche had swept over their heads. The whole of the road, with the exception of a narrow piece four feet in width, had been carried away. Looking upwards, they saw that the forest had been swept clear, not a tree remaining in a wide track as far as they could see up the hill. The great boulders which had strewn the hill-side, and many of which were as large as houses, had been swept away like straws before the rush of snow, and for a moment they feared that the refuge had also been carried away. Turning the corner, however, they saw to their delight that the limits of the avalanche had not extended so far, the refuges, as they afterwards learned, being so placed as to be sheltered by over-hanging cliffs from any catastrophe of this kind.

They found the guide upon his knees, muttering his prayers before a cross, which he had formed of two sticks laid crosswise on the ground before him; and he could scarce believe his eyes when they entered, so certain had he considered it that they were lost. There were no longer any signs of the wolves. The greater portion, indeed, of the pack had been overwhelmed by the avalanche, and the rest, frightened and scared, had fled to their fastnesses in the woods. The knight now removed his helmet, and discovered a handsome young man of some four-or-five-and-twenty years old.

"I am," he said, "Baron Ernest of Kornstein. To whom do I owe my life?"

"In spite of my red cross," Cuthbert said, "I am English. My name is Sir Cuthbert, and I am Earl of Evesham. I am on my return from the Holy Land with my followers; and as we are passing through countries where many of the people are hostile to England, we have thought it as well for a time to drop our nationality. But to you I do not hesitate to tell the truth."

"You do well," the young knight said, "for, truth to say, the people of these parts bear but little love to your countrymen. You have saved my life when I was in the sorest danger. I had given myself up for lost, for even my armour could not have saved me long from these wretches; and my sword and life are at your disposal. You are young indeed," he said, looking with surprise at Cuthbert, who had now thrown back the hood of his cloak, "to have gained the honour of knighthood. You scarce look eighteen years of age, although, doubtless, you are older."

"I am scarce seventeen," Cuthbert said; "but have had the good fortune to attract the notice of King Richard, and to have received the knighthood from his sword."

"None more worthy," said the young knight, "for although King Richard may be fierce and proud, he is the worthiest knight in Christendom, and resembles the heroes of romance rather than a Christian king."

"He is my lord and master," Cuthbert said, "and I love him beyond all men, and would give my life for his. He is the kindest and best of masters; and although it be true that he brooks no opposition, yet is it only because his own bravery and eagerness render hateful to him the indolence and cowardice of others."

They now took their seats round the fire. The archers, by the advice of the guide, rubbed their wounds with snow, and then applied bandages to them. The wallets were opened, and a hearty supper eaten; and all, wrapping themselves in their fur cloaks, were soon asleep.

For four days the gale continued, keeping the party prisoners in the hut. On the fifth, the force of the wind abated, and the snow ceased to fall. They were forced to take the door off its hinges to open it, for the snow had piled up so high that the chimney alone of the hut remained above its surface. With great difficulty and labour they cleared a way out, and then the guide again placing himself at their head, they proceeded on their way. The air was still and cold, and the sky of a deep, dark blue, which seemed even darker in contrast with the whiteness of the snow. At times they had great difficulty in struggling through the deep drifts; but for the most part the wind had swept the path clear. Where it was deepest, the tops of the posts still showed above the snow, and enabled the guide to direct their footsteps. They were, however, obliged to travel slowly, and it was three days before they gained the village on the northern slope of the mountains, having slept at refuges by the road.

"What are your plans?" the knight asked Sir Cuthbert

that night, as they sat by the fire of the hostelry. "I would warn you that the town which you will first arrive at is specially hostile to your people, for the baron, its master, is a relation of Conrad of Montferat, who is said to have been killed by order of your king."

"It is false," Cuthbert said. "King Richard had appointed him King of Jerusalem; and, though he liked him not, thought him the fittest of those there to exercise sovereignty. He was the last man who would have had an enemy assassinated; for so open is he of disposition, that he would have fought hand to hand with the meanest soldier of his army, had he desired to kill him."

"I doubt not that it is so, since you tell me," the knight said courteously. "But the people here have taken that idea into their minds, and it will be hard to disabuse them. You must therefore keep up your disguise as a French knight while passing through this neighbourhood. Another week's journeying, and you will reach the confines of Saxony, and there you will, as you anticipate, be safe. But I would not answer for your life were you discovered here to be of English birth. And now tell me if there is aught that I can do for you. I will myself accompany you into the town, and will introduce you as a French knight, so that no suspicion is likely to lie upon you, and will, further, ride with you to the borders of Saxony. I am well known, and trust that my company will avert all suspicion from you. You have told me that your purse is ill-supplied; you must suffer me to replenish it. One knight need not fear to borrow of another; and I know that when you have returned to your home, you will bestow the sum which I now give you upon some holy shrine in my name, and thus settle matters between us."

Cuthbert without hesitation accepted the offer, and was well pleased at finding his purse replenished, for its emptiness had caused him serious trouble. Cuthbert's steed was led by one of the archers, and he himself walked gaily alongside of Sir Ernest, followed by his retainers. Another long day's march brought them down to Innsbruck, where they remained quietly for a week. Then they journeyed on until they emerged from the mountains, crossed the Bavarian frontier, and arrived at Fussen, a strong city, with well-built walls and defences.

They at once proceeded to the principal hostelry, where the young baron was well known, and where great interest was excited by the news of the narrow escape which he had had from the attack of the wolves. A journey across the Alps was in those days regarded as a very perilous enterprise in the winter season, and the fact that he should have been rescued from such a strait appeared almost miraculous. They stayed for two days quietly in the city, Cuthbert declining the invitation of the young noble to accompany him to the houses of his friends, as he did not wish that any suspicion should be excited as to his nationality, and preferred remaining quiet to having forced upon him the necessity of making false statements. As to his followers, there was no fear of the people among whom they mixed detecting that they were English. To the Bavarian inhabitants, all languages, save their native German, were alike unintelligible; and, even had French been commonly spoken, the dialects of that tongue, such as would naturally be spoken by archers and men-at-arms, would have been as Greek to those accustomed only to Norman French.

Upon the third day, however, an incident occurred which upset Cuthbert's calculations, and nearly involved the whole party in ruin. The town was, as the young baron had said, governed by a noble who was a near relation of Conrad of Montferat, and who was the bitter enemy of the English. A great fête had been given in honour of the marriage of his daughter, and upon this day the young pair were to ride in triumph through the city. Great preparations had been made; masques and pageants of various kinds manufactured; and the whole townspeople, dressed in their holiday attire, were gathered in the streets. Cuthbert had gone out, followed by his little band of retainers, and taken their station to see the passing show. First came a large body of knights and men-at-arms, with gay banners and trappings. Then rode the bridegroom, with the bride carried in a litter by his side. After this came several allegorical representations. Among these was the figure of a knight bearing the arms of Austria. Underneath his feet, on the car, lay a figure clad in a royal robe, across whom was thrown a banner with the Leopards of England. The knight stood with his foot on this figure.

This representation of the dishonour of England at the

hands of Austria elicited great acclamations from the crowd. Cuthbert clenched his teeth and grasped his sword angrily, but had the sense to see the folly of taking any notice of the insult. Not so with Cnut. Furious at the insult offered to the standard of his royal master, Cnut, with a bound, burst through the ranks of the crowd, leaped on to the car, and with a buffet smote the figure representing Austria, into the road, and lifted the flag of England from the ground. A yell of indignation and rage was heard. The infuriated crowd rushed forward. Cnut, with a bound, sprang from the car, and, joining his comrades, burst through those who attempted to impede them, and darted down a by-street.

Cuthbert, for the moment amazed at the action of his follower, had on the instant drawn his sword and joined the archers. In the crowd, however, he was for a second separated from them; and before he could tear himself from the hands of the citizens who had seized him, the men-at-arms accompanying the procession surrounded him, and he was led away by them to the castle, the guards with difficulty protecting him from the enraged populace. Even at this moment Cuthbert experienced a deep sense of satisfaction at the thought that his followers had escaped. But he feared that alone, and unacquainted with the language of the country, they would find it difficult indeed to escape the search which would be made for them, and to manage to find their way back to their country. For himself, he had little hopes of liberty, and scarcely more of life. The hatred of the baron towards the English would now be heightened by the daring act of insult to the arms of Austria, and this would give a pretext for any deed of violence which might be wrought.

Cuthbert was, after a short confinement, brought before the lord baron of the place, in the great hall of the castle.

"Who art thou, sir," the noble exclaimed, "who darest to disturb the marriage procession of my daughter, and to insult the standard of the emperor my master?"

"I am Sir Cuthbert, Earl of Evesham, a baron of England," Cuthbert said fearlessly, "and am travelling homeward from the Holy Land. My garb as a crusader should protect me from all interruption; and the heedless conduct of my retainer was amply justified by the insult offered to the arms of England. There is not one of the knights assembled round you who would not in like manner have avenged an insult offered to those of Austria; and I am ready to do battle in the lists with any who choose to say that the deed was a foul or improper one. In the Holy Land,

Austrians and English fought side by side; and it is strange indeed to me that on my return, journeying through the country of the emperor, I should find myself treated as an enemy, and see the arms of King Richard exposed to insult and derision by the burghers of this city."

As Cuthbert had spoken, he threw down his mailed glove, and several of the knights present stepped forward to pick it up. The baron, however, waved them back.

"It is no question," he said, "of honourable fight. This is a follower of the murderer of my good cousin of Montferat, who died under the hands of assassins set upon him by Richard of England."

"It is false!" Cuthbert shouted. "I denounce it as a foul lie, and will maintain it with my life."

"Your life is already forfeited," the baron said, "both by your past connexion with Richard of England and as the insulter of the arms of Austria. You die, and to-morrow at noon your head shall be struck off in the great square before my castle."

Without another word Cuthbert was hurried off to his cell, and there remained, thinking moodily over the events of the day, until nightfall. He had no doubt that his sentence would be carried out, and his anxiety was rather for his followers than for himself. He feared that they would make some effort on his behalf, and would sacrifice their own lives in doing so, without the possibility of assisting him.

The next morning he was led out to the square before the castle. It was a large flagged courtyard. Upon one side was the entrance to the castle, one of whose wings also formed a second side to the square. The side facing this was formed by the wall of the city, and the fourth opened upon a street of the town. This side of the square was densely filled with citizens, while the men-at-arms of the baron and a large number of knights were gathered behind a scaffold erected in the centre. Upon this was a block, and by the side stood a headsman. As Cuthbert was led forward a thrill of pleasure ran through him at perceiving no signs of his followers, who he greatly feared might have been captured in the night, and brought there to share his fate.

As he was led forward, the young noble whose life he had saved advanced to the baron, and dropping on one knee before him, craved the life of Cuthbert, relating the event by which he had saved his life in the passage of the mountains. The baron frowned heavily.

"Though he had saved the life of every noble in Bavaria," he said, "he should die. I have sworn an oath that every Englishman who fell into my hands should expiate the murder of my kinsman; and this fellow is, moreover, guilty of an outrage to the arms of Austria."

The young Sir Ernest drew himself up haughtily.

"My lord baron," he said, "henceforth I renounce all allegiance to you, and I will lay the case before the emperor, our common master, and will cry before him at the outrage which has thus been passed upon a noble gentleman. He has thrown down the glove, and challenged any of your knights, and I myself am equally ready to do battle in his cause."

The baron grew red with passion, and he would have ordered the instant arrest of the young man, but as Sir Ernest was connected by blood with many present, and was indeed one of the most popular among the nobles of the province, the baron simply waved him aside, and ordered Cuthbert to be led to the block. The young Englishman was by the executioner divested of his armour and helmet, and stood in the simple attire worn by men of rank at that time. He looked around, and holding up his hand, conveying alike a farewell and a command to his followers to remain in concealment, he gazed round the crowd, thinking that he might see among them in some disguise or other the features of Cnut, whose tall figure would have rendered him conspicuous in a crowd. He failed, however, to see any signs of him, and turning to the executioner, signified by a gesture that he was ready.

At this instant an arrow from the wall above pierced the

brain of the man, and he fell dead in his tracks. A roar of astonishment burst from the crowd. Upon the city wall at this point was a small turret, and on this were five figures. The wall around was deserted, and for the moment these men were masters of the position.

"Seize those insolent varlets!" the baron shouted, shaking his sword with a gesture of fury at them.

His words, however, were arrested, for at that moment another arrow struck him in the throat, and he fell back into the arms of those around him.

Quickly now the arrows of the English archers flew into the courtyard. The confusion which reigned there was indescribable. The citizens with shouts of alarm took to their heels. The

men-at-arms were powerless against this rain of missiles, and the knights, hastily closing their visors, shouted contradictory orders, which no one obeyed.

In the confusion no one noticed the prisoner. Seizing a moment when the attention of all was fixed upon the wall, he leaped from the platform, and making his way unnoticed through the excited crowd of men-at-arms darted down a narrow lane that divided the castle from the wall. He ran along until, 100 yards farther, he came to a staircase by which access to the battlements was obtained. Running lightly up this, he kept along the wall until he reached the turret.

"Thanks, my noble Cnut!" he exclaimed, "and you, my brave fellows. But I fear you have forfeited your lives. There is no escape. In a minute the whole force of the place will recover from their confusion, and be down upon us from both sides."

"We have prepared for that," Cnut said. "Here is a rope hanging down into the moat."

Glancing over, Cuthbert saw that the moat was dry; and after a final discharge of arrows into the crowd, the six men slid one after another down the rope and made their way at full speed across the country.

CHAPTER XIX.

DRESDEN.

IT was some ten minutes before the men-at-arms rallied sufficiently from their surprise to obey orders. Two bodies were then drawn up, and proceeded at a rapid pace towards the staircases leading to the wall, one on each side of the turret in which they believed that the little body of audacious assailants were still lying. Having reached the wall, the soldiers advanced, covering themselves with their shields, for they had learnt the force with which an English clothyard shaft drawn by a strong hand flies. Many had been killed by these missiles passing through and through the cuirass and backpiece.

No reply being obtained to the summons to surrender, they proceeded to break in with their battle-axes the door of the little turret. Rushing in with axe and pike, they were astonished to find the place empty. A glance over the wall showed the rope still hanging, and the manner of the escape became manifest. The fugitives were already out of sight, and the knights, furious at the escape of the men who had bearded them in the heart of the city with such audacity, and had slain the lord baron and several of his knights, gave orders that an instant pursuit should be organized. It was, however, a full half hour before the city gates were thrown open, and a strong troop of knights and mounted men issued out.

Cuthbert had been certain that an instant pursuit would be set on foot, and the moment that he was out of sight of the battlements, he changed the direction in which he had started, and turning at right angles, swept round the city, still keeping at a distance, until he reached the side next the mountains, and then plunged into the woods on the lower slopes of the hills.

"They will," he said, as they halted breathless from their run, "follow the road towards the south, and scour the country for awhile before it occurs to their thick German skulls that we have doubled back on our tracks. Why, what is it, Cnut?"

This exclamation was provoked by the forester throwing himself on his knees before Sir Cuthbert, and imploring his pardon for the dire strait into which his imprudence had drawn him.

"It was a dire strait, certainly, Cnut. But if you got me into it, at least you have extricated me; and never say more about it, for I myself was near committing the imprudence to which you gave way, and I can well understand that your English blood boiled at the sight of the outrage to the flag of England. Now, let us waste no time in talk, but, keeping to the foot of this mountain, make along as far as we can to the west. We must cling to the hills for many days' march before we venture again to try to cross the plains. If possible, we will keep on this way until we reach the confines of the country of the Swiss, who will assuredly give us hospitality, and who will care little for any threats of these German barons, should they hear that we have reached their asylum."

By nightfall they had already travelled many leagues, and making a fire in the wood, Cuthbert asked Cnut for an account of what had taken place on the previous day.

"We ran for life, Sir Cuthbert, and had not noticed that you had been drawn into the fray. Had we done so, we would have remained, and sold our lives with yours; but hoping that you had passed unnoticed in the crowd, and that you would find some means to rejoin us, we kept upon our way. After running down three streets, we passed a place where a courtyard with stables ranged round it was open. There were none about, and we entered, and, taking refuge in a loft, hid ourselves beneath some provender. There we remained all night, and then borrowing some apparel which some of the stablemen had hung up on the walls, we issued into the town. As we neared the great square we saw some men employed in erecting a platform in the midst, and a suspicion that all might not be right, and that you might have fallen into the hands of these German dogs, beset our minds. After much consultation we determined to see what the affair meant, and making our way on to the walls, which, indeed, were entirely deserted, we took refuge in that turret where you saw us.

Seeing the crowd gather, and being still more convinced that some misfortune was about to occur, I again went back to the stables, where I had noticed a long rope used by the carters for fastening their loads to the waggons. With this I returned, for it was clear that if we had to mingle in this business it would be necessary to have a mode of escape. Of the rest you are aware. We saw the knights coming out of the castle, with that portly baron, their lord, at their head. We saw the block and the headsman upon the platform, and were scarcely surprised when you were led out, a prisoner, from the gates. We judged that what did happen would ensue. Seeing that the confusion wrought by a sudden attack from men perched up aloft as we were, commanding the courtyard, and being each of us able to hit a silver mark at the distance of 100 yards, would be great indeed, we judged that you might be able to slip away unobserved, and were sure that your quick wit would seize any opportunity which might offer. Had you not been able to join us, we should have remained in the turret and sold our lives to the last, as, putting aside the question that we could never return to our homes, having let our dear lord die here, we should not, in our ignorance of the language and customs of the country, have ever been able to make our way across it. We knew, however, that before this turret was carried we could show these Germans how five Englishmen, when brought to bay, can sell their lives."

They had not much difficulty in obtaining food in the forest, for game abounded, and they could kill as many deer as seemed fit to them. As Cnut said, it was difficult to believe that they were not back again in the forest near Evesham, so similar was their life to that which they had led three years before. To Cnut and the archers, indeed, it was a pleasanter time than any which they had passed since they had left the shores of England, and they blithely marched along, fearing little any pursuit which might be set on foot, and, indeed, hearing nothing of their enemies. After six days' travel they came upon a rude village, and here Cuthbert learnt from the people—with much difficulty, however, and pantomime, for neither could understand a word spoken by the other—that they were now in one of the Swiss cantons, and therefore secure from all pursuit by the Germans. Without much difficulty Cuthbert engaged one of the young men of the village to act as their guide to Basle, and here, after four days' travelling, they arrived safely. Asking for the residence of the Burgomaster, Cuthbert at once proceeded thither, and stated that he was an English knight on the return from the Crusades; that he had been foully entreated by the Lord of Fussen, who had been killed in a fray by his followers; and that he besought hospitality and refuge from the authorities of Basle.

"We care little," the Burgomaster said, "what quarrel you may have had with your neighbours. All who come hither are free to come and go as they list, and you, as a knight on the return from the Holy Land, have a claim beyond that of an ordinary traveller."

The Burgomaster was himself able to speak French, and summoning several of the councillors of the town, he requested Cuthbert to give a narrative of his adventures; which he did. The councillors agreed with the Burgomaster that Cuthbert must be received hospitably; but the latter saw that there was among many of them considerable doubt as to the expediency of quarrelling with a powerful neighbour. He therefore said to the Burgomaster,—

"I have no intention, honourable sir, of taking up a prolonged residence here. I only ask to be furnished with a charger and arms, and in payment of these I will leave this gold chain, the gift of King Richard himself, as a gage, and will on my return to my country forward to you the value of the arms and horse, trusting that you will return the chain to me."

The Burgomaster, however, said that the city of Basle was not so poor that it need take the gage of an honourable knight, but that the arms and charger he required should be given him in a few hours, and that he might pay the value in London to a Jew merchant there who had relations

with one at Basle. Full instructions were given to him, and he resolved to travel down upon the left bank of the Rine, until he reached Lorraine, and thence to cross into Saxony. The same afternoon the promised horse and arms were provided, and Cuthbert, delighted again to be in harness, and thanking courteously the Burgomaster and council for their kindness, started with his followers on his journey north. These latter had been provided with doublets and other garments suitable to the retinue of a knight, and made a better show than they had done since they first left England.

Leaving Basle, they travelled along the left side of the Rhine by easy stages. The country was much disturbed, owing to the return and disbandment of so many of the troops employed in the Crusades. These, their occupation being gone, scattered over the country, and France and Germany alike were harassed by bands of military robbers. The wild country between the borders of Switzerland and Lorraine was specially vexed, as the mountains of the Vosges afforded shelter, into which the freebooters could not be followed by the troops of the duke.

Upon the evening of the third day they reached a small inn standing in a lonely position near the foot of the mountains.

"I like not the look of this place," Cuthbert said; "but as we hear that there is no other within a distance of another ten miles, we must e'en make the best of it."

The host received them with extreme and even fawning civility, which by no means raised him in the estimation of Cuthbert or Cnut. A rough meal was taken, and they then ascended to the rude accommodation which had been provided. It was one large room barely furnished. Upon one side straw was thickly littered down—for in those days beds among the common people were unknown. In a sort of alcove at the end was a couch with a rough mattress and coverlet. This Cuthbert took possession of, while his followers stretched themselves upon the straw.

"Methinks," Cnut said, "that it were well that one should keep watch at the door. I like not the look of our host, and we are near the spot where the bands of the robbers are said to be busy."

Towards morning the archer on guard reported that he could hear the sound of many approaching footsteps. All at once sprang to their feet, and betook themselves to their arms. Looking from the window they saw a large party of rough men, whose appearance at once betokened that they were disbanded soldiers—a title almost synonymous in those days with that of robber. With the united strength of the party the truckle bed was carried from the alcove and placed against the door. Cuthbert then threw open the window, and asked in French what they wanted. One of the party, who appeared to be the leader, said that the party had better surrender immediately. He promised them good treatment, and said that the knight would be put to ransom, should it be found

that the valuables upon his person were not sufficient to pay the worshipful company present for the trouble which they had taken in waiting upon him. This sally was received with shouts of laughter. Cuthbert replied quietly that he had no valuables upon his person; that if they took him there were none would pay as much as a silver mark for the ransom of them all; and that the only things that they had to give were sharp arrows and heavy blows.

"You talk bravely, young sir," the man said. "But you have to do with men versed in fight, and caring but little either for knocks or for arrows. We have gone through the Crusades, and are therefore held to be absolved from all sin, even that so great as would be incurred in the cutting of your knightly throat."

"But we have gone through the Crusades also," Cuthbert said, "and our persons are sacred. The sin of slitting our weazands, which you speak of, would therefore be so great that even the absolution of which you rely would barely extend to it."

"We know most of those who have served in the Holy Land," the man said more respectfully than he had yet spoken, "and would fain know with whom we speak."

"I am an Englishman, and a follower of King Richard," Cuthbert said, "and am known as Sir Cuthbert of Evesham. As I was the youngest among the knights who fought for the holy sepulchre, it may be that my appearance is known to you?"

"Ah," the other said, "you are he whom they called the Boy Knight, and who was often in the thick of the fray, near to Richard himself. How comes it, Sir Cuthbert, that you are here?"

"The fleet was scattered on its return," Cuthbert replied, "and I landed with my followers, well-nigh penniless, at Zara, and have since made my way across the Tyrol. I have, then, as you may well suppose, neither silver nor gold about my person; and assuredly neither Phillip of France nor John of Austria would give a noble for my ransom; and it would be long, methinks, to wait ere John of England would care to ransom one of King Richard's followers."

The brigands spoke for awhile among themselves, and then the leader said,—

"You speak frankly and fairly, Sir Knight, and as you have proved yourself indeed a doughty giver of hard blows, and as I doubt not that the archers with you can shoot as straight and as fast as the rest of the Saxon breed, we will e'en let you go on your way, for your position is but little better than ours, and dog should not rob dog."

"Thanks, good fellow," Cuthbert said. "We trust that in any case we might have made a strong defence against you;

but it would be hard if those who have fought together in the Holy Land, should slay each other in this lonely corner of Lorraine."

"Are you seeking adventures or employment, Sir Knight? For if so, myself and comrades here would gladly take service with you; and it may be that with a clump of spears you might obtain engagement, either under the Duke of Lorraine or he of Cleves."

"Thanks for your offer," Cuthbert replied; "but at present my face is turned towards England. King Richard needs all his friends; and there is so little chance of sack or spoil, even should we have—which God forfend—civil war, that fear I could ill reward the services which you offer me."

The leader and his men shouted an adieu to Cuthbert, and departed for the mountains, leaving the latter well pleased with his escape from a fight of which the result was doubtful.

Journeying on without further adventure, they came to Nancy, and were there kindly received by the duke, who was not at that time upon good terms with Phillip of France, and was therefore well disposed towards the English. Cuthbert inquired from him whether any news had been heard of King Richard? but received as a reply that the duke had heard nothing of him since he sailed from Palestine.

"This is strange," Cuthbert said, "for I myself have journeyed but slowly, and have met with many delays. King Richard should long ere this have reached Saxony; and I fear much that some foul treatment has befallen him. On our way, we found how bitter was the feeling among those related to Conrad of Montferat against him; and the Archduke John is still smarting from the blow which King Richard struck him at Ascalon. But surely they would not be so unknightly as to hinder so great a champion of Christendom as King Richard on his homeward way?"

"The Archduke John is crafty and treacherous," the duke said; "and the emperor himself would, I think be not sorry to lay hand upon the King of England, were it only to do pleasure to Phillip of France. Assuredly, however, the anger and indignation of all Christendom will be aroused should the king's passage be interrupted, for it were indeed gross breach of hospitality to seize upon a man who has the double claim of being a champion of Christendom and a shipwrecked man. However, it is early yet to be uneasy, and it may be that in a few days we may have news of the arrival of the King in Saxony. He may have encountered difficulties similar to those which you yourself have met with. The country is everywhere disturbed, and it is not only in my forests that bands of outlawed men are to be met with. At

present there is peace in Europe. It may last indeed but a short time. But so long as it continues, so long must the mountains and woods be full of desperate men. Were war declared between any two princes these would flock to the banners of him who would pay them highest, and a war which could end in the entire destruction of the armies of both combatants would be a blessing to Europe."

After entertaining Cuthbert courteously for three days, the Duke of Lorraine bade him adieu, and gave him an escort of men-at-arms to the borders of the Rhine, where he would find the way open to the domains of the Duke of Saxony. Without adventure Cuthbert and his followers arrived at Dresden, and he immediately presented himself at the castle of the duke. The instant that he sent in his name as Sir Cuthbert of Evesham, a knight of King Richard, he was conducted to the presence of the duke and of his wife, the sister of King Richard,

"Are you bearer of news of my brother Richard?" the duke said, advancing a step to meet the young knight as he entered the hall.

"Alas! my lord duke, I am not," Cuthbert said; "but had hoped to gain tidings from you."

"From me?" the duke said in surprise. "What should lead you to believe that I have any news of King Richard later than that which others have received? The last I heard of him was upon the day of his departure from the Holy Land, before the storm arose which scattered his fleet, and I am ignorant whether he has foundered at sea, or whether, as some suppose, his vessel may have been taken captive by the Moors."

"I bear you later tidings," Cuthbert said, "than those you have received. I was on board the ship with King Richard. We were wrecked upon the Island of Corfu, and there hiring a small ship, we proceeded to Zara. King Richard determined to make his way across the Tyrol to this place; but he thought that it would attract attention to him were he accompanied by so large a party. Therefore he, with Sir Baldwin of Béthune, and a few followers, started north, while I with my men kept west through the north of Italy, and then crossed by the pass over Trent."

"How long is it since you left my brother?" the duchess asked anxiously.

"It is now over a month since I bade him adieu," Cuthbert answered.

"Then he should have been heard of long since," the duchess said. "What fate can have befallen him?"

"Judging from my own experience," Cuthbert said, "I fear that he may have come to harm at the hands of the friends of Conrad of Montferat, who falsely allege that the death of their kinsman was caused by King Richard. The

Archduke John, too, owes him no good-will; and even the emperor is evilly disposed towards him. The king travelled under an assumed name; but it might well be that he would be recognized upon the way. His face was known to all who fought in the East; and his lordly manner and majestic stature could ill be concealed beneath a merchant's garb. Still, lady, as I have been so long in making my way across, it may be that King Richard has been similarly delayed without danger befalling him, and it could hardly be that so important a man as the King of England would be detained, or come to any misfortune, without the news being bruited abroad."

In spite of Cuthbert's reassuring words, the duke and duchess were greatly alarmed at the news of King Richard's disappearance, although indeed console to find that their previous fears, that he had been drowned in the storm or captured by the Moorish corsairs, were unfounded.

They now requested from Cuthbert the story of what had befallen him since he left the king; and this he related at some length. The duke was greatly interested, and begged Cuthbert at least to remain at his court until some news might arrive of King Richard.

For a month Cuthbert tarried at the castle of the Duke of Saxony, where he was nobly entertained, and treated as a guest of much honour. Cnut and the archers were delighted at the treatment they received, for never in their lives had they been so royally entertained. Their Saxon tongue was nigh enough akin to the language spoken here to be understood; and their tales of adventure in the Holy Land rendered them as popular among the retainers of the duke as their master became with the duke and duchess.

CHAPTER XX.

UNDER THE GREENWOOD.

AT the end of a month, news came from England that Sir Baldwin of Béthune had returned there, bearing the news that the King had been arrested at Gortz, only two days' journey north of the Adriatic—that he had been recognized, and at once captured. He had offered no resistance, finding indeed that it would be hopeless so to do. Sir Baldwin had been permitted to depart without molestation. He believed that the folk into whose hands he had fallen were retainers of the Archduke John. This news, although sad in itself, was yet in some degree reassuring to the duke and his wife; for they felt that while the followers of Conrad of Montferat would not hesitate to put King Richard

to death should he fall into their hands, the Archduke John
would not dare to bring upon himself the indignation of
Europe by such treatment of his royal captive. Cuthbert at
once determined to return to England to see Sir Baldwin,
and to ascertain what steps were being taken for the
discovery of the prison in which King Richard was confined,
and for his release therefrom; and also to establish himself
in his new dignity as Earl of Evesham. Therefore, bidding
adieu to the duke and duchess, he started north. The duke
furnished him with letters of introduction to the princes
through whose countries he would travel; and again crossing
the Rhine, he journeyed through the territories of the Dukes
of Cleves and Brabant, and reached the mouth of the
Scheldt without interruption. There taking ship, he sailed for
London.

It was a long and stormy passage between the mouth of
the Scheldt and London. The vessel in which Cuthbert had
shipped was old and somewhat unseaworthy, and several
times in the force of the gale all on board gave up hope for
their lives. At last, however, they reached the mouth of the
Thames, and dropping up with the tide, reached London
eight days after their embarcation. The noble charger which
the King of Saxony had presented to Cuthbert, had suffered
greatly, and he feared at one time, that the poor animal
would succumb to the effects of the tempest. However, after
entering into smooth water it recovered itself, and on
landing near the Tower he found that it was able to support
his weight. Cnut and the archers were, like Cuthbert,
delighted to have their feet again upon English soil; and
although London did not now strike them with the same
wonder which it would have done had they first visited it
before starting on their journey—for in many respects it was
greatly behind some of the continental cities—yet the feeling
of home, and the pleasure of being able to understand the
conversation of those around them, made the poor fellows
almost beside themselves with joy. Beyond the main

political incidents, Cuthbert had heard little of what had passed in England since his departure; and putting up at a hostelry, he inquired of the host whether Sir Baldwin of Béthune was in London, or whether he was away on his estates. The landlord did not know. There were, he said, but few nobles at court, and London was never so dull as at present. As Cuthbert did not wish his coming home to be known to John until he had learnt something of the position of affairs, he despatched Cnut to the Tower to inquire privately of some of the officials about the place whether Sir Baldwin was there. Cnut soon returned with the news that he had not been at the court since his return from the Holy Land, and that he was living at his castle down in Dorsetshire. After some hesitation, Cuthbert resolved to set out to see his friend, and after six days' travel he arrived at the castle of the knight.

Sir Baldwin received him with immense joy. He had not heard of him since they parted at Zara, and he feared that a fate similar to that which had befallen King Richard had overtaken Cuthbert, even if he were still alive.

"Have you seen aught of the king, our master?" the good knight inquired.

"Nothing," Cuthbert said. "I know no more than yourself. Indeed, I hoped to have learnt something from you as to the king."

"I was separated from him at Gortz, and while he was taken a prisoner to the archduke, I was allowed to pursue my way. I had many difficulties and dangers, and was some weeks in finding my way back. Nothing was known of the king when I returned. Indeed, I was the first bearer of any definite news concerning him since the day when he sailed from Acre. Three weeks ago, as you may have learnt, the news came that he is now detained in captivity by the emperor who demanded his delivery by the Archduke John, into whose hands he first fell. But where he is, no one exactly knows. The news has created an immense excitement in the kingdom, and all are resolved to sacrifice any of their treasures which may be demanded in order to satisfy the ransom which the recreant emperor has placed upon the king. Shame is it indeed that a Christian sovereign should hold another in captivity. Still more, when that other was returning through his dominions as a crusader coming from the Holy Land, when his person should be safe, even to his deadliest enemy. It has long been suspected that he was in the hands either of the emperor, or of the archduke, and throughout Europe the feeling of indignation has been strong; and I doubt not, now that the truth is known, this feeling will be stronger than ever."

"But, now that it is known," Cuthbert said, "I suppose there will be no delay in ransoming the king."

"There will be no delay in raising the ransom," Sir Baldwin said. "But the kingdom is very impoverished by war, by the exactions of Prince John, and by those of Langley, who held it for King Richard. He was a loyal servant of the king, but an exacting and rapacious prelate. However, I doubt not that the rents of the English nobles will soon be charged with sums sufficient for the ransom; and if this avail not, not one of them will grudge their silver flagons and vessels to melt down to make the total required. But we must not flatter ourselves that he will obtain his liberty so soon as the money is raised. Prince John has long been yearning for sovereignty. He has long exercised the real, if not the nominal, power, and he has been intriguing with the Pope and Phillip of France for their support for his seizing the crown. He will throw every obstacle in the way, as, we may be sure, will Phillip of France, Richard's deadly enemy. And now about yourself, Sir Cuthbert; tell me what has befallen you since we last met."

Cuthbert related the adventures which had befallen him, and heard those of Sir Baldwin.

"You have not, I suppose," the latter remarked, "as yet seen Prince John?"

"No," Cuthbert replied, "I thought it better to come down to ask you to advise me on the position of affairs before I attempted to see him."

"You did well," Sir Baldwin said. "When I arrived, I found that the proper officials, had, according to King Richard's instructions, drawn up the patent conferring upon you the lands and title of Earl of Evesham, before leaving Acre, and had received the king's signature to it. This was attested by several of the nobles who were with us and who returned safely to England. Prince John, however, declared that he should not give any heed to the document; that King Richard's power over this realm had ceased before he made it; and that he should bestow the earldom upon whomsoever he chose. As a matter of fact, it has been given to Sir Rudolph Fleming, a Norman knight and a creature of the prince. The king has also, I hear promised to him the hand of the young Lady Margaret, when she shall become of marriageable age. At present she is placed in a convent in Worcester. The abbess is, I believe, a friend of the late earl, and the girl had been with her for some time previously.

"Indeed she went there, I think, when her father left England. This lady was ordered to give up her charge to the guardianship of Sir Rudolph; but she refused to do so, saying that it would not be convenable for a young lady to be under the guardianship of a bachelor knight having no lady at the head of his establishment, and that therefore she should retain her, in spite of the orders of the Prince. Prince John, I hear, flew into a fury at this; but he did not dare to provoke the anger of the whole of the clergy by ordering the convent to be violated. And indeed, not only would the clergy have been indignant, but many of the great nobles would also have taken their part, for there can be no doubt that the contention of the abbess was reasonable; and there is among all the friends of King Richard a very strong feeling of anger at your having been deprived of the earldom. This, however, has, so far, not found much vent in words, for as it was uncertain whether you would ever return to claim your rights, it was worth no one's while to embroil himself unnecessarily with the prince upon such a subject. God knows that there are subjects enough of dispute between John Lackland and the English barons without any fresh ones arising. The whole kingdom is in a state of disturbance. There have been several risings against Prince John's authority; but these have been, so far, suppressed. Now that we know where King Richard is, and hope for his return ere very long, it is probable that peace will be maintained; but should treachery prevail, and King Richard's return be prevented, you may be sure that John will not be permitted to mount the throne without the determined resistance of a large number of the nobles."

"But," Cuthbert said, "John is not the successor to the throne. Prince Arthur of Brittany was named by King Richard from the first as his successor. He is so by blood and by right, and John can have no pretence to the throne so long as he lives."

"That is so," Sir Baldwin said. "But, unhappily, in England at present might makes right, and you may be sure that at King Richard's death, be it when it may, Prince John will make a bold throw for the throne, and, aided as he will be by the pope and by Phillip of France, methinks that his chances are better than those of the young prince. A man's power, in warlike times, is more than a boy's. He can intrigue and promise and threaten, while a boy must be in the hands of partisans. I fear that Prince Arthur will have troubled times indeed before he mounts the throne of England. Should Richard survive until he becomes of age to take the field himself and head armies, he may succeed, for all speak well of him as a boy of singular sweetness of disposition, while Prince John is detested by all save those who flatter and live by him. But enough for the present of politics, Cuthbert; let us now to table. It is long since we two feasted together; and, indeed, such meals as we took in the

Holy Land could scarcely have been called feasts. A boar's head and a good roasted capon are worthy all the strange dishes that we had there. I always misdoubted the meat, which seemed to me to smack in flavour of the Saracens, and I never could bring myself to inquire whence that strange food was obtained. A stoup of English ale, too, is worth all the Cyprus wines, especially when the Cyprus wines are half full of the sand of the desert. Pah ! it makes my throat dry to think of those horrible meals. So you have brought Cnut and your four archers safely back with you?"

"Yes," Cuthbert said, smiling. "But they were, I can assure you, a heavy weight on me, in spite of their faithfulness and fidelity. Their ignorance of the language brought most of my troubles upon me, and Cnut had something of the nature of a bull in him. There are certain things which he cannot stomach, and when he seeth them he rageth like a wild beast, regardless altogether of safety or convenience."

In the evening, the two knights again talked over the course which Cuthbert should adopt. The elder knight's opinion was that his young friend had best formally claim the title by writing to the king-at-arms, and should also announce his return to Prince John, signing himself "Sir Cuthbert, Earl of Evesham;" but that, in the present state of things, it would be unwise for him to attempt to regain his position, should, as was certain to be the case, Prince John refuse to recognize him.

"You are very young yet," Sir Baldwin said, "not eighteen, I think, and can afford to wait at any rate, to see whether King Richard returns. Should he come back, he will see all these wrongs are righted; and one of his first cares would assuredly be to cast this usurper out of his stolen dignities. How old is the Lady Margaret?"

"She is fifteen," Cuthbert said. "She was three years younger than I."

"I wish she had been younger," Sir Baldwin said. "At

fifteen she is not by custom fairly marriageable; but men can strain these points when they choose; and I fear that the news of your coming will hasten both the prince and Sir Rudolph in their determination to strengthen the claim of this usurper by marriage with the heiress of Evesham. The Lady Margaret and her friends can of course claim that she is a royal ward, and that as such the king alone can dispose of her person and estates. But, unfortunately, force overrides argument."

"But surely," Cuthbert said, "they will never venture to take her by force from the convent?"

"They venture a great many strange things in England now," Sir Baldwin said; "and Worcester is perilously near to Evesham. With a clump of twenty spears, Sir Rudolph might break into the convent and carry off the young lady, and marry her by force; and although the Church might cry out, crying would be of little avail when the deed was done; and a handsome present on the part of Sir Rudolph might go far to shut the mouths of many of the complainants, especially as he will be able to say that he has the king's sanction for what he did."

"Methinks," Cuthbert said, "that if such be the case it would be perilous indeed to wait for King Richard's return. Assuredly Sir Rudolph would not tarry until she attained the age of seventeen, and it may well be that two years may yet pass before King Richard comes back. It seems to me the wiser part will be that I should give Prince John no notice that I am in England. As you say, such notice would be of no avail in recovering my lands and title, but it would put the prince upon his guard; and assuredly he and his minions would press forward their measures to obtain possession of the person of the Lady Margaret; while, on the other hand, no harm can come of my maintaining silence."

"I think that you are right, Sir Cuthbert. It were indeed best that your enemies should suppose you either dead or in some dungeon in the Tyrol. What would you then do?"

"I would return to my old home," Cuthbert said. "My lady mother is, I trust, still alive. But I will not appear at her house, but will take refuge in the forest there. Cnut, and the archers with him, were all at one time outlaws living there, and I doubt not that there are many good men and true still to be found in the woods. Others will assuredly join when they learn that Cnut is there, and that they are wanted to strike a blow for my rights. I shall then bide my time. I will keep a strict watch over the castle and over the convent. As the abbess is a friend and relative of Lady Margaret's, I may obtain an interview with her, and warn her of the dangers that await her, and ask if she be willing to fulfil the promise of her father, and King Richard's will, in accepting me as her husband when due time shall arrive, and whether she will be willing that I should take such steps as I may to deliver her from the persecution of Sir Rudolph. If, as I trust, she assents to this, I will keep a watch over the convent as well as the castle, and can then either attack the latter, or carry her off from the former, as the occasion may appear to warrant. There are plenty of snug cottages round the forest, where she can remain in concealment in the care of some good farmer's wife for months, and we shall be close at hand to watch over her. With the aid of the forest men, Sir Walter took the castle of Sir John of Wortham; and although Evesham is a far grander pile than that, yet methinks it could be carried by a sudden assault; and we know more of war now than we did then. Prince John may deny me the right of being the Earl of Evesham; but methinks before many months I can, if I choose, become its master."

"Be not too hasty in that matter," Sir Baldwin said. "You might capture the castle with the aid of your outlaws; but you could scarcely hold it. The prince has, ere now, with the aid of those faithful to him and his foreign mercenaries, captured stronger holds than that of Evesham; and if you turn his favourite out, you would have a storm of hornets around you such as the walls of Evesham could not keep out. It would therefore be worse than useless for you to attempt what would be something like an act of rebellion against Prince John's authority, and would give him what now he has no excuse for, a ground for putting a price upon your head—and cutting it off if he got the opportunity. You might now present yourself boldly at court, and although he might refuse to recognize your title of earl, yet, as a knight and a crusader who has distinguished himself greatly in the Holy Land, he dare not interfere with your person, for this would be resented by the whole of the chivalry of England. Still, I agree with you that your best course is to keep your return a secret. You will then be unwatched and unnoticed,

and your enemies will take their time in carrying their designs into effect."

Two days later Cuthbert, attended by his faithful retainers, left Sir Baldwin's castle, and travelled by easy stages through Wiltshire and the confines of Gloucestershire up to Worcester. He had been supplied by Sir Baldwin with suitable attire for himself and his followers, and now rode as a simple knight, without arms or cognizance, journeying from one part to another. All the crosses and other crusading signs were laid aside, and there was nothing to attract any attention to him upon his passage. Cuthbert had at first thought of going direct to the convent of Worcester, and asking for an interview with Lady Margaret; but he reflected that it might be possible that some of the myrmidons of Sir Rudolph might be keeping a watch over that building, to see that Lady Margaret was not secretly removed to some other place of refuge, and that the appearance of a knight before its doors would excite comment and suspicion. He therefore avoided the town, and journeyed straight to the forest, where he had so often roamed with Cnut and the outlaws.

Here he found that matters had but little changed since he was last there. Many of those who had fought with him in the Holy Land, and who had returned by sea, had again taken to the forest, joined by many new men whom the exactions of Sir Rudolph had already goaded into revolt. Cnut was received with enthusiasm, and when he presented Cuthbert to them as the rightful heir of Evesham and the well-known friend of the foresters, their enthusiasm knew no bounds. They at once accepted him as their lord and master, and promised to obey his orders, and to lay down their lives, if necessary, in his cause, as they knew that it was he who had formerly obtained the pardon of the forest band, and who had fought with them in their attack on Wortham Castle.

To Cuthbert's great delight he heard that his mother was in good health, although she had for some months been grievously fretting over his disappearance and supposed death. Cuthbert hesitated whether he should proceed at once to see her; but he feared that the shock of his appearance might be too much for her, and that her expressions of joy might make the retainers and others aware of his arrival, and the news might in some way reach the ears of those at the castle. He therefore despatched Cnut to see her, and break the news to her cautiously, and to request her to arrange for a time when she would either see Cuthbert at some place at a distance from the house, or

would so arrange that the domestics should be absent and
that he would have an interview with her there unobserved.

Cnut was absent some hours, and on his return told
Cuthbert that he had seen Dame Editha, and that her joy on
hearing of her son's safe arrival had caused her no harm,
but rather the reverse. The news that King Richard had
bestowed upon him the title and lands of Evesham was new
to her, and she was astonished indeed to hear of his
elevation. Having heard much of the character of the
pretending earl, she had great fears for the safety of
Cuthbert, should his residence in the neighbourhood get to
his ears; and although sure of the fidelity of all her retainers,
she feared that in their joy at their young master's return
they might let slip some incautious word which would come
to the ears of some of those at the castle. She therefore
determined to meet him at a distance. She had arranged that
upon the following day she would give out that she intended
to make a pilgrimage to the shrine of St. Dunstan, which lay
at the edge of the forest, to thank him for her recovery from

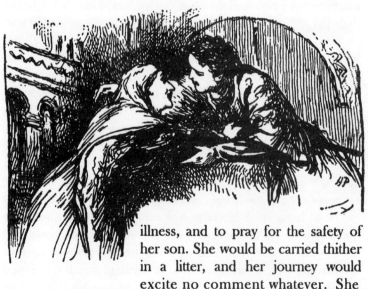

illness, and to pray for the safety of
her son. She would be carried thither
in a litter, and her journey would
excite no comment whatever. She

would take with her four of her most trusted retainers, and would on her arrival at the shrine send them to a distance, in order to pay her devotions undisturbed. Cuthbert was to be near, and the moment he saw them depart, to enter.

This arrangement was carried out, and the joy of Dame Editha at again meeting her son was deep indeed. He had left her a lad of fifteen. He now returned a youth of nearly eighteen, stout and strong beyond his age, and looking far older than he was, from the effect of the hot sun of Syria and of the hardships through which he had gone. That he should win his spurs upon the first opportunity the earl had promised her, and she doubted not that he would soon attain the rank which his father had held. But that he should return to her a belted earl was beyond her wildest thoughts. This, however, was but little in her mind then. It was her son, and not the Earl of Evesham, whom she clasped in her arms.

As the interview must necessarily be a short one, Cuthbert gave her but a slight outline of what had happened since they parted, and the conversation then turned upon the present position, and upon the steps which had best be taken.

"Your peril is, I fear, as great here as when you were fighting the infidels in the Holy Land," she said. "Sir Rudolph has not been here long; but he has proved himself a cruel and ruthless master. He has driven forth many of the old tenants and bestowed their lands upon his own servants and retainers. The forest laws he carries out to the fullest severity, and has hung several men who were caught infringing them. He has laid such heavy burdens on all the tenants that remain that they are fairly ruined, and if he stay here long he will rule over a desert. Did he dream of your presence here, he would carry fire and sword through the forest. It is sad indeed to think that so worthless a knave as this should be a favourite of the ruler of England. But all men say that he is so. Thus were you to attack him, even did

you conquer and kill him, you would have the enmity of
Prince John to contend with; and he spareth none, man or
woman, who stand in his way. It will be a bad day indeed for
England should our good King Richard not return. I will, as
you wish me, write to my good cousin, the Lady Abbess of
St. Anne's, and will ask that you may have an interview with
the Lady Margaret, to hear her wishes and opinions
concerning the future, and will pray her to do all that she
can to aid your suit with the fair young lady, and to keep her
at all events safe from the clutches of the tyrant of
Evesham."

Three days later, a boy employed as a messenger by
Dame Editha brought a note to Cuthbert, saying that she
had heard from the Abbess of St. Anne's, who would be
glad to receive a visit from Cuthbert. The abbess had asked
his mother to accompany him; but this she left for him to
decide. Cuthbert sent back a message in reply, that he
thought it would be dangerous for her to accompany him, as
any spy watching would report her appearance, and
inquiries were sure to be set on foot as to her companion.
He said that he himself would call at the convent on the
following evening after night-fall, and begged her to send
word to the abbess to that effect, in order that he might,
when he presented himself, be admitted at once.

CHAPTER XXI.

THE ATTEMPT ON THE CONVENT.

UPON the following evening Cuthbert proceeded to Worcester. He left his horse some little distance outside the town, and entered on foot. Having no apprehension of an attack, he had left all his pieces of armour behind, and was in the quiet garb of a citizen. Cnut attended him—for that worthy follower considered himself as responsible that no harm of any sort should befall his young master. The consequences of his own imprudence in the Tyrol were ever before his mind, and he determined that from henceforth. there should be no want of care on his part. He accompanied Cuthbert to within a short distance of the convent, and took up his position in the shade of a house. whence he could watch should any one appear to be observing Cuthbert's entrance.

Upon ringing the bell, Cuthbert told the porteress, as had been arranged, that he had called on a message from Dame Editha, and he was immediately ushered into the parlour of the convent, where, a minute or two later, he was joined by the lady abbess. He had when young been frequently to the convent, and had always been kindly received.

"I am indeed glad to see you, Sir Cuthbert," she said, "though I certainly should not have recognized the lad who used to come here with my cousin, in the stalwart young knight I see before me. You are indeed changed and improved. Who would think that my gossip Editha's son would come to be the Earl of Evesham! The Lady Margaret is eager to see you; but I think that you exaggerate the dangers of her residence here. I cannot think that even a minion of Prince John would dare to violate the sanctity of a convent."

"I fear, good mother," Cuthbert said, "that when ambition and greed are in one scale, reverence for the holy church will not weigh much in the other. Had King Richard been killed upon his way home, or so long as nothing was heard of him, Sir Rudolph might have been content to allow matters to remain as they were, until at least Lady Margaret attained an age which would justify him in demanding that the espousal should be carried out. But the news which has now positively been ascertained, that the king is in the hands of the emperor, and the knowledge that sooner or later his freedom will be obtained, will hasten the friends of the usurper to make the most of their advantage. He knows that the king would at once upon his return annul the nomination of Sir Rudolph to the earldom which had previously been bestowed upon me. But he may well think that if before that time he can secure in marriage the person of the late earl's daughter, no small share of the domains may be allotted to him as her dowry, even if he be obliged to lay by his borrowed honours. You will, unless I am greatly mistaken, hear from him before long."

The abbess looked grave.

"There is much in what you say, Sir Cuthbert; and indeed a certain confirmation is given to it by the fact that only yesterday I received a letter from Sir Rudolph, urging that now the Lady Margaret is past the age of fifteen, and may therefore be considered marriageable, the will of the prince should be carried into effect, and that she should for the present be committed to the charge of the Lady Clara Boulger, who is the wife of a friend and associate of Sir Rudolph. He says that he should not wish to press the marriage until she attains the age of sixteen, but that it were well that his future wife should become accustomed to the outside world, so as to take her place as Castellan of Evesham with a dignity befitting the position. I wrote at once to him saying, that in another year it would, in my poor judgment, be quite time to think about such worldly matters; that at the present the Lady Margaret was receiving an education suitable to her rank; that she was happy here; and that unless constrained by force—of which, I said, I could not suppose that any possibility existed—I should not surrender the Lady Margaret into any hands whatsoever, unless, indeed, I received the commands of her lawful guardian, King Richard."

"You said well, holy mother," Sir Cuthbert said. "But you see the hawks scent the danger from afar, and are moving uneasily already. Whether they consider it so pressing that they will dare to profane the convent, I know not. But I am sure that should they do so, they will not hesitate a moment at the thought of the anger of the church. Prince John has already shown that he is ready, if need be, to oppose the authority of the holy father, and he may well, therefore, despise any local wrath that might be excited by an action which he can himself disavow, and for which, even at the worst, he need only inflict some nominal punishment upon his vassal. Bethink thee, lady, whether it would not be safer to send the Lady Margaret to the care of some person, where she may be concealed from the search of Sir Rudolph."

"I would gladly do so," the abbess said, "did I know of such a person or such a place. But it is difficult indeed for a young lady of rank to be concealed from such sharp searchers as Sir Rudolph would be certain to place upon her track. Your proposal that she should take refuge in the house of some small franklin near the forest, I cannot agree to. In the first place, it would demean her to be so placed; and in the second, we could never be sure that the report of her residence there might not reach the ears of Sir Rudolph. As a last resource, of course such a step would be justifiable, but not until at least overt outrages have been attempted. Now I will call Lady Margaret in."

The young girl entered with an air of frank gladness, but was startled at the alteration which had taken place in her former playfellow, and paused and looked at the abbess, as

if inquiring whether this could be really the Cuthbert she had known. Lady Margaret was fifteen in years; but she looked much younger. The quiet seclusion in which she had lived in the convent had kept her from approaching that maturity which as an earl's daughter, brought up in the stir and bustle of a castle, she would doubtless have attained.

"This is indeed Sir Cuthbert," the abbess said, "your old playfellow, and the husband destined for you by your father and by the will of the king."

Struck with a new timidity, the girl advanced, and, according to the custom of the times, held up her cheek to be kissed. Cuthbert was almost as timid as herself.

"I feel, Lady Margaret," he said, "a deep sense of my own unworthiness of the kindness and honour which the dear lord your father bestowed upon me; and were it not that many dangers threaten, and that it were difficult under the circumstances to find one more worthy of you, I would gladly resign you into the hands of such a one were it for your happiness. But believe me that the recollection of your face has animated me in many of the scenes of danger in which I have been placed; and although even in fancy my thought scarcely ventured to rise so high, yet I felt as a true knight might feel for the lady of his love."

"I always liked you, Sir Cuthbert," the girl said frankly, "better than any one else next to my father, and gladly submit myself to his will. My own inclinations indeed, so far as is maidenly, go with his. These are troubled times," she said anxiously, "and our holy mother tells me that you fear some danger is overhanging me."

"I trust that the danger may not be imminent," Cuthbert answered. "But knowing the unscrupulous nature of the false Earl of Evesham, I fear that the news that King Richard is found will bestir him to early action. But you can rely, dear lady, on a careful watch being kept over you night and day; and should any attempt be made to carry you away, or to put force upon you, be assured that assistance will be at hand. Even should any attempt succeed, do not lose heart, for rescue will certainly be attempted; and I must be dead, and my faithful followers crushed, before you can become the bride of Sir Rudolph."

Then turning to other subjects, he talked to her of the life he had led since he last saw her. He told her of the last moments of her father, and of the gallant deeds he had done in the Holy Land.

After waiting for two hours, the abbess judged that the time for separation had arrived; and Cuthbert, taking a respectful adieu of his young mistress, and receiving the benediction of the abbess, departed.

He found Cnut on guard at the point where he had left him.

"Have you seen aught to give rise to suspicion" Cuthbert asked.

"Yes," Cnut said, "the place is undoubtedly watched. Just after you had entered, a man came from that house yonder and went up to the gate, as if he would fain learn by staring at its iron adornments the nature of him who had passed in. Then he reentered his house, and if I mistake not is still on the watch at that casement. If we stand here for a minute or two, perchance he may come out to see what delays you in this dark corner, in which case I may well give him a clout with my axe which will settle his prying."

"Better not," Cuthbert said. "We can retire round this corner and so avoid his observation; and were his body found slain here, suspicion would be at once excited in the mind of his employer. At present he can have no ground for any report which may make the knight uneasy, for he can but know that a gentleman has entered, and remained for two hours at the convent, and he will in no way connect my visit with the Lady Margaret."

They had just turned the corner which Cuthbert indicated, when a man came up rapidly behind them and almost brushed them as he passed, half-turning round and trying to gaze into their faces. Cnut at once assumed the aspect of an intoxicated person, and stretching forth his foot with a dexterous shove pushed the stranger into the gutter. The latter rose with a fierce cry of anger; but Cnut with a blow of his heavy fist again stretched him on the ground, this time to remain quiet until they had walked on and passed out of sight.

"A meddling fool," Cnut grumbled. "He will not, methinks, have much to report to Sir Rudolph this time. Had I thought that he had seen your face, I would have cleft his skull with no more hesitation than I send an arrow into the brain of a stag in the forest."

As they journeyed along, Cuthbert informed Cnut of what the abbess had told him; and the latter agreed that a watch must be placed on the convent, and that a force must be kept as near as possible at hand so as to defeat any attempt which might be made.

The next day one of the forest men who had been a peaceable citizen, but who had been charged with using false weights and had been condemned to lose his ears, repaired to Worcester. His person was unknown there, as he had before lived at Gloucester. He hired a house in the square in which the convent was situated, giving out that he desired to open a house of business for the sale of silks, and for articles from the Low Countries. As he paid down earnest-money for the rent, no suspicion whatever was excited. He at once took up his abode there, having with him two stout serving-men, and a 'prentice boy; and from that time two sets of watchers observed without ceasing what passed at the Convent of St. Anne.

At a distance of half a mile from the road leading between Worcester and Evesham, stood a grange, which had for some time been disused, the ground belonging to it having been sequestrated and given to the lord of an adjoining estate, who did not care to have the grange occupied. In this, ten men, headed by Cnut, took up their residence, blocking up the window of the hall with hangings, so that the light of the fire kindled within would not be observed.

Two months passed on without any incident of importance. The feeling between the outlaws in the forest and the retainers of the false Earl of Evesham was becoming much embittered. Several times the foresters of the latter, attempting pursuit of men charged with breaking the game laws, were roughly handled. These on making their report were sent back again, supported by a force of footmen; but these, too, were driven back, and the authority of Sir Rudolph was openly defied.

Gradually it came to his ears that the outlaws were commanded by a man who had been their leader in times gone by, but who had been pardoned, and had, with a large number of his band, taken service in the army of the crusaders; also, that there was present a stranger, whose manner and the deference paid to him by Cnut proclaimed him to be of gentle blood. This news awakened grave uneasiness on the part of Sir Rudolph. The knight caused inquiries to be made, and ascertained that Cnut had been especially attached to the young Cuthbert, and that he had fought under the Earl of Evesham's banner. It seemed possible then that with him had returned the claimant for the earldom; and in that case Sir Rudolph felt that danger menaced him, for the bravery of the Earl of Evesham's adopted son had been widely spoken of by those who had returned from the Holy Land.

Sir Rudolph was a man of forty, tall and dark, with Norman features. He held the Saxons in utter contempt, and treated them as beings solely created to till the land for the benefit of their Norman lords. He was brave and fearless, and altogether free from the superstition of the times. Even the threats of the pope, which although Prince John defied them yet terrified him at heart, were derided by his follower, who feared no one thing in the world, save, perhaps, the return of King Richard from captivity.

No sooner had the suspicion that his rival was in the neighbourhood possessed him, than he determined that one of two things must be carried out: either Sir Cuthbert must be killed, or the Lady Margaret must be carried off and

forced to accept him as her husband. First he endeavoured
to force Sir Cuthbert to declare himself, and to trust to his
own arm to put an end to his rival. To that end he caused a
proclamation to be written, and to be affixed to the door of
the village church at the fair of Evesham.

Cnut and several of his followers were there, all quietly
dressed as yeomen. Seeing a crowd round the door of the
church, he pressed forward. Being himself unable to read
writing, he asked one of the burgesses what was written upon
the paper which caused such excitement.

"It is," the burgess said, "in the nature of a cartel or
challenge from our present lord, Sir Rudolf. He says that it
having come to his ears that a Saxon serf, calling himself Sir
Cuthbert, Earl of Evesham, is lurking in the woods and
consorting with outlaws and robbers, he challenges him to

appear, saying that he will himself, grievously although he
would demean himself by so doing, yet condescend to meet
him in the lists with sword and battle-axe, and to prove upon
his body the falseness of his averments. Men marvel much,"
the burgess continued, "at this condescension on the earl's
part. We have heard indeed that King Richard, before he
sailed for England, did, at the death of the late good earl,
bestow his rank and the domains of Evesham upon Sir
Cuthbert, the son of the Dame Editha. Whether it be true

or not, we cannot say; but it seems strange that such honour should have been bestowed upon one so young. In birth indeed he might aspire to the rank, since his father, Sir Walter, was a brave knight, and the mother, Dame Editha, was of good Saxon blood, and descended from those who held Evesham before the arrival of the Normans."

Cnut's first impulse was to stride forward and to tear down the proclamation. But the remembrance of his solemn determination not in future to act rashly, came across him, and he decided to take no steps until he had reported the facts to his master, and taken his counsel thereon.

Cuthbert received the news with much indignation.

"There is nought that I should like better," he said, "than to try my strength against that of this false traitor. But although I have proved my arm against the Saracens, I think not that it is yet strong enough to cope against a man who, whatsoever be his faults, is said to be a valiant knight. But that would not deter me from attempting the task. It is craftily done on the part of Sir Rudolph. He reckons that if I appear he will kill me; that if I do not appear, I shall be branded as a coward, and my claims brought into disrepute. It may be, too, that it is a mere ruse to discover if I be in the neighbourhood. Some rumours thereof may have reached him, and he has taken this course to determine upon their truth. He has gone too far, and honest men will see in the cartel itself a sign that he misdoubts him that my claims are just; for were I, as he says, a Saxon serf, be sure that he would not condescend to meet me in the lists as he proposes. I trust that the time will come when I may do so. But, at present, I will submit to his insult rather than imperil the success of our plans, and, what is of far greater importance, the safety and happiness of the Lady Margaret, who, did aught befall me, would assuredly fall into his hands."

After some thought, however, Cuthbert drew up an

answer to the knight's proclamation. He did not in this speak in his own name, but wrote as if the document were the work of Cnut. It was worded as follows: "I, Cnut, a free Saxon and a leader of bowmen under King Richard in the Holy Land, do hereby pronounce and declare the statements of Sir Rudolph, miscalled the Earl of Evesham, to be false and calumnious. The earldom was, as Rudolph well knows, and as can be proved by many nobles and gentlemen of repute who were present with King Richard, granted to Sir Cuthbert, King Richard's true and faithful follower. When the time shall come, Sir Cuthbert will doubtless be ready to prove his rights. But at present right has no force in England, and until the coming of our good King Richard must remain in abeyance. Until then, I support the title of Sir Cuthbert, and do hereby declare Sir Rudolph a false and perjured knight; and warn him that if he falls into my hands it will fare but badly with him, as I know it will fare but badly with me should I come into his."

At nightfall the cartel of Sir Rudolph was torn down from the church and that of Cnut affixed in its place. The reading thereof caused great astonishment in Evesham, and the rage of Sir Rudolph, when the news came to his ears, was very great. Cuthbert was sure that this affair would quicken the intentions of Sir Rudolph with regard to the Lady Margaret, and he received confirmation of this in a letter which the abbess sent him, saying that she had received another missive from Sir Rudolph, authoritatively demanding in the king's name the instant surrender of Lady Margaret to him. That night forty archers stole, one by one quietly into Worcester, entering the town before the gates were shut, and so mingling with the citizens that they were unobserved. When it was quite dark they quietly took their way, one by one, to the square in which stood the convent, and were admitted into the shop of Master Nicholas, the silk merce.

The house was a large one, with its floors overhanging each the one beneath it, as was the custom of the time, and with large casements running the whole width of the house.

The mercer had laid by a goodly store of provisions, and for three days the troop, large as it was, was accommodated there. Cuthbert himself was with them, Cnut remaining at the grange with the ten men originally sent there.

On the third day Sir Rudolph, with a number of knights and men-at-arms, arrived in the town, giving out that he was passing northwards, but he would abide that night at the hostelry. A great many of his men-at-arms did, as those on the watch observed, enter one by one into the town. The people of Worcester were somewhat surprised at this large accompaniment of the earl, but thought no harm. The Abbess of St. Anne's, however, was greatly terrified, as she feared that some evil design might be intended against her. She was, however, reassured in the evening by a message brought by a boy, to the effect that succour would be near, whatsoever happened.

At midnight a sudden uproar was heard in the streets of Worcester.

A party of men fell upon the burgesses guarding the gate of the town, disarmed them, and took possession of it. At the same time those who had put up at the hostelry with Sir Rudolph suddenly mounted their horses, and with a great clatter rode down the streets to the Convent of St. Anne. Numbers of men on foot also joined, and some sixty in all suddenly appeared before the great gate of the convent. With a thundering noise they knocked at the door, and upon the grating being opened Sir Rudolph himself told the porteress who looked through it, that she was to go at once to the abbess and order her to surrender the body of the Lady Margaret to him, in accordance with the order of Prince John; adding, that if within the space of five minutes the order was not complied with, he would burst in the gates of the convent and take her for himself. In another minute a casement opened above, and the abbess herself appeared.

"Rash man," she said to Sir Rudolph, "I warn you against

committing the sin of sacrilege. Neither the orders of Prince John nor of any other potentate can over-ride the rights of the holy church; and should you venture to lay the hand of force upon this convent you will be placed under the anathema of the church, and its spiritual terrors will be directed against you."

"I am prepared to risk that, holy mother," Sir Rudolph said, with a laugh. "So long as I am obeying the orders of my prince, I care nought for those of any foreign potentate, be he pope or be he emperor. Three minutes of the time I gave you have elapsed, and unless within two more the Lady Margaret appears at the gate I will batter it down; and you may think yourself lucky if I do not order my men to set light to it and to smoke you out of your hole."

The abbess closed the window, and as she did so the long row of casements in the house of Master Nicholas were opened from top to bottom, and a volley of sixty clothyard arrows was poured into the group closely standing round the gate. Many fell, killed outright, and shouts of rage and pain were heard arising.

Furious at this unexpected attack, Sir Rudolph turned, and commanded those with him to attack the house whence this volley of missiles had come. But even while he spoke another flight of arrows, even more deadly than the last, was poured forth. One of the knights standing by the side of Sir Rudolph fell, shot through the brain. Very many of the common men, undefended by harness, fell shot through and through; and an arrow piercing the joint of the armour of Sir Rudolph, wounded him in the shoulder. In vain the knight stormed and raged and ordered his men to advance. The suddenness of the attack seemed to his superstitious followers a direct answer from heaven to the words of the abbess. Their number was already seriously lessened, and those who were in case to do so at once took flight and scattered through the city, making for the gate, which had already been seized by Sir Rudolph's men.

Finding himself alone with only a few of his knights and principal men-at-arms remaining, while the storm of arrows continued unabated, Sir Rudolph was forced to order his men to retreat, with many fierce threats of the vengeance which he would hereafter take.

CHAPTER XXII.

A DASTARDLY STRATAGEM.

THE return of Sir Rudolph's party to Evesham was not unmarked by incident, for as they passed along the road, from an ambush in a wood other archers, whose numbers they could not discover, shot hard upon them, and many fell here who had

escaped from the square at Worcester. When the list was called upon the arrival at the castle, it was found that no less than thirty of those who had set out were missing, while many others were grievously wounded.

The noise of the tumult in the square of the convent aroused the whole town of Worcester. Alarm bells were rung; and the burgesses, hastily arming themselves, poured into the streets. Directed by the sound, they made their way to the square, and were astonished at finding it entirely deserted, save for some twenty men, lying dead or dying in front of the gate of the convent, pierced with long arrows. They speedily found that Sir Rudolph and his troop had departed; and further inquiry revealed the fact that the burgher guard at one of the gates had been overpowered and were prisoners in the watchroom. These could only say that they were suddenly seized, all being asleep save the one absolutely on guard. They knew nothing more than that a few minutes later there was a great clatter of horsemen and men on foot leaving the city. Unable to find any solution to this singular circumstance, but satisfied that Sir Rudolph had departed, and that no more disturbance was likely to arise that night, the burgesses again betook themselves to their beds, having closed the gates and placed a strong guard over them, determining next morning to sift the affair to the bottom.

In the morning the leading burgesses met in council, and finding, none who could give them any information, the mayor and two of the councillors repaired to the convent, where they asked for an interview with the lady abbess. Mightily indignant were they at hearing that Sir Rudolph had attempted to break into the convent, and to carry off a boarder residing there. But the abbess herself could give them no further news. She said that after she retired from the window, she heard great shouts and cries, and that almost immediately afterwards the whole of the party in front hastily retired.

That Sir Rudolph had been attacked by a party of archers was evident; but whence they had shot, or how they had come upon the spot at the time, or whither they had gone, were mysteries that could not be solved. In the search which the authorities made, however, it was discovered that the house of the draper, Master Nicholas, was closed. Finding that summonses to open were unanswered, the door was broken in, and the premises were found in confusion. No goods of any kind were discovered there, but many bales filled with dried leaves, bark of trees, and other worthless matters. Such goods as had been displayed in the window had clearly been carried away. Searching the house, they found signs that a considerable number of men had been concealed there, and although not knowing whence the body of archers could have come, they concluded that those who defeated the attempt of Sir Rudolph must have been hidden in the draper's house. The singularity of this incident gave rise to great excitement; but the indignation against Sir Rudolph was in no way lessened by the fact that his attempt had been defeated, not by the townsmen themselves, but by some unknown force.

After much consultation on the part of the council, it was resolved that a deputation, consisting of the mayor and the five senior councillors, should resort to London, and there demand from the prince redress for the injury put upon their town by Sir Rudolph. These worthy merchants betook themselves to London by easy stages, and upon their arrival there were kept for some days before they could obtain an interview with King John. When they appeared before him and commenced telling their story, the prince fell into sudden rage.

"I have heard of this matter before," he said, "and am mightily angry with the people of Worcester, inasmuch as they have dared to interfere to prevent the carrying out of my commands. The Earl of Evesham has written to me, that thinking to scare the abbess of St. Anne's into a compliance with the commands which I had laid upon her, and to secure the delivery of a contumacious ward of the crown, he had pretended to use force, having, however, no idea of carrying his threats into effect. When, as he doubted not, the abbess was on the point of yielding up the ward, the good knight was suddenly set upon by the rascals of the town, who slew some of his companions and followers, and did grievously ill-treat the remainder. This," said the prince, "you now pretend was done by a party of men of whose presence in the town you had no cognizance. Your good sense must be small, if you think that I should believe such a tale as this. It is your rascaldom at Worcester which interfered to prevent my will being carried out, and I have a goodly mind to order the troop of Sir Charles Everest, which is now marching towards Evesham, to sack the town, as a punishment for its rebellion. As, however, I am willing to believe that you and the better class of burgesses were in ignorance of the doings of the rougher kind, I will extend

mercy towards the city, and will merely inflict a fine of 3000 golden marks upon it."

The mayor attempted humbly to explain and to entreat; but the prince was seized with a sudden passion, and threatened if he said more he would at once cast him and his fellows into durance. Therefore, sadly crestfallen at the result of their mission, the mayor and councillors returned to Worcester, where their report caused great consternation. This was heightened by the fact that upon the following day Sir Charles Everest, with 500 mercenaries of the prince, together with Sir Rudolph and his following, and several other barons favourable to the cause of the prince, were heard to be approaching the town.

Worcester was capable of making a stout defence, but seeing that no help was likely to be forthcoming, and fearing the utter ruin of the town should it be taken by storm, the council, after sitting many hours in deliberation, determined to raise the money required to pay the fine inflicted by the prince. The bolder sort were greatly averse to this decision, especially as a letter had been received, signed "Cuthbert, Earl of Evesham," offering, should the townspeople decide to resist the unjust demands of Prince John, to enter the town with 150 archers to take part in its defence. With this force, as the more ardent spirits urged, the defeat of any attempt to carry it by storm would be assured. But the graver men argued that even if defeated for the first time, further attempts would be made, and as it was likely that King Richard would not return for a long time, and that Prince John might become Sovereign of England, sooner or later the town must be taken, and, in any case, its trade would for a long time be destroyed, and great suffering inflicted upon all; therefore, that it was better to pay the fine now than to risk all these evils, and perhaps the infliction of a heavier impost upon them.

The abbess was kept informed by friends in the council of the course of the proceedings. She had in the meantime had another interview with Sir Cuthbert, and had determined, seeing that Prince John openly supported the doings of his minion, it would be better to remove the Lady Margaret to some other place, as no one could say how the affair might terminate; and with 500 mercenaries at his back, Sir Rudolph would be completely master of the city that he would be able in broad daylight, did he choose, to force the gates of the convent and carry off the king's ward.

Accordingly, two days before the arrival of the force before the walls of Worcester, Lady Margaret left the convent by a postern gate in the rear, late in the evening.

She was attended by two of the sisters, both of whom, as well as herself, were dressed as countrywomen. Mules were in readiness outside the city gates, and here Sir Cuthbert, with an escort of archers, was ready to attend them. They travelled all night, and arrived in the morning at a small convent situated five miles from the city of Hereford. The abbess here was a cousin of the Superior of St. Anne's, and had already consented to receive Lady Margaret. Leaving her at the door, and promising that, as far as possible, he would keep watch over her, and that even in the worst she need never despair, Sir Cuthbert left her and returned to the forest.

The band there assembled varied considerably in numbers, for provisions could not be found continually for a large body of men. The forest was indeed very extensive, and the number of deer therein large. Still, for the feeding of 150 men many animals are required and other food. The franklins in the neighbourhood were all hostile to Sir Rudolph, whom they regarded as a cruel tyrant, and did their utmost in the way of supplies for those in the forest. Their resources, however, were limited, and it was found necessary to scatter the force, and for a number of them to take up their residence in places a short distance away, forty only remaining permanently on guard.

Sir Rudolph and his friends entered Worcester, and there received with great hauteur the apologies of the mayor and council, and the assurance that the townspeople were in nowise concerned in the attack made upon him. To this he pretended disbelief. The fine demanded was paid, the principal portion in gold, the rest in bills signed by the leading merchants of the place; for after every effort it had been found impossible to collect such a sum within the city.

The day after he arrived, he again renewed his demand to the abbess for the surrender of the Lady Margaret; this time, however, coming to her attended only by two squires, and by pursuivant bearing the king's order for the delivery of the damsel. The abbess met him at the gate, and informed him that the Lady Margaret was no longer in her charge.

" Finding," she said, in a fearless tone, "that the holy wall of this convent were insufficient to restrain lawless men, and fearing that these might be tempted to acts of sacrilege, which might bring down upon them the wrath of the church and the destruction of their souls, I have sent her away."

"Whither has she gone?" Sir Rudolph demanded, half mad with passion.

"That I decline to say," the lady abbess replied. "She is in good hands; and when King Richard returns, his ward shall be delivered to him at once."

"Will you take oath upon the Bible that she is not within these walls?" Sir Rudolph exclaimed.

"My word is sufficient," the lady abbess replied calmly. "But should it be necessary, I should be ready to swear upon the relics that she is not here."

A few hours later Sir Rudolph, attended by his own party and by 100 of Sir Charles Everest's mercenaries, returned to his castle.

Three days afterwards, as Cuthbert was sitting at a rude but hearty meal in the forest, surrounded by Cnut and his followers, a hind entered breathless. Cuthbert at once recognized him as one of the servitors of his mother.

"What is it?" he exclaimed, leaping to his feet.

"Terrible news, Master Cuthbert, terrible news!" exclaimed the man. "The wicked earl came down this morning, with fifty of his men, set fire to the house, and all its buildings and stacks, and has carried off the lady, your mother, a prisoner to the castle, on a charge, as he said, of harbouring traitors."

A cry of fury broke from Cnut and his men.

"The false traitor shall bitterly regret this outrage," Cuthbert exclaimed.

He had in the first excitement seized his arms, and his followers snatched up their bows, as if for instant warfare. A few moments' reflection, however, showed to Cuthbert the impossibility of his attacking a fortress like Evesham, garrisoned by a strong body of well-armed men, with only the archers of the forest, without implements necessary for such an assault.

"Send at once, Cnut," he said, "and call in all the band. We cannot take the castle; but we will carry fire and sword round its walls. We will cut off all communication from within or from without. If attacked by large forces, we will retire upon the wood, returning to our posts without the walls as soon as the force is withdrawn. These heavily armed men can move but slowly; while we can run at full speed. There cannot be more than some twenty horsemen in the castle; and methinks with our arrows and pikes we can drive these back if they attempt to fall upon us."

Cnut at once sent off swift-footed messengers to carry out Cuthbert's orders, and on the following day the whole of the band were again assembled in the woods. Just as Cuthbert was setting them in motion, a distant blast of a horn was heard.

"It is," Cuthbert exclaimed, "the note calling for a parley. Do you, Cnut, go forward, and see what is demanded. It is probably a messenger from Sir Rudolph."

After half-an-hour's absence, Cnut returned, bringing with him a pursuivant or herald. The latter advanced at once towards Cuthbert, who, now in his full knightly armour, was evidently the leader of the party.

"I bear to you, Sir Cuthbert, falsely calling yourself Earl of Evesham, a message from Sir Rudolph. He bids me tell you that the traitress, Dame Editha, your mother, is in his hands, and that she has been found guilty of aiding and abetting you in your war against Prince John, the Regent of this kingdom. For that offence she has been condemned to die."

Here he was interrupted by a cry of rage which broke from the assembled foresters. Continuing unmoved, he

said,—

"Sir Rudolph, being unwilling to take the life of a woman, however justly forfeited by the law, commands me to say, that if you will deliver yourself up to him by to-morrow at twelve, the Dame Editha shall be allowed to go free. But that if by the time the dial points to noon you have not delivered yourself up, he will hang her over the battlements of the castle."

Cuthbert was very pale, and he waved his hand to restrain the fury which animated the outlaws.

"This man," he said to them, "is a herald, and, as such, is protected by all the laws of chivalry. Whatsoever his message, it is none of his. He is merely the mouthpiece of him who sent him." Then, turning to the herald, he said, "Tell the false knight, your master, on my part, that he is a foul ruffian, perjured to all the vows of knighthood; that this act of visiting upon a woman the enmity he bears her son, will bring upon him the execration of all men; and that the offer which he makes me is as foul and villainous as himself. Nevertheless, knowing his character, and believing that he is capable of keeping his word, tell him that by to-morrow at noon I will be there; that the lady, my mother, is to leave the castle gates as I enter them; and that though by his foul device he may encompass my death, yet that the curse of every good man will light upon him, that he will be shunned as the dog he is, and that assuredly heaven will not suffer that deeds so foul should bring with them the prize he seeks to gain."

The herald bowed, and, escorted by two archers to the edge of the forest, returned to Evesham Castle.

After his departure, an animated council took place. Cnut and the outlaws, burning with indignation, were ready to attempt anything. They would, had Cuthbert given the word, have attacked the castle that very night. But Cuthbert pointed out the absolute impossibility of their carrying so strong a place by such an assault, unprovided with engines for battering down the gates. He said that surprise would be impossible, as the knight would be sure to take every precaution against it; and that in the event of such an attack being attempted, he would possibly carry his threat into execution, and murder Dame Editha before their eyes. Cnut was like a madman, so transported with fury was he; and the archers were also beside themselves. Cuthbert alone retained his calmness. Retiring apart from the others, he paced slowly backwards and forwards among the trees, deliberating upon the best course to be pursued. The archers gathered round the fire and passed the night in long and angry talk, each man agreeing that in the event of their beloved leader being sacrificed by Sir Rudolph, they would one and all give their lives to avenge him by slaying the oppressor whensoever he ventured beyond the castle gates.

After a time, Cuthbert called Cnut to him, and the two talked long and earnestly. Cnut returned to his comrades with a face less despairing than that he had before worn, and sent off at once a messenger with all speed to a franklin near the forest to borrow a stout rope some fifty feet in length, and without telling his comrades what the plans of Sir Cuthbert were, bade them cheer up, for that desperate as the position was, all hope was not yet lost.

"Sir Cuthbert," he said, "has been in grievous straits before now, and has gone through them. Sir Rudolph does not know the nature of the man with whom he has to deal, and we may trick him yet."

At eleven o'clock the next day, from the walls of Evesham Castle a body of archers 150 strong were seen advancing in solid array.

"Think you, Sir Rudolph," one of his friends, Sir Hubert of Gloucester, said to him, "that these varlets think of attacking the castle?"

"They might as well think of scaling heaven," Sir Rudolph said. "Evesham could resist a month's siege by a force well equipped for the purpose; and were it not that good men are wanted for the king's service, and that these villains shoot straight and hard, I would open the gates of the castle and launch our force against them. We are two to one as strong as they, and our knights and mounted men-at-arms could alone scatter that rabble."

Conspicuous upon the battlements a gallows had been erected.

The archers stopped at a distance of a few hundred yards from the castle, and Sir Cuthbert advanced alone to the edge of the moat. "Sir Rudolph of Eresby, false knight and perjured gentleman," he shouted in a loud voice, "I, Sir Cuthbert of Evesham, do denounce you as foresworn and dishonoured, and do challenge you to meet me here before the castle in sight of your men and mine, and decide our quarrel as heaven may judge with sword and battle-axe."

Sir Rudolph leant over the battlements, and said,—

"It is too late, varlet. I condescended to challenge you before, and you refused. You cannot now claim what you then feared to accept. The sun on the dial approaches noon, and unless you surrender yourself before it reaches the mark, I will keep my word, and the traitress, your mother, shall swing from that beam."

Making a sign to two men-at-arms, these brought forward Dame Editha and so placed her on the battlements that she could be seen from below. Dame Editha was still a very fair woman, although nigh forty years had rolled over her head. No sign of fear appeared upon her face, and in a firm voice she cried to her son,—

"Cuthbert, I beg—nay, I order you to retire. If this unknightly lord venture to carry out his foul threats against me, let him do so. England will ring with the dastardly deed, and he will never dare show his face again where Englishmen congregate. Let him do his worst. I am prepared to die."

A murmur rose from the knights and men-at-arms standing round Sir Rudolph.

Several of his companions had from the first, wild and reckless as they were, protested against Sir Rudolph's course, and it was only upon his solemn assurance that he intended but to frighten Sir Cuthbert into surrender, and had no intention of carrying his threats against the lady into effect, that they had consented to take part in the transaction. Even now, at the fearless words of the Saxon lady several of them hesitated, and Sir Hubert of Gloucester stepped forward to Sir Rudolph.

"Sir knight," he said, "you know that I am your true comrade and the faithful servant of Prince John. Yet in faith would I not that my name should be mixed up in so foul a deed. I repent me that I have for a moment consented to it. But the shame shall not hang upon the escutcheon of Hubert of Gloucester that he stood still when such foul means were tried. I pray you, by our long friendship, and for the sake of your own honour as a knight, to desist from this endeavour. If this lady be guilty, as she well may be, of aiding her son in his assault upon the soldiers of Prince John, then let her be tried, and doubtless the court will confiscate her estates. But let her son be told that her life is in no danger, and that he is free to go, being assured that harm will not come to her."

"And if I refuse to consent to allow my enemy, who is now almost within my hand, to escape," Sir Rudolph said, "what then?"

"Then," said the knight, "I and my following will at once leave your walls, and will clear ourselves to the brave young knight yonder of all hand in this foul business."

A murmur of agreement from several of those standing round showed that their sentiments were in accordance with those of Sir Hubert.

"I refuse," said Rudolph passionately. "Go, if you will. I am master of my actions, and of this castle."

Without a word, Sir Hubert and two others of the knights present turned, and briefly ordering their men-at-arms to follow them, descended the staircase to the courtyard below. Their horses were brought out, the men fell into rank, and the gates of the castle were thrown open.

"Stand to arms!" Sir Cuthbert shouted to the archers. "They are going to attempt a sortie." And hastily he retired to the main body of his men.

CHAPTER XXIII.

THE FALSE AND PERJURED KNIGHT.

AS the band of knights and their retainers issued from the gate, a trumpeter blew a parley, and the three knights advanced alone towards the group of archers.

"Sir Cuthbert de Lance," Sir Hubert said, "in the name of myself and my two friends here we ask your pardon for having so far taken part in this foul action. We did so believing only that Sir Rudolph intended the capture of your lady mother as a threat. Now that we see he was in earnest, we wash our hands of the business; and could we in any way atone for our conduct in having joined him, we would gladly do so, consistently only with our allegiance to the Prince Regent."

Cuthbert bowed courteously.

"Thanks for your words, Sir Hubert. I had always heard yourself and the knights here spoken of as brave and gallant gentlemen, whose sole fault was that they chose to take part with a rebel prince, rather than with the King of England. I rejoice that you have cleared your name of so foul a blot as this would have placed upon it, and I acknowledge that your conduct now is knightly and courteous. But I can no more parley. The sun is within a few minutes of twelve, and I must surrender, to meet such fate as may befall me."

So saying, with a bow he left them, and again advanced to the castle gate.

"Sir Rudolph," he shouted, "the hour is at hand. I call upon you to deliver, outside the gate, the lady, my mother. Whether she wills it or not, I call upon you to place her beyond the gate, and I give you my knightly word that as she leaves it I enter it."

Dame Editha would then have attempted resistance; but she saw that it would be useless. With a pale face she descended the steps, accompanied by the men-at-arms. She knew that any entreaty to Sir Rudolph would be vain, and with the courage of her race she mentally vowed to devote the rest of her life to vengeance for her son:

As the gate opened and she was thrust forth, for a moment she found herself in the arms of her son.

"Courage, mother!" he whispered; "all may yet be well."

Cnut was waiting a few paces behind, and offering his hand to Dame Editha, he led her to the group of archers, while Cuthbert, alone, crossed the drawbridge, and entered the portal, the heavy portcullis falling after him.

Cnut immediately ordering four of his men to escort Dame Editha to the wood with all speed, advanced with his men towards the walls. All had strung their bows and placed their arrows on the ground in front of them in readiness for instant use. Cnut himself, with two others carrying the rope, advanced to the edge of the moat. None observed their doings, for all within the castle were intent upon the proceedings there.

In the courtyard Sir Rudolph had taken his post, with the captain of the mercenaries beside him, and the men-at-arms drawn up in order. He smiled sardonically as Cuthbert entered.

"So, at last," he said, "this farce is drawing to an end. You are in my power, and for the means which I have taken to capture you, I will account to the prince. You are a traitor to him; you have attacked and slaughtered many of my friends; you are an outlaw defying the law; and for each of these offences your head is forfeited."

"I deny," Cuthbert said standing before him, "your right to be my judge. By my peers only can I be tried. As a knight of England and as rightful lord of this castle, I demand to be brought before a jury of my equals."

"I care nothing for rights or for juries," said Sir Rudolph. "I have the royal order for your execution, and that order I shall put into effect, although all the knights and barons in England objected."

Cuthbert looked round to observe the exact position in which he was standing. He knew, of course, every foot of the castle, and saw that but a short distance behind a single row of armed men was the staircase leading to the battlements.

"False and perjured knight," he said, taking a step forward, "I may die; but I would rather a thousand deaths than such a life as yours will be when this deed is known in England. But I am not yet dead. For myself, I could pardon you; but for the outrage to my mother—"and with a sudden movement he struck Sir Rudolph in the face with all his strength, with his mailed hand.

With the blood gushing from his nostrils, the knight fell backwards, and Sir Cuthbert, with a bound, before the assembly could recover from their astonishment at the deed, burst through the line of men-at-arms, and sprang up the narrow staircase. A score of men-at-arms started in pursuit; but Sir Cuthbert gained the battlements first, and without a moment's hesitation sprang upon them and plunged forward, falling into the moat fifty feet below. Here he would have perished miserably, for in his heavy armour he was of course unable to swim a stroke, and his weight took him at once into the mud of the moat. At its margin, however, Cnut stood awaiting him, with one end of the rope in his hand. In an instant he plunged in, and diving to the bottom, grasped Cuthbert by the body, and twisted the rope round him. The two archers on the bank at once hauled upon it, and in a minute Sir Cuthbert was dragged to the bank.

By this time a crowd of men-at-arms appeared upon the battlements. But as they did so the archers opened a storm of arrows upon them, and quickly compelled them to find shelter. Carried by Cnut and the men with him—for he was insensible—Sir Cuthbert was quickly conveyed to the centre of the outlaws, and these at once in a compact body began their retreat to the wood. Cuthbert quickly recovered consciousness, and was soon able to walk. As he did so, the gates of the castle were thrown open, and a crowd of men-at-arms, consisting of the retainers of the castle and the mercenaries of Prince John sallied forth. So soon as Cuthbert was able to move, the archers started at a brisk run, several of them carrying Cuthbert's casque and sword, and others assisting him to hurry along. The rear ranks turned as they ran and discharged flights of arrows at the enemy, who, more heavily armed and weighted, gained but slowly upon them.

Had not Sir Rudolph been stunned by the blow dealt him by Cuthbert, he would himself have headed the pursuit, and in that case the foresters would have had to fight hard to make their retreat to their fastness. The officer in command of the mercenaries, however, had no great stomach for the matter. Men were hard to get, and Prince John would not have been pleased to hear that a number of the men whom he had brought with such expense from foreign parts had been killed in a petty fray. Therefore after following for a short time he called them off, and the archers fell back into the forest.

Here they found Dame Editha, and for three days she abode among them, living in a small hut in the centre of the forest. Then she left, to take up her abode, until the troubles were past, with some kin who lived in the south of Gloucestershire.

Although the lady abbess had assured Cuthbert that the retreat of Lady Margaret was not likely to be found out, he himself, knowing how great a stake Sir Rudolph had in the matter, was still far from being easy. It would not be difficult for the latter to learn through his agents that the lady superior of the little convent near Hereford was of kin to her of St. Anne's, and, close as a convent is, yet the gossiping of the servants who go to market was certain to let out an affair so important as the arrival of a young lady to reside under the charge of the superior. Cuthbert was not mistaken as to the acuteness of his enemy. The relationship between the two lady superiors was no secret, and after having searched all the farm-houses and granges near the forest, and being convinced that the lady abbess would have sent her charge rather to a religious house than to that of a franklin, Sir Rudolph sought which of those within the circuit of a few miles would be likely to be the one selected. It was not long before he was enabled to fix upon that near Hereford, and spies going to the spot soon found out from the country people that it was a matter of talk that a young lady of rank had been admitted by the superior. Sir Rudolph hesitated whether to go himself at the head of a strong body of men and openly to take her, or to employ some sort of device. It was not that he himself feared the anathema of the church; but he knew Prince John to be weak and vacillating, at one time ready to defy the thunder of the pope, the next cringing before the spiritual authority. He therefore determined to employ some of his men to burst into the convent and carry off the heiress, arranging that he himself, with some of his men-at-arms, should come upon them in the road, and make a feigned rescue of her, so that, if the lady superior laid her complaint before the pope's legate, he could deny that he had any hand in the matter, and could even take credit for having rescued her from the men who had profaned the convent. That his story would be believed mattered but little. It would be impossible to prove its falsity, and this was all that he cared for.

This course was followed out. Late one evening, the lady superior was alarmed by a violent knocking at the door. In reply to questions asked through the grill, the answer was given, "We are men of the forest, and we are come to carry the Lady Margaret of Evesham off to a secure hiding-place. The lord of Evesham has discovered her whereabouts, and will be here shortly, and we would fain remove her before he arrives."

"From whom have you warrant?" the lady superior said. "I surrender her to no one, save to the lady abbess of St. Anne's. But if you have a written warrant from Sir Cuthbert, the rightful lord of Evesham, I will lay the matter before the Lady Margaret, and will act as it may seem fit to her."

"We have no time for parleying," a rough voice said. "Throw open the gate at once, or we will break it down."

"Ye be no outlaws," the lady superior said, "for the outlaws are men who fear God and respect the church. Were ye what ye say, ye would be provided with the warrants that I mention. I warn you, therefore, that if you use force, you will be excommunicated, and placed under the ban of the church."

The only answer was a thundering assault upon the gate, which soon yielded to the blows. The sisters and novices ran shrieking through the corridors at this rude uproar. The lady superior, however, stood calmly awaiting the giving way of the gate.

"Where is the Lady Margaret?" the leader of the party, who were dressed in rough garb, and had the seeming of a band of outlaws, demanded.

"I will say nothing," she said, "nor do I own that she is here."

"We will soon take means to find out," the man exclaimed. "Unless in five minutes she is delivered to us, we will burn your place to the ground."

The lady abbess was insensible to the threat; but the men rushing in, seized some sisters, who, terrified out of their wits by this irruption, at once gave the information demanded, and the men made their way to the cell where the Lady Margaret slept.

The girl had at once risen when the tumult commenced, doubting not in her mind that this was another attempt upon the part of her enemy to carry her off. When, therefore, she heard heavy footsteps approaching along the gallery—having already hastily attired herself—she opened the door and presented herself.

"If you seek the Lady Margaret of Evesham," she said calmly, "I am she. Do not harm any of the sisters here. I am in your power, and will go with you at once. But I beseech you add not to your other sins that of violence against holy women."

The men, abashed by the calm dignity of this young girl, abstained from laying hands upon her, but merely motioned to her to accompany them. Upon their way they met the man who appeared to be their leader, and he, well pleased that the affair was over, led the way to the courtyard.

"Farewell, my child," the abbess exclaimed. "God will deliver you from the power of these wicked men. Trust in Him, and keep up your courage. Wickedness will not be permitted to triumph upon the earth; and be assured that

the matter shall be brought to
the ears of the pope's legate,
and of Prince John himself."

She could say no more, for
the men closing round the
weeping girl, hurried her out
from the convent. A litter awaited them without, and in this
the young lady was placed, and, borne upon the shoulders
of four stout men, she started at a fast pace, surrounded
closely by the rest of the band.

It was a dark night, and the girl could not see the
direction in which she was being taken; but she judged from
the turn taken upon leaving the convent, that it was towards
Evesham. They had proceeded some miles, when a
trampling of horses was heard, and a body of armed men
rode up. For a moment Lady Margaret's heart gave a leap,
for she thought that she had been rescued by her friends.
There was a loud and angry altercation, a clashing of

swords, and a sound of shouting and cries outside the litter. Then it was placed roughly on the ground, and she heard the sound of the footsteps of her first captors hurrying away. Then the horsemen closed round the litter, and the leader dismounted.

"I am happy indeed, Lady Margaret," he said

approaching the litter, "to have been able to save you from the power of these villains. Fortunately, word came to me that the outlaws in the forest were about to carry you off, and that they would not hesitate even to desecrate the walls of the convent. Assembling my men-at-arms, I at once rode to your rescue, and am doubly happy to have saved you, first, as a gentleman, secondly, as being the man to whom our gracious prince has assigned you as a wife. I am Sir Rudolph, Earl of Evesham."

As from the first the girl had been convinced that she had fallen into the power of her lawless suitor, this came upon her as no surprise.

"Whether your story is true, Sir Rudolph," she said, "or not, God knows, and I, a poor weak girl, will not pretend to venture to say. It is between you and your conscience. If, as you say, you have saved me from the power of the outlaws, I demand that, as a knight and a gentleman, you return with me at once to the convent from which I was taken by force."

"I cannot do that," Sir Rudolph said. "Fortune has placed you in my hands, and has enabled me to carry out the commands of the prince. Therefore, though I would fain yield to your wishes and so earn your goodwill, which above all things I wish to obtain, yet my duty towards the prince commands me to utilize the advantage which fate has thrown in my hands."

"You must do as you will, Sir Rudolph," the girl said with dignity. "I believe not your tale. You sought before, in person, to carry me off; but failed, and you have now employed other means to do so. The tale of your conduct to Dame Editha has reached my ears, and I hold you a foresworn knight and a dishonoured man, and as such I would rather die than become your wife, although as yet I am but a child, and have no need to talk of weddings for years to come."

"We need not parley here," the knight said coldly, we shall have plenty of time when at my castle."

The litter was now lifted, placed between two horses, and proceeded rapidly on its journey. Although the hope was but faint, yet until the gates of the castle closed upon them the Lady Margaret still hoped that rescue might reach her. But the secret had been too well kept, and it was not until the following day that the man who had been placed in a cottage near the convent arrived in all haste in the forest, to say that it was only in the morning that he had learnt that the convent had been broken open by men disguised as archers, and the Lady Margaret carried off.

Four days elapsed before Sir Rudolph presented himself before the girl he had captured. So fearfully was his face bruised and disfigured by the blow from the mailed hand of Cuthbert three weeks before, that he did not wish to appear before her under such unfavourable circumstances, and the captive passed the day gazing from her casement in one of the rooms in the upper part of the keep, towards the forest whence she hoped rescue would come.

Within the forest hot discussions were going on as to the best course to pursue. An open attack was out of the question, especially as upon the day following the arrival there of Lady Margaret, 300 more mercenaries had marched in from Worcester, so that the garrison was now raised to 500 men.

"Is there no way," Cnut exclaimed furiously, "by which we might creep into this den, since we cannot burst into it openly?"

"There is a way from the castle," Cuthbert said, "for my dear lord told me of it one day when we were riding together in the Holy Land. He said then that it might be that he should never return, and that it were well that I should know of the existence of this passage, which few beside the earl himself knew of. It is approached by a very heavy slab of stone in the great hall. This is bolted down, and as it stands under the great table passes unnoticed, and appears part of the ordinary floor. He told me the method in which, by touching a spring, the bolts were withdrawn and the stone could be raised. Thence, a passage a quarter of a mile long leads to the little chapel standing in the hollow, and which, being hidden among the trees, would be unobserved by any party besieging the castle. This of course was contrived in order that the garrison, or any messenger thereof, might make an exit in case of siege."

"But if we could escape," Cnut asked, "why not enter by this way?"

"The stone is of immense weight and strength," Cuthbert replied, "and could not be loosed from below save with great labour and noise. There are, moreover, several massive doors in the passage, all of which are secured by heavy bolts within. It is therefore out of the question that we could enter the castle by that way. But were we once in, we could easily carry off the lady through this passage."

The large force which Sir Rudolph had collected was not intended merely for the defence of the castle, for the knight considered that with his own garrison he could hold it against a force tenfold that which his rival could collect. But he was determined if possible to crush out the outlaws of the forest, for he felt that so long as this formidable body remained under an enterprising leader like Sir Cuthbert, he would never be safe for a moment, and would be a prisoner in his own castle.

Cuthbert had foreseen that the attack was likely to be made, and had strengthened his band to the utmost. He felt, however, that against so large a force of regularly armed men, although he might oppose a stout resistance and kill many, yet that in the end he must be conquered. Cnut, however, suggested to him a happy idea, which he eagerly grasped.

"It would be rare sport," Cnut said, "when this armed force comes out to attack us, if we could turn the tables by slipping in, and taking their castle."

"The very thing," Cuthbert exclaimed. "It is likely that he will use the greater portion of his forces, and that he will not keep above fifty or sixty men, at the outside, in the castle. When they sally out we will at first oppose a stout resistance to them in the wood, gradually falling back. Then, at a given signal, all save twenty men shall retire hastily, and sweeping round, make for the castle. Their absence will not be noticed, for in this thick wood it is difficult to tell whether twenty men or two hundred are opposing you among the bushes; and the twenty who remain must shoot thick and fast to make believe that their numbers are great, retiring sometimes, and leading the enemy on into the heart of the wood."

"But supposing, Sir Cuthbert, that they should have closed the gates and lifted the drawbridge? We could not gain entrance by storming, even if only twenty men held the walls, until long after the main body would have returned."

Cuthbert thought for some time, and then said, "Cnut, you shall undertake this enterprise. You shall fill a cart high with faggots, and in it shall conceal a dozen of your best men. You, dressed as a serf, shall drive the oxen, and when you reach the castle shall say, in answer to the hail of the sentry, that you are bringing in the tribute of wood of your master the franklin of Hopeburn. They will then lower the drawbridge and open the gates; and when you have crossed the bridge and are under the portcullis, spring out suddenly, cut loose the oxen so that they will not draw the cart further in, cut the chains of the drawbridge so that it cannot be drawn off, and hold the gate for a minute or two until we arrive."

"The plan is capital," Cnut exclaimed. "We will do the proud Norman yet. How he will storm when he finds us masters of his castle. What then will you do, Sir Cuthbert?"

"We can hold the castle for weeks," Cuthbert said, "and every day is in our favour. If we find ourselves forced to yield to superior numbers, we can at last retire through the passage I have spoken of, and must then scatter and each shift for himself until these bad days be past."

CHAPTER XXIV

THE SIEGE OF EVESHAM CASTLE.

UPON the day before starting out to head the expedition against the outlaws, Sir Rudolph sent word to the Lady Margaret that she must prepare to become his wife at the end of the week. He had provided two tiring maids for her by ordering two of the franklins to send in their daughters for that purpose, and these mingled their tears with Margaret's at the situation in which they were placed. She replied firmly to the messenger of the knight that no power on earth could oblige her to marry him. He might drive her to the altar; but though he killed her there, her lips should refuse to say the words which would unite them.

The following morning, early, the castle rang with the din of preparation. The great portion of the mercenaries were encamped in tents outside the walls, for, spacious as it was, Evesham could hardly contain 400 men in addition to its usual garrison. The men-at-arms were provided with heavy axes to cut their way through the bushes. Some carried bundles of straw, to fire the wood should it be found practicable to do so; and as it was now summer and the wind was blowing high, Sir Rudolph hoped that the dry grass and bushes would catch, and would do more even than his men-at-arms in clearing the forest of those whom he designated the villains infesting it. They had, too, with them several fierce dogs trained to hunting the deer, and these, the knight hoped, would do good service in tracking the outlaws. He and the knights and the men-at-arms with him were all dismounted, for he felt that horses would in the forest be an encumbrance, and he was determined himself to lead the way to the men-at-arms.

When they reached the forest, they were saluted by a shower of arrows; but as all were clad in mail, these at a distance effected but little harm. As they came closer, however, the clothyard arrows began to pierce the coarse and ill-made armour of the foot soldiers, although the finer armour of the knights kept out the shafts which struck against it. Sir Rudolph and his knights leading the way, they entered the forest, and gradually pressed their invisible foe backwards through the trees. The dogs did good service, going on ahead and attacking the archers; but, one by one, they were soon shot, and the assailants left to their own devices. Several attempts were made to fire the wood. But these failed, the fire burning but a short time and then dying out of itself. In addition to the fighting men, Sir Rudolph had impressed into the service all the serfs of his domain, and these, armed with axes, were directed to cut down the trees as the force proceeded, Sir Rudolph declaring that he would not cease until he had levelled the whole forest, though it might take him months to do so.

The assailants gained ground steadily, the resistance being less severe than Sir Rudolph had anticipated. Several small huts and clearings in the forest which had been used by the outlaws, and round which small crops had been planted, were destroyed, and all seemed to promise well for the success of the enterprise.

It was about two hours after they had left the castle, when a heavy cart filled with faggots was seen approaching its gates. The garrison, who had not the least fear of any attack, paid no attention to it until it reached the edge of the moat. Then the warder, seeing that it contained faggots, lowered the drawbridge without question, raised the portcullis, and opened the gates.

"From whom do you bring this wood?" he asked, as the man driving the oxen began to cross the bridge.

"From the franklin of Hopeburn."

"It is well," said the warder, "for he is in arrears now, and should have sent in the firewood two months since. Take it to the wood-house at the other end of the court."

The heavy waggon crossed the drawbridge, but as it was entering the gate it came suddenly to a stop. With a blow of his ox goad Cnut levelled the warder to the ground, and cutting the cords of the bullocks, drove them into the yard ahead. As he did so the pile of faggots fell asunder, and twelve men armed with bow and pike leaped out. The men-at-arms standing near, lounging in the courtyard, gave a shout of alarm, and the garrison, surprised at this sudden cry, ran to their arms. At first they were completely panic-stricken. But seeing after a time how small was the number of their assailants, they took heart and advanced against them. The passage was narrow, and the twelve men formed a wall across it. Six of them with their pikes advanced, the other six with bent bows standing behind them and delivering their arrows between their heads. The garrison fought stoutly, and although losing many, were pressing the little band backwards. In vain the assistant-warder tried to lower the portcullis, or to close the gates. The former fell on to the top of the waggon, and was there retained. The gates also were barred by the obstacle. The chains of the drawbridge had at once been cut. Cnut encouraged his followers by his shouts, and armed with a heavy axe, did good service upon the assailants. But four of his party had fallen, and the rest were giving way, when a shout was heard, and over the drawbridge poured Cuthbert and 150 of the outlaws of the forest. Struck with terror at this attack, the garrison drew back, and the foresters poured into the yard. For a few minutes there was a fierce fight; but the defenders of the castle, disheartened and taken by surprise, were either cut down or, throwing down their arms, cried for quarter.

Ten minutes after the waggon had crossed the drawbridge, the castle was safely in possession of Sir Cuthbert. The bridge was raised, the waggon removed, the portcullis lowered, and to the external eye all remained as before.

Cuthbert at once made his way to the chamber where the Lady Margaret was confined, and her joy at her deliverance was great indeed. So unlimited was her faith in Sir Cuthbert that she had never lost confidence; and although it did not seem possible that in the face of such disparity of numbers he could rescue her from the power of Sir Rudolph, yet she had not given up hope. The joy of the farmers' daughters who had been carried off to act as her attendants was little inferior to her own; for once in the power of this reckless baron, the girls had small hopes of ever being allowed to return again to their parents.

The flag of Sir Rudolph was thrown down from the keep, and that of the late earl hoisted in its stead; for Cuthbert himself, although he had assumed the cognizance which King Richard had granted him, had not yet any flag or pennon emblazoned with it.

No words can portray the stupefaction and rage of Sir Rudolph when a man who had managed to slip unobserved from the castle at the time of its capture, bore the news to him in the forest. All opposition there had ceased, and the whole of the troops were engaged in aiding the peasants in cutting wide roads through the trees across the forest, so as to make it penetrable by horsemen in every direction. It was supposed that the outlaws had gradually stolen away through the thickets and taken to the open country, intending to scatter to their homes, or other distant hiding-places; and the news that they had by a ruse captured the castle, came as a thunderclap. Sir Rudolph's first impulse was to call his men together and to march towards the castle. The drawbridge was up, and the walls bristled with armed men. It was useless to attempt a parley; still more useless to think of attacking the stronghold without the proper machines and appliances. Foaming with rage, Sir Rudolph took possession of a cottage near, camped his men around and prepared for a siege.

There were among the mercenaries many men accustomed to the use of engines of war. Many, too, had aided in making them; and these were at once set to work to construct the various machines in use at that time. Before the invention of gunpowder, castles such as those of the English barons were able to defy any attack by an armed force for a long period. Their walls were so thick that even the balistas, casting huge stones, were unable to breach them except after a very long time. The moats which surrounded them were wide and deep, and any attempt at storming by ladders was therefore extremely difficult; and these buildings were consequently more often captured by famine than by other means. Of provisions, as Sir Rudolph knew, there was a considerable supply at present in the castle, for he had collected a large number of bullocks in order to feed the strong body who had been added to the garrison. The granaries, too, were well stored; and with a groan Sir Rudolph thought of the rich stores of French wines which he had collected in his cellars. After much deliberation with the knights with him and the captain of the mercenaries, it was agreed in the first instance to attempt to attack the place by filling up a portion of the moat and ascending by scaling ladders. Huge screens of wood were made, and these were placed on waggons; the waggons themselves were filled with bags of earth, and a large number of men getting beneath them shoved the ponderous machines forward to the edge of the moat. The bags of stones and earth were then thrown in, and the waggons pushed backwards to obtain a fresh supply. This operation was of course an exceedingly slow one, a whole day being occupied with each trip of the waggons. They were not unmolested in their advance, for, from the walls, mangonels and other machines hurled great stones down upon the wooden screens, succeeding sometimes, in spite of their thickness, in crashing through them, killing many of the men beneath. The experiment was also tried of throwing balls of Greek fire down upon the wood; but as this was green and freshly felled it would not take fire, but the flames dropping through, with much boiling pitch and other materials, did grievously burn and scald the soldiers working below it. Upon both sides every device was tried. The crossbow men among the mercenaries kept up a fire upon the walls to hinder the defenders from interfering with the operations, while the archers above shot steadily, and killed many of those who ventured within range of their bows.

After ten days' labour, a portion of the moat some twenty yards in length was filled with bags of earth, and all was ready for the assault. The besiegers had prepared great numbers of strong ladders, and these were brought up under shelter of the screens. Then, all being ready, the trumpets sounded for the assault, and the troops moved forward in a close body, covering themselves with their shields so that no man's head or body was visible, each protecting the one before him with his shield held over him. Thus the body presented the appearance of a great scale-covered animal.

In many respects, indeed, the warfare of those days was changed in no way from that of the time of the Romans. In the 1200 years which had elapsed between the siege of Jerusalem and the days of the crusades there had been but little change in arms or armour, and the operations which Titus undertook for the reduction of the Jewish stronghold differed but little from those which a Norman baron employed in besieging his neighbour's castle.

Within Evesham Castle all was contentment and merriment during these days. The garrison had no fear whatever of being unable to repel the assault when it should be delivered. Huge stones had been collected in numbers on the walls, cauldrons of pitch, beneath which fires kept simmering, stood there in readiness. Long poles with hooks with which to seize the ladders and cut them down were laid there; and all that precaution and science could do was prepared.

Cuthbert passed much of the day, when not required upon the walls, chatting with the Lady Margaret, who, attended by her maidens, sat working in her bower. She had learnt to read from the good nuns of the convent—an accomplishment which was by no means general, even among the daughters of nobles; but books were rare, and Evesham boasted but few manuscripts. Here Margaret

learnt in full all the details of Cuthbert's adventures since leaving England, and the fondness with which as a child she had regarded the lad grew gradually into the affection of a woman.

The courage of the garrison was high, for although they believed that sooner or later the castle might be carried by the besiegers, they had already been told by Cnut that there was a means of egress unknown to the besiegers, and that when the time came they would be able to escape unharmed. This, while it in no way detracted from their determination to defend the castle to the last, yet rendered their task a far lighter and more agreeable one than it would have been had they seen the gallows standing before them as the end of the siege.

As the testudo, as it was called in those days, advanced towards the castle, the machines upon the walls—catapults, mangonels, and arbalasts—poured forth showers of stones and darts upon it, breaking up the array of shields and killing many; and as these openings were made, the archers, seizing their time, poured in volleys of arrows. The mercenaries, however, accustomed to war, advanced steadily, and made good their footing beneath the castle wall, and proceeded to rear their ladders. Here, although free from the action of the machines, they were exposed to the hand missiles, which were scarcely less destructive. In good order, and with firmness, however, they reared the ladders, and mounted to the assault, covering themselves as well as they could with their shields. In vain, however, did they mount. The defenders poured down showers of boiling pitch and oil, which penetrated the crevices of their armour, and caused intolerable torment. Great stones were toppled over from the battlements upon them; and sometimes the ladders, seized by the poles with hooks, were cast backwards, with all upon them, on the throng below. For half-an-hour, encouraged by the shouts of Sir Rudolph and their leaders, the soldiers strove gallantly; but were at last compelled to draw off; having lost nigh 100 men, without one gaining a footing upon the walls.

That evening another council of war was held without. Already some large machines for which Sir Rudolph had sent had arrived. In anticipation of the possibility of failure, two castles upon wheels had been prepared, and between these a huge beam with an iron head was hung. This was upon the following day pushed forward on the newly-formed ground across the moat. Upon the upper part of each tower were formed men who worked machines casting sheaves of arrows and other missiles. Below were those who worked the ram. To each side of the beam were attached numerous cords, and with these it was swung backwards and forwards, giving heavy blows each stroke upon the wall. The machines for casting stones, which had arrived, were also brought in play, and day and night these thundered against the walls; while the ram repeated its ceaseless blows upon the same spot, until the stone crumbled before it.

Very valiantly did the garrison oppose themselves to these efforts. But each day showed the progress made by the besiegers. Their forces had been increased, Prince John having ordered his captain at Gloucester to send another 100 men to the assistance of Sir Rudolph. Other towers had now been prepared. These were larger than the first, and overtopped the castle walls. From the upper story were drawbridges, so formed as to drop from the structures upon the walls, and thus enable the besiegers to rush upon them. The process was facilitated by the fact that the battlements had been shot away by the great stones, and there was a clear space on which the drawbridges could fall. The attack was made with great vigour; but for a long time the besieged maintained their post, and drove back the assailants as they poured out across the drawbridges on to the wall. At last Cuthbert saw that the forces opposed to him were too numerous to be resisted, and gave orders to his men to fall back upon the inner keep.

Making one rush, and clearing the wall of those who had gained a footing, the garrison fell back hastily, and were safely within the massive keep before the enemy had mustered in sufficient numbers upon the wall to interfere with them. The drawbridge was now lowered, and the whole of the assailants gained footing within the castle. They were still far from having achieved a victory. The walls of the keep were massive and strong, and its top far higher than the walls, so that from above a storm of arrows poured down upon all who ventured to show themselves. The keep had no windows low enough down for access to be gained; and those on the floors above were so narrow, and protected by bars, that it seemed by scaling the walls alone could an entry be effected. This was far too desperate an enterprise to be attempted, for the keep rose eighty feet above the courtyard. It was upon the door, solid and studded with iron, that the attempt had to be made.

Several efforts were made by Sir Rudolph, who fought with a bravery worthy of a better cause, to assault and batter down the door. Protected by wooden shields from the rain of missiles from above, he and his knights hacked at the door with their battle-axes. But in vain. It had been strengthened by beams behind, and by stones piled up against it. Then fire was tried. Faggots were collected in the forest, and brought; and a huge pile having been heaped against the door, it was lighted. "We could doubtless prolong the siege for some days, Lady Margaret," said Cuthbert, "but the castle is ours; and we wish not, when the time comes that we shall again be masters of it, that it should be a mere heap of ruins. Methinks we have done enough. With but small losses on our side, we have killed great numbers of the enemy, and have held them at bay for a month. Therefore, I think that tonight it will be well for us to leave the place."

Lady Margaret was rejoiced at the news that the time for escape had come, for the perpetual clash of war, the rattling of arrows, the ponderous thud of heavy stones, caused a din very alarming to a young girl; and although the room in which she sat, looking into the inner court of the castle, was not exposed to missiles, she trembled at the thought that brave men were being killed, and that at any moment a shot might strike Cuthbert, and so leave her without a friend or protector.

Content with having destroyed the door, the assailants made no further effort that evening, but prepared in the morning to attack it, pull down the stones filled behind it, and force their way into the keep. There was, with the exception of the main entrance, but one means of exit, a small postern door behind the castle, and throughout the siege a strong body of troops had been posted here, to prevent the

garrison making a sortie.
Feeling secure therefore
that upon the following
day his enemies would
fall into his power, Sir Rudolph
retired to rest.

An hour before midnight
the garrison assembled in the
hall. The table was removed, and
Cuthbert having pressed the
spring, which was at a distance from the stone and could not
be discovered without a knowledge of its existence, the stone
turned aside by means of a counterpoise, and a flight of
steps was seen. Torches had been prepared. Cnut and a
chosen band went first; Cuthbert followed, with Lady
Margaret and her attendants; and the rest of the archers
brought up the rear, a trusty man being left in charge at last
with orders to swing back the stone into its place, having first
hauled the table over the spot, so that their means of escape
should be unknown.

The passage was long and dreary, the walls were damp
with wet, and the massive doors so swollen by
moisture that it was with the greatest difficulty they
could be opened. At last, however, they emerged into
the little friary in the wood. It was deserted, the priest
who usually dwelt there having fled when the siege began.

The stone which there, as in the castle, concealed the exit, was carefully closed, and the party then emerged into the open air. Here Cuthbert bade adieu to his comrades. Cnut had very anxiously begged to be allowed to accompany him and share his fortunes, and Cuthbert had promised him that if at any time he should again take up arms in England, he would summon him to his side, but that at present as he knew not whither his steps would be turned, it would be better that he should be unattended. The archers had all agreed to scatter far and wide through the country, many of them proceeding to Nottingham and joining the bands in the forest of Sherwood.

Cuthbert himself had determined to make his way to the castle of his friend, Sir Baldwin, and to leave the Lady Margaret in his charge. Cnut hurried on at full speed to the house of a franklin some three miles distant. Here horses were obtained and saddled, and dresses prepared; and when Cuthbert with Lady Margaret arrived there, no time was lost. Dressed as a yeoman, with the Lady Margaret as his sister, he mounted a horse, with her behind him on a pillion. The other damsels also mounted, as it would not have been safe for them to remain near Evesham. They therefore purposed taking refuge in a convent near Gloucester for the present. Bidding a hearty adieu to Cnut, and with thanks to the franklin who had aided them, they set forward on their journey. By morning they had reached the convent, and here the two girls were left, and Cuthbert continued his journey. He left his charge at a convent a day's ride distant from the castle of Sir Baldwin, as he wished to consult the knight first as to the best way of her entering the castle without exciting talk or suspicion.

Sir Baldwin received him with joy. He had heard something of his doings, and the news of the siege of Evesham had been noised abroad. He told him that he was in communication with many other barons, and that ere long they hoped to rise against the tyranny of Prince John, but that at present they were powerless, as many, hoping that King Richard would return ere long, shrank from involving the country in a civil war. When Cuthbert told him that the daughter of his old friend was at a convent but a day's ride distant, and that he sought protection for her, Sir Baldwin instantly offered her hospitality.

"I will," he said, "send my good wife to fetch her. Some here know your presence, and it would be better therefore that she did not arrive for some days, as her coming will then seem to be unconnected with yourself. My wife and I will, a week hence, give out that we are going to fetch a cousin of my wife's to stay here with her; and when we return no suspicion will be excited that she is other than she seems. Should it be otherwise, I need not say that Sir Baldwin of Béthune will defend his castle against any of the minions of Prince John. But I have no fear that her presence here will be discovered. What think you of doing in the meantime?"

"I am thinking," Cuthbert said, "of going east. No news has been obtained of our lord the king save that he is a prisoner in the hands of the emperor; but where confined, or how, we know not. It is my intent to travel to the Tyrol, and to trace his steps from the time that he was captured. Then, when I obtain knowledge of the place where he is kept, I will return, and consult upon the best steps to be taken. My presence in England is now useless. Did the barons raise the standard of King Richard against the prince, I should at once return and join them. But without land or vassals I can do nothing here, and shall be indeed like a hunted hare, for I know that the false earl will move heaven and earth to capture me."

Sir Baldwin approved of the resolution; but recommended Cuthbert to take every precaution not to fall himself into the hands of the emperor; "for," he said, "if we cannot discover the prison of King Richard, I fear that it would be hopeless indeed ever to attempt to find that in which a simple knight is confined."

CHAPTER XXV.

IN SEARCH OF THE KING.

THE following day, with many thanks Cuthbert started from the castle, and in the first place visited the convent, and told Lady Margaret that she would be fetched in a few days by Sir Baldwin and his wife. He took a tender adieu of her, not without many forebodings and tears upon her part; but promising blithely that he would return and lead her back in triumph to her castle, he bade adieu and rode for London.

He had attired himself as a merchant, and took up his abode at a hostelry near Cheapside. Here he remained quietly for some days, and, mixing among the people, learnt that in London as elsewhere the rapacity of Prince John had rendered him hateful to the people, and that they would gladly embrace any opportunity of freeing themselves from his yoke. He was preparing to leave for France, when the news came to him that Prince John had summoned all the barons faithful to him to meet him near London, and had recalled all his mercenaries from different parts of the country, and was gathering a large army; also, that the barons faithful to King Richard, alarmed by the prospect, had raised the royal standard, and that true men were hurrying to their support. This entirely destroyed the plans that he had formed. Taking horse again, and avoiding the main road, by which he might meet the hostile barons on their way to London, he journeyed down to Nottingham.

Thence riding boldly into the forest, he sought the outlaws, and was not long ere he found them. At his request he was at once taken before their leader, a man of great renown both for courage and bowmanship, one Robin Hood. This bold outlaw had long held at defiance the Sheriff of Nottingham, and had routed him and all bodies of troops who had been sent against him. With him Cuthbert found many of his own men; and upon hearing that the royal standard had been raised, Robin Hood at once agreed to march with all his men to join the royal force. Messengers were despatched to summon the rest of the forest band from their hiding places, and a week later Cuthbert, accompanied by Robin Hood and 300 archers, set out for the rendezvous. When they arrived there they found that Sir Baldwin had already joined with his retainers, and was by him most warmly received, and introduced to the other barons in the camp, by whom Cuthbert was welcomed as a brother. The news that Prince John's army was approaching was brought in, a fortnight after Cuthbert had joined the camp, and the army in good order moved out to meet the enemy.

The forces were about equal. The battle began by a discharge of arrows; but Robin Hood and his men shot so true and fast that they greatly discomfited the enemy; and King John's mercenaries having but little stomach for the fight, and knowing how unpopular they were in England, and that if defeated small mercy was likely to be shown to them, refused to advance against the ranks of the loyal barons, and falling back declined to join in the fray. Seeing their numbers so weakened by this defection, the barons on the prince's side hesitated, and surrounding the prince advised him to make terms with the barons while there was yet time. Prince John saw that the present was not a favourable time for him, and concealing his fury under a mask of courtesy, he at once acceded to the advice of his followers, and despatched a messenger to the barons with an inquiry as to what they wanted of him. A council was held, and it was determined to demand the dismissal of the mercenaries and their despatch back to their own country; also that John would govern only as his brother's representative; that the laws of the country should be respected; that no taxes should be raised without the assent of the barons; that all men who had taken up arms against his authority should be held free; and that the barons on Prince John's side should return peaceably home and disband their forces. Seeing, under the circumstances, that there was no way before him but to yield to these demands, Prince John accepted the terms. The mercenaries were ordered to march direct to London, and orders were given that ships should be at once prepared to take them across to Normandy, and the barons marched for their homes. Satisfied, now that the mercenaries were gone, that they could henceforth hold their ground against Prince John, the royal barons also broke up their forces. Robin Hood with his foresters returned to Sherwood; and Cuthbert, bidding adieu to Sir Baldwin, rode back to London, determined to carry out the plan which he had formed. He was the more strengthened in this resolution, inasmuch as in the royal camp he had met a friend from whom he parted last in the Holy Land. This was Blondel, the minstrel of King Richard, whose songs and joyous music had often lightened the evening after days of fighting and toil in Palestine. To him Cuthbert confided his intention, and the minstrel instantly offered to accompany him.

"I shall," he said, "be of assistance to you. Minstrels are like heralds. They are of no nationality, and can pass free where a man at arms would be closely watched and hindered. Moreover, it may be that I might aid you greatly in discovering the prison of the king. So great is the secrecy with which this has been surrounded, that I question if any inquiries you could make would enable you to trace him. My voice, however, can penetrate into places where we cannot enter. I will take with

me my lute, and as we journey I will sing outside the walls of each prison we come to one of the songs which I sang in Palestine. King Richard is himself a singer and knows my songs as well as myself. If I sing a verse of some song which I wrote there and which, therefore, would be known only to him, if he hears it he may follow with the next verse, and so enable us to know of his hiding place."

Cuthbert at once saw the advantages which such companionship would bring him, and joyfully accepted the minstrel's offer, agreeing himself to go as serving man to Blondel. The latter accompanied him to London. Here their preparations were soon made, and taking ship in a merchantman bound for the Netherlands, they started without delay upon their adventure.

The minstrels and troubadours were at that time a privileged race in Europe, belonging generally to the south of France, although produced in all lands. They travelled over Europe singing the lays which they themselves had composed, and were treated with all honour at the castles where they chose to alight. It would have been considered as foul a deed to use discourtesy to a minstrel as to insult a herald. Their persons were, indeed, regarded as sacred, and the knights and barons strove to gain their good will by hospitality and presents, as a large proportion of their ballads related to deeds of war; and while they would write lays in honour of those who courteously entertained them, they did not hesitate to heap obloquy upon those who received them discourteously, holding them up to the gibes and scoffs of their fellows. In no way, therefore, would success be so likely to attend the mission of those who set out to discover the hiding place of King Richard as under the guise of a minstrel and his attendant. No questions would be asked them; they could halt where they would, in castle or town, secure of hospitality and welcome. Blondel was himself a native of the south of France, singing his songs in the soft language of Languedoc. Cuthbert's Norman French would pass muster anywhere as being that of a native of France; and although when dressed as a servitor attention might be attracted by his bearing, his youth might render it probable that he was of noble family, but that he had entered the service of the minstrel in order to qualify himself some day for following that career. He carried a long staff; a short sword, and at his back the lute or small harp played upon by the troubadour. Blondel's attire was rich, and suitable to a person of high rank.

They crossed to the Scheldt, and thence travelled by the right bank of the Rhine as far as Mannheim, sometimes journeying by boat, sometimes on foot. They were also hospitably entertained, and were considered to more than repay their hosts by the songs which Blondel sang. At Mannheim they purchased two horses, and then struck east for Vienna. The journey was not without danger, for a large portion of this part of Europe was under no settled govern-

ment, each petty baron living in
his own castle, and holding but
slight allegiance to any feudal lord, making
war upon his neighbour on his own
account, levying blackmail from travellers,
and perpetually at variance with the burghers of the towns.
The hills were covered with immense forests, which
stretched for many leagues in all directions, and these were
infested by wolves, bears, and robbers. The latter, however,
although men without pity or religion, yet held the
troubadours in high esteem, and the travellers without fear
entered the gloomy shades of the forest.

They had not gone far when their way was barred by a
number of armed men.

"I am a minstrel," Blondel said, "and as such doubt not
that your courtesy will be extended to me."

"Of a surety," the leader said, "the gay science is as much
loved and respected in the greenwood as in the castle; and
moreover, the purses of those who follow it are too light to

offer any temptation to us. We would pray you, however, to accompany us to our leader, who will mightily rejoice to see you, for he loves music, and will gladly be your host so long as you will stay with him."

Blondel, without objection, turned his horse's head and accompanied the men, followed by Cuthbert. After half an hour's travelling, they came to a building which had formerly been a shrine, but which was now converted to the robbers' headquarters. The robber chief on hearing from his followers the news that a minstrel had arrived, came forward to meet him, and courteously bade him welcome.

"I am Sir Adelbert, of Rotherheim," he said, "although you see me in so poor a plight. My castle and lands have been taken by my neighbour, with whom for generations my family have been at feud. I was in the Holy Land with the emperor, and on my return found that the baron had taken the opportunity of my absence, storming my castle and seizing my lands. In vain I petitioned the emperor to dispossess this traitorous baron of my lands, which by all the laws of Christendom should have been respected during my absence. The emperor did indeed send a letter to the baron to deliver them up to me; but his power here is but nominal, and the baron contemptuously threw the royal proclamation into the fire, and told the messenger that what he had taken by the sword he would hold by the sword; and the emperor, having weightier matters on hand than to set troops in motion to redress the grievances of a simple knight, gave the matter no further thought. I have therefore been driven to the forest, where I live as best I may with my followers, most of whom were retainers upon my estate, and some my comrades in the Holy Land. I make war upon the rich and powerful, and beyond that do harm to no man. But, methinks," he continued, "I know your face, gentle sir."

"It may well be so, Sir Adelbert," the minstrel said, "for I too was in the Holy Land. I followed the train of King Richard, and mayhap at some of the entertainments given by him you have seen my face. My name is Blondel."

"I remember now," the knight said. "It was at Acre that I first saw you, and if I remember rightly you can wield the sword as well as the lute."

"One cannot always be playing and singing," Blondel said, "and in lack of amusement I was forced to do my best against the infidel, who indeed would have but little respected my art had I fallen into his hands. The followers of the prophet hold minstrels but in slight reverence."

"What is the news of King Richard?" the knight said. "I have heard that he was lost on the voyage homewards."

"It is not so," Blondel said. "He landed safely on the coast, and was journeying north with a view of joining his sister at the Court of Saxony, when he was foully seized and imprisoned by the Archduke John."

"That were gross shame indeed," the knight said, "and black treachery on the part of Duke John. And where is the noble king imprisoned?"

"That," said Blondel, "no man knows. On my journey hither I have gathered that the emperor claimed him from the hand of the Archduke, and that he is imprisoned in one of the royal fortresses; but which, I know not. And indeed, sir knight, since you are well disposed towards him, I may tell you that the purport of my journey is to discover if I can the place of his confinement. He was a kind and noble master, and however long my search may be, I will yet obtain news of him."

The knight warmly applauded the troubadour's resolution, and was turning to lead him into his abode, when his eye fell upon Cuthbert.

"Methinks I know the face of your attendant as well as your own; though where I can have seen him I know not. Was he with you in the Holy Land?"

"Yes," Blondel said, "the youth was also there; and doubtless you may have noticed him, for he is indeed of distinguished and of good family."

"Then let him share our repast," the knight said, "if it seems good to you. In these woods there is no rank, and I myself have long dropped my knightly title, and shall not reassume it until I can pay off my score to the Baron of Rotherheim, and take my place again in my castle."

The minstrel and Cuthbert were soon seated at the table with the knight and one or two of his principal companions. A huge venison pasty formed the staple of the repast, but hares and other small game were also upon the table. Nor was the generous wine of the country wanting.

The knight had several times glanced at Cuthbert, and at last exclaimed, "I have it now. This is no attendant, sir minstrel, but that valiant young knight who so often rode near King Richard in battle. He is, as I guess, your companion in this quest; is it not so?"

"It is," Cuthbert replied frankly. "I am like yourself, a disinherited knight, and my history resembles yours. Upon my return to England I found another in possession of the land and titles that belonged to the noble I followed, and which King Richard bestowed upon me. The Earl of Evesham was doubtless known to you, and before his death King Richard, at his request, bestowed upon me as his adopted son—although but a distant connexion—his title and lands and the hand of his daughter. Prince John, who now rules in England, had however granted these things to one of his favourites, and he having taken possession of the land and title, though not, happily, of the lady, closed his door somewhat roughly in my face. I found means, however, to make my mark upon him; but as our quarrel could not be fought out to the end, and as the false knight had the aid of Prince John, I am forced for a while to postpone our settlement, and meeting my good friend the minstrel, agreed to join him in his enterprise to discover our lord the king."

The knight warmly grasped Cuthbert's hand.

"I am glad," he said, "to meet so true and valiant a knight. I have often wondered at the valour with which you, although so young, bore yourself; and there were tales afloat of strange adventures which you had undergone in captivity for a time among the infidels."

At Sir Adelbert's request, Cuthbert related the story of his adventures among the Saracens; and then Blondel tuning his lute, sang several canzonets which he had composed in the Holy Land, of feats of arms and adventure.

"How far are you," Cuthbert asked presently, when Blondel laid his lute aside, "from the estates which were wrongfully wrested from you?"

"But twenty leagues," the knight said. "My castle was on the Rhine, between Coblentz and Mannheim."

"Does the baron know that you are so near?" Cuthbert asked.

"Methinks that he does not," the knight replied, "but that he deems me to have gone to the court of the emperor to seek for redress—which, he guesses, I shall certainly fail to obtain."

"How many men have you with you?" Cuthbert asked.

"Fifty men, all good and true," the knight said.

"Has it never entered your thoughts to attempt a surprise upon his castle?" Cuthbert said.

The knight was silent for a minute.

"At times," he said at length, "thoughts of so doing have occurred to me; but the castle is strong, and a surprise would be difficult indeed."

"If the baron is lulled in security at present," Cuthbert said, "and deems you afar off, the watch is likely to be relaxed, and with a sudden onslaught you might surely obtain possession. Blondel and myself are not pressed for time, and the delay of a few days can make but little difference. If, therefore, you think we could be of assistance to you in such an attempt, my sword, and I am sure that of my friend, would be at your disposal."

The knight sat for some time in silence.

"Thanks, generous knight," he said at last, "I am sorely tempted to avail myself of your offer; but I fear that the enterprise is hopeless. The aid, however, of your arm and knowledge of war would greatly add to my chances, and if it pleases you we will ride to-morrow to a point where we can obtain a sight of the baron's castle. When you see it, you shall judge yourself how far such an enterprise as you propose is possible."

"Is your own castle intact?" Cuthbert asked.

"The walls are standing," he said; "but a breach has been made in them, and at present it is wholly deserted."

"Do you think," Cuthbert asked, "that if you succeeded in surprising and defeating the garrison of the castle that you could then regain your own, and hold it against your enemy?"

"I think that I could," Sir Adelbert said. "The baron's domains are but little larger than my own. Many of my retainers still live upon the estate, and would, I am sure, gladly join me, if I were to raise my flag. The baron, too, is hated by his neighbours, and could I inflict a crushing blow upon him, methinks it would be so long a time before he could assemble a force, that I might regain my castle and put it in an attitude of defence before he could take the field against me."

"If," Cuthbert said, "we could surprise the castle, it might well be that the baron would fall into your hands, and in that case you might be able to make your own terms with him. How strong a force is he likely to have in his castle?"

"Some fifty or sixty men," the knight replied; "for with such a force he could hold the castle against an attack of ten times their number, and he could in twelve hours call in his retainers, and raise the garrison to 300 or 400 men."

Blondel warmly assented, to Cuthbert's scheme, and it was settled that at daybreak they should start to view the Castle of Rotherheim. At early dawn they were in the saddle,

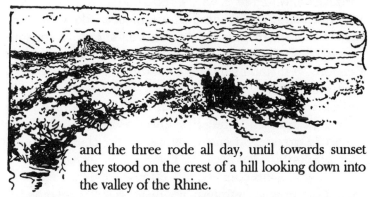

and the three rode all day, until towards sunset they stood on the crest of a hill looking down into the valley of the Rhine.

The present aspect of that valley affords but a slight idea of its beauty in those days. The slopes are now clad with vineyards, which, although picturesque in idea, are really, to look at from a distance, no better than so many turnip fields. The vines are planted in rows and trained to short sticks, and as these rows follow the declivities of the hillside, they are run in all directions, and the whole mountain side, from the river far up, is cut up into little patches of green lines. In those days the mountains were clad with forests, which descended nearly to the river side. Here and there, upon craggy points, were situate the fortalices of the barons. Little villages nestled in the woods, or stood by the river bank, and a fairer scene could not be witnessed in Europe.

"That is Rotherheim," the knight said, pointing to a fortress standing on a crag, which rose high above the woods around it; "and that," he said, pointing to another some four miles away, similarly placed, "is my own."

Cuthbert examined closely the fortress of Rotherheim. It was a large building, with towers at the angles, and seemed to rise almost abruptly from the edge of the rock. Inside rose the gables and round turrets of the dwelling-place of the baron; and the only access was by a steep winding path on the river side.

"It is indeed a strong place," Cuthbert said, "and difficult to take by surprise. A watch no doubt is always kept over the entrance, and there we can hope for no success. The only plan will be to scale the wall by means of a ladder; but how the ladder is to be got to so great a height, I own at present passes my comprehension." After much thought, Cuthbert went on, "It might, methinks, be practicable for an archer to approach the walls, and to shoot an arrow over the angle of the castle so that it would pass inside the turret there, and fall in the forest beyond. If to this arrow were attached a light cord, it could be gained by one on the other side, and a stronger cord hauled over. To this could be attached a rope ladder, and so this could be raised to the top of the wall. If a sentinel were anywhere near he might hear the rope pulled across the battlements; but if as we may hope, a watch is kept only over the entrance, the operation might be performed without attracting notice."

The knight was delighted with the project, which seemed perfectly feasible, and it was agreed that the attempt should be made.

"It will need," Sir Adelbert said, "an archer with a strong arm indeed to shoot an arrow with a cord attached to it, however light, over the corner of the castle."

"Methinks," Cuthbert said, "that I can do that, for as a lad I was used to the strong bows of my country. The first thing, however, will be to obtain such a bow; but doubtless one can be purchased in one of the towns, which, if not so strong as those to which I was accustomed, will at any rate suffice for us."

The party bivouacked in the woods for the night, for the horses had already done a very long journey, and needed rest before starting back for the Black Forest. At daybreak, however, they started, and at nightfall rejoined their band.

These were delighted when they heard the scheme that had been set on foot, and all avowed their eagerness to join in the attempt to restore their lord to his rights.

Two days later they set out, having already procured from the nearest town a strong bow, some arrows, a very light rope, and a stronger one from a portion of which they manufactured a rope ladder capable of reaching from the top of the wall to the rock below. The journey this time occupied two days, as the men on foot were unable to march at the pace at which the mounted party had traversed the ground. The evening of the second day, however, saw them in sight of the castle. By Cuthbert's advice, Sir Adelbert determined to give them twenty-four hours of rest, in order that they might have their full strength for undertaking the task before them. During the day, Cuthbert, guided by the knight, made his way through the woods to the foot of the rocks on which the castle stood. They were extremely steep, but could be mounted by active men if unopposed from above. Cuthbert measured the height with his eye from the top of the castle wall to the place which he selected as most fitting from which to shoot the arrow, and announced to the knight that he thought there would be no difficulty in discharging an arrow over the angle.

At nightfall the whole party made their way silently through the woods. Three men were sent round to the side of the castle opposite that from which Cuthbert was to shoot. The length of light string was carefully coiled on the ground, so as to unwind with the greatest facility, and so offer as little resistance to the flight of the arrow as might be. Then, all being in readiness, Cuthbert attached the end to an arrow, and drawing the bow to its full compass, let fly the arrow. All held their breath; but no sound followed the discharge. They were sure, therefore, that the arrow had not struck the wall, but that it must have passed clear over it. Half-an-hour elapsed before they felt that the cord was pulled, and knew that the men upon the other side had succeeded in finding the arrow and string attached. The stronger cord was now fastened to that which the arrow had carried, and this gradually disappeared in the darkness. A party now stole up the rock, and posted themselves at the foot of the castle wall. They took with them the coil of rope-ladder and the end of the rope. At length the rope tightened, and to the end they attached the ladder. This again ascended until the end only remained upon the ground, and they knew that it must have reached the top of the wall. They now held fast, and knew that those on the other side, following the instructions given them, would have fastened the rope to a tree upon the opposite side. They were now joined by the rest of the party, and Sir Adelbert leading the way, and followed by Cuthbert and Blondel, began cautiously to ascend the rope ladder.

All this time no sound from the castle proclaimed that their intention was suspected, or that any alarm had been given, and in silence they gained the top of the wall. Here they remained quiet until the whole band were gathered there, and then made their way along until they reached the stairs leading to the courtyard. These they descended, and then, raising his war cry, Sir Adelbert sprang upon the men who, round a fire, were sitting by the gate. These were cut down before they could leap to their feet, and the party then rushed at the entrance to the dwelling-house. The retainers of the castle, aroused by the sudden din, rushed from their sleeping places, but taken completely by surprise, were unable to offer any resistance whatever to the strong force which had, as if by magic, taken possession of the castle. The surprise was complete, and with scarce a blow struck they found themselves in possession. The baron himself was seized as he rose from his bed, and his rage at finding himself in the power of his enemy was so great as for some time to render him speechless. Sir Adelbert briefly dictated to him the conditions upon which only he should desist from using his power to hang him over his own gate.

The baron was instantly to issue orders to all his own retainers and tenantry to lend their aid to those of Sir Adelbert in putting the castle of the latter into a state of defence and mending the breach which existed. A sum of money, equal to the revenues of which he had possessed himself, was to be paid at once, and the knight was to retain possession of Rotherheim and of the baron's person until these conditions were all faithfully carried out. The baron had no resource but to assent to these terms, and upon the following day Cuthbert and Blondel departed upon their way, overwhelmed with thanks by Sir Adelbert, and confident that he would now be able to regain and hold the possession of his estate.

CHAPTER XXVI.

KING RICHARD'S RETURN TO ENGLAND.

JOURNEYING onward, Blondel and his companion stopped at many castles, and were everywhere hospitably entertained. Arriving at Vienna they lingered for some time, hoping there to be able to obtain some information of the whereabouts of King Richard. Blondel in his songs artfully introduced allusions to the captive monarch and to the mourning of all Christendom at the imprisonment of its champion. These allusions were always well received, and he found that the great bulk of the nobles of the empire were indignant and ashamed at the conduct of the emperor in imprisoning his illustrious rival. The secret of his prison place, however, appeared to have been so well kept that no information whatever was obtainable.

"We must carry out our original plan," he said at length, "and journey into the Tyrol. In one of the fortresses there he is most likely to be confined."

Leaving the capital they wandered up into the mountains for weeks, visiting one castle after another. It was no easy matter in all cases to get so near to these prisons as to give a hope that their voice might be heard within, or an answer received without. More than once cross-bow bolts were shot at them from the walls when they did not obey the sentinel's challenge and move further away. Generally, however, it was in the day time that they sang. Wandering carelessly up, they would sit down within earshot of the castle, open their wallets, and take out provisions from their store, and then,

having eaten and drunk, Blondel would produce his lute and sing, as if for his own pleasure. It needed, however, four visits to each castle before they could be sure that the captive was not there; for the song had to be sung on each side. Sometimes they would cheat themselves with the thought that they heard an answering voice; but it was not until the end of the fourth week, when singing outside the castle of Diernstein, that a full rich voice, when

Blondel ceased, sang out the second stanza of the poem. With difficulty Blondel and Cuthbert restrained themselves from an extravagant exhibition of joy. They knew, however, that men on the prison wall were watching them as they sat singing, and Blondel, with a final strain taken from a ballad of a knight who, having discovered the hiding place of his ladylove, prepared to free her from her oppressors, shouldered his lute, and they started on their homeward journey.

There was no delay now. At times they sang indeed at castles; but only when their store was exhausted, for upon these occasions Blondel would be presented with a handsome goblet or other solid token of the owner's approval, and the sale of this at the next city would take them far on their way. They thought it better not to pass through France, as Phillip, they knew, was on the watch to prevent any news of King Richard reaching England.

They therefore again passed through Brabant, and so by ship to England. Hearing that Longchamp, Bishop of Ely, one of Richard's vicegerents, was over in Normandy, and rightly deeming him the most earnest of his adherents, they at once recrossed the sea, and found the warlike prelate at Rouen. Greatly delighted was he at hearing that Richard's hiding-place had been discovered. He at once sent across the news to England, and ordered it to be published far and wide, and himself announced it to the barons of Normandy. Then with a gorgeous retinue, including Cuthbert and Blondel, he started for Vienna, and arriving there demanded an interview with the emperor.

The news that it was now certain that Richard was imprisoned in a castle of the emperor, had already spread through Europe, and the bishop had been received everywhere with tokens of sympathy; and so great was the feeling shown by the counts and barons of the empire, that the Emperor Henry felt that he could no longer refuse to treat for the surrender of his captive. Therefore he granted the interview which Longchamp demanded. The English envoy was received by the emperor surrounded by his nobles. The prelate advanced with great dignity.

"I come," he said, "in the name of the people of England to demand the restoration of King Richard, most unjustly and unknightly detained a prisoner in his passage through your dominions."

"King Richard was my foe," the emperor said, "open and secret, and I was justified in detaining one who is alike my enemy and a scourge to Europe as a prisoner, when fortune threw him in my hands. I am, however, willing to put him to a ransom, and will upon the payment of 150,000 marks allow him to go free."

"I deny your right to detain him or to put him to ransom," the bishop said. "But as you have the power, so my denial is useless. England is poor, impoverished with war and by the efforts which she made in the service of our holy religion. Nevertheless, poor as she is, she will raise the sum you demand. There is not an Englishman who will not furnish all he can afford for the rescue of our king. But once again, in the presence of your nobles, I denounce your conduct as base and unkingly."

The emperor could with difficulty restrain his passion; but the sight of the sombre visages of his nobles showed that they shared in no slight degree the feelings which the English envoy had so boldly announced.

"Before, however," the emperor said, "I surrender King Richard, he must be tried by my peers of many and various crimes of which he is accused. Should he be found guilty of these, no gold can purchase his release. Should he, however, be acquitted, then as my word is given so shall it be."

"Although," the prelate said, "I deny your right to try our king, and believe that he himself will refuse to accept your jurisdiction, yet I fear not the result if our lord be left in the hands of the nobles or the empire and not in yours. I can trust their honour and courtesy."

And turning upon his heel, without another word he quitted the apartment.

An hour later the bishop and his following took horse and rode with all speed to the north coast, and thence sailed for England. The news of the amount of ransom filled the people with consternation; but preparations were at once made for collecting the sum demanded. Queen Eleanor was unceasing in her efforts to raise the money for the release of her favourite son. The nobles contributed their jewels and silver; the people gave contributions of goods, for money was so scarce in England that few had the wherewithal to pay in coin. Prince John placed every obstacle in the way of the collection; but the barons had since their successful stand obtained the upper hand, and it was by intrigue only that he could hinder the collection.

In the meantime, popular opinion throughout Europe was strong upon the side of King Richard. The pope himself wrote to the emperor on his behalf. The barons of the empire were indignant at the shame placed upon their country; and the emperor, although he would fain have thrown further delays in the way, was obliged at last to order the first step to be taken.

A solemn diet was ordered to assemble at Worms. Here were collected all the nobles of the empire, and before them King Richard was brought. It was a grand assembly. Upon a raised throne on the dais sat the emperor himself, and beside him and near him were the great feudatories of the empire, and along the sides of the walls were ranged in long rows the lesser barons. When the doors were opened and King Richard entered, the whole assembly, save the emperor, rose in respect to the captive monarch. Although pale from his long confinement, the proud air of Richard was in

no way abated, and the eyes that had flashed so fearlessly upon the Saracens looked as sternly down the long lines of the barons of Germany. Of splendid stature and physique, King Richard was unquestionably the finest man of his time. He was handsome, with a frank face, but with a fierce and passionate eye. He wore his moustache with a short beard and closely-cut whisker. His short curly hair was cropped closely to his head, upon which he wore a velvet cap with gold coronet, while a scarlet robe lined with fur fell over his coat of mail, for the emperor had deemed it imprudent to excite the feeling of the assembly in favour of the prisoner by depriving him of the symbols of his rank. King Richard strode to the place prepared for him, and then turning to the assembly he said, in a voice which rang through the hall,—

"Counts and lords of the Empire of Germany, I, Richard, King of England, do deny your right to try me. I am a king, and can only be tried by my peers and by the pope, who is the head of Christendom. I might refuse to plead, refuse to take any part in this assembly, and appeal to the pope, who alone has power to punish kings. But I will waive my rights. I rely upon the honour and probity of the barons of Germany. I have done no man wrong, and would appear as fearlessly before an assembly of peasants as before a gathering of barons. Such faults as I may have, and none are without them, are not such as those with which I am charged. I have slain many men in anger, but none by treachery. When Richard of England strikes, he strikes in the light of day. He leaves poison and treachery to his enemies, and I hurl back with indignation and scorn in the teeth of him who makes them the charges brought against me."

So saying King Richard took his seat amidst a murmur of applause from the crowded hall.

The trial then commenced. The accusations against Richard were of many kinds. Chief among them was the murder of Conrad of Montferat; but there were charges of having brought the crusade to naught by thwarting the general plans, by his arrogance in refusing to be bound by the decision of the other leaders, and by having made a peace contrary to the interests of the crusaders. The list was a long one; but the evidence adduced was pitiably weak. Beyond the breath of suspicion, no word of real evidence connecting him with the murder of Conrad of Montferat was adduced, and the other charges were supported by no better evidence. Many of the German barons who had been at the crusades themselves came forward to testify to the falsity of these charges, and the fact that Richard had himself placed Conrad of Montferat upon the throne, and had no possible interest in his death, was alone more than sufficient to nullify the vague rumours brought against him. Richard himself in a few scornful words disposed of this accusation. The accusation that he, Richard of England, would stoop to poison a man whom he could have crushed in an instant, was too absurd to be seriously treated.

"I am sure," the king said, "that not one person here believes this idle tale. That I did not always agree with the other leaders is true; but I call upon every one here to say whether, had they listened to me and followed my advice, the crusade would not have had another ending. Even after Phillip of France had withdrawn; even after I had been deserted by John of Austria, I led the troops of the crusaders from every danger and every difficulty to within sight of the walls of Jerusalem. Had I been supported with zeal, the holy city would have been ours; but the apathy, the folly, and the weakness of the leaders brought ruin upon the army. They thought not of conquering Jerusalem, but of thwarting me; and I retort upon them the charge of having sacrificed the success of the crusade. As to the terms of peace, how were they made? I, with some fifty knights and 1000 followers alone remained in the Holy Land. Who else, I ask, so circumstanced, could have obtained any terms whatever from Saladin? It was the weight of my arm alone which saved Jaffa and Acre, and the line of seacoast, to the Cross. And had I followed the example set me by him of Austria and the Frenchman, not one foot of the Holy Land would now remain in Christian hands."

The trial was soon over, and without a single dissentient the King of England was acquitted of all the charges brought against him. But the money was not yet raised, and King Richard was taken back into the heart of Germany. At length, by prodigious exertions, half the amount claimed was collected, and upon the solicitations of the pope and of the counts of his own empire, the emperor consented to release Richard upon receipt of this sum and his royal promise that the remainder should be made up.

Not as yet, however, were the intrigues at an end. Prince John and King Phillip alike implored the emperor to retain his captive, and offered to him a larger sum than the ransom if he would still hold him in his hands. Popular opinion was, however, too strong. When the news of these negotiations became bruited abroad, the counts of the empire, filled with indignation, protested against this shame and dishonour being brought upon the country. The pope threatened him with excommunication; and at last the emperor, feeling that he would risk his throne did he further insist, was forced to open the prison gates and let the king free. Cuthbert, Blondel, and a few other trusty friends were at hand, and their joy at receiving their long-lost sovereign was indeed intense. Horses had been provided in readiness, and without a moment's delay the king started, for even at the last moment it was feared that the emperor might change his mind. This indeed was the case. The king had not started many hours, when the arrival of fresh messengers from Phillip and John induced the emperor once more to change his intentions, and a body of men were sent in pursuit of the king. The latter fortunately made no stay on the way, but changing horses frequently—for everywhere he was received with honour and attention—he pushed forward for the coast of the North Sea, and arrived there two or three hours only before his oppressors. Fortunately it was night, and taking a boat he embarked without a moment's delay; and when the emissaries of the emperor arrived the boat was already out of sight, and in the darkness pursuit was hopeless.

On landing at Dover, the first to present himself before him was Prince John, who, in the most abject terms

besought pardon for the injuries he had inflicted. King Richard waved him contemptuously aside.

"Go," he said, "and may I forget your injuries as speedily as you will forget my pardon."

Then taking horse, he rode on to London, where he was received with the most lively acclamation by his subjects.

The first step of King Richard was to dispossess all the minions of John from the castles and lands which had been taken from his faithful adherents. Some of these resisted; but their fortresses were speedily stormed. Sir Rudolph was not one of these. Immediately the news of King Richard's arrival in England reached him, feeling that all was now lost, he rode to the seacoast, took ship, and passed into France, and Cuthbert, on his arrival at Evesham, found himself undisputed lord of the place. He found that the hiding-place of his mother had not been discovered, and, after a short delay to put matters in train, he, attended by a gallant retinue, rode into Wiltshire to the castle of Sir Baldwin of Béthune. Here he found the Lady Margaret safe and sound, and mightily pleased to see him. She was now seventeen, and offered no objections whatever to the commands of King Richard that she should at once bestow her hand upon the Earl of Evesham. By the king's order, the wedding took place at London, the king himself bestowing the bride upon his faithful follower, whom we may now leave to the enjoyment of the fortune and wife he had so valiantly won.

THE END

Preston Speed RR#4, Box 705, Mill Hall, PA 17751

ublications   www.prestonspeed.com   (717) 726-7844

Available Henty Titles:
Ancient Civilizations
The Young Carthaginian: A Story of The Times of Hannibal
(Hardcover, 321 pages, 12 illustrations)
For the Temple: A Tale of the Fall of Jerusalem
(hardcover; 333 pages, 10 illustrations, map/plan illustrating the siege of Jersualem)
Beric the Briton: A Story of the Roman Invasion
(hardcover, 398 pages, 12 illustrations)
The Cat of Bubastes: A Tale of Ancient Egypt
(hardcover, pages, 8 illustrations, Special Foreword by Douglas Wilson)

Middle Ages
The Dragon and the Raven: Or the Days of King Alfred
(hardcover, 238 pages, 9 illustrations)
Winning His Spurs: A Tale of the Crusades
(Hardcover, 326 pages, numerous illustrations, Foreword by J. Byron Snapp)
In Freedom's Cause: A Story of Wallace and Bruce
(hardcover, 351 pages, 12 illustrations)
Reformation Times
By Pike and Dyke: A Tale of the Rise of the Dutch Republic
(hardcover, 366 pages, 10 illustrations, 4 maps)
St. Bartholomew's Eve: A Tale of the Huguenot Wars
(hardcover, 376 pages, 12 illustrations, fold out map of France)
Under Drake's Flag: A Tale of the Spanish Main
(hardcover, 298 pages, 12 illustrations, Special Foreword by Rev. Dale Dykema)

more...

American Continents Exploits

By Right of Conquest: or with Cortez in Mexico
(Hardcover, 375 pages, 10 illustrations, 2 maps, Special Foreword by Rev. J. Steven Wilkins)

With Lee in Virginia: A Story of the American Civil War
(hardcover, 337 pages, 12 illustrations, 2 maps (1 of which is a fold out map of Virginia), 4 battle plan maps, includes both British and the extremely rare American 'My Dear Lads' Prefaces, Special Foreword by George M. Calhoun)

Preston/Speed Publications takes great pride in re-printing the complete works of G. A. Henty. New titles are regularly being released. Our editions contain the complete text along with all maps and/or illustrations. In order to ensure the most complete Henty editions, we review all previous releases for the most comprehensive version. Preston/Speed Publications maintains the original vocabulary that Mr. Henty first penned as this will open up to American students the necessary vocabulary skills when conversing with British or other European cultures and/or reading their literature.

The New Captain

Our newsletter, *The New Captain,* will be available soon.